'A STRANGE T(

Tradition, Language and the Appropriation of Mystical Experience
in late fourteenth-century England and sixteenth-century Spain

STUDIES IN SPIRITUALITY SUPPLEMENTS
Edited by Titus Brandsma Instituut - Nijmegen - The Netherlands

2. Imoda, F., *Human Development. Psychology and Mystery*, 1998, 397 p., ISBN: 90-429-0028-8.

3. van Baest, M., *Poetry of Hadewijch*, 1998, VIII-330 p., ISBN: 90-429-0667-7.

4. Keller, H.E., *My Secret is Mine. Studies on Religion and Eros in the German Middle Ages*, 2000, VIII-294 p., ISBN: 90-429-0871-8.

5. Imoda, F., *A Journey to Freedom. An Interdisciplinary Approach to the Anthropology of Formation*, 2000, XIV-482 p., ISBN: 90-429-0894-7.

6. Classen, A., *'Mein Seel fang an zu singen'. Religiöse Frauenlieder des 15.-16. Jahrhunderts. Kritische Studien und Textedition*, 2002, 395 p., ISBN: 90-429-1098-4.

7. Baird, M.L., *On the Side of the Angels. Ethics and Post-Holocaust Spirituality*, 2002, 143 p., ISBN: 90-429-1156-5.

8. Waaijman, K., *Spirituality. Forms, Foundations, Methods*, 2002, 967 p., ISBN: 90-429-1183-2.

9. Green, J.D., *'A Strange Tongue'. Tradition, Language and the Appropriation of Mystical Experience in late fourteenth-century England and sixteenth-century Spain*, 2002, VIII - 227 p., ISBN: 90-429-1236-7

STUDIES IN SPIRITUALITY
Supplement 9

'A STRANGE TONGUE'

Tradition, Language and the Appropriation of Mystical Experience
in late fourteenth-century England and sixteenth-century Spain

JOHN D. GREEN

PEETERS

LEUVEN - PARIS - DUDLEY, MA
2002

Library of Congress Cataloging-in-Publication Data

Green, John D., 1932-
A strange tongue : tradition, language, and the appropriation of mystical experience in late fourteenth-century England and sixteenth-century Spain / John D. Green.
    p. cm. -- (Studies in spirituality. Supplement; 9)
  Includes bibliographical references.
  ISBN 9042912367 (alk. paper)
    1. Mysticism--England--History--Middle Ages, 600-1500. 2. Discernment of spirits--History of doctrines--Middle Ages, 600-1500. 3. Julian, of Norwich, b. 1343. 4. Hilton, Walter, d. 1396. 5. Mysticism--Spain--History--16th century. 6. Discernment of spirits--History of doctrines--16th century. 7. Ignatius, of Loyola, Saint, 1491-1556. 8. John of the Cross, Saint, 1542-1591. I. Title. II. Series.

BV5077.G7 G74 2002
248.2'2'0942--dc21

                                                                2002035462

© Peeters, Bondgenotenlaan 153, B-3000 Leuven 2002

ISBN 90-429-1236-7
D. 2002/0602/150

An Allegory of 'Love' in the Tradition of 'Desert Spirituality'

The summit of Mt Sinai hidden in clouds depicting the awesome mystery of the God who, hidden from the gaze of onlookers, only reveals Himself to contemplatives. The contemplatives have successfully completed the ascent which places them as close to Heaven as is possible in this life. They have conquered both their 'animality' and 'rationality' by 'love' and have become 'spiritualis'.

El Greco, Mount Sinai (back of the Modena Polyptych), before 1570.

TABLE OF CONTENTS

Figures

ACKNOWLEDGEMENTS

The El Grecos are reproduced from the Skira publication on *El Greco*; *a Biographical and Critical Study* by Paul Guinard from 'The Taste of Our Time' series, a collection planned and directed by Albert Skira 1956, by kind permission of Editions d'Art Albert Skira S.A of Geneva.

Figures 4 and 5 are reproduced from *John of the Cross: Selected Writings*. Edited with an Introduction by Kiernan Kavanaugh, O.C.D. and Preface by Ernest E. Larkin, O. Carm. in the Classics of Western Spirituality series, pages 44/45, by kind permission of the publishers Paulist Press, New York, Mahwah.

---

1   Skira: El Greco No.38, Galleria Estense, Modena.
2   *Ibid.* No.92, Salas Capitulares, Convent of the Escorial.
3   *Ibid.* No.12, Central Panel of the Modena Polyptych, Galleria Estense, Modena.
4   *Ibid.* No.17. Salas Capitulares, Convent of the Escorial.

PREFACE

The remote origins of this book extend to the days when I was reading history at Oxford and struggling to understand my own religious convictions. The influence of St Augustine of Hippo began to pervade both my historical studies and my search for an understanding of the process of religious conviction.

Many years later, the opportunity arose for further study and coincided with the reading of Peter Brown's masterly biography of Augustine. I was reminded of my earlier puzzlement about the way in which Augustine's influence projected itself into the Christian mind-set not only in the mediaeval period but also to the present day. The outcome was a study of how Augustine influenced the spirituality of the mediaeval church as reflected in the spiritual teaching of mystics at different points in the mediaeval period.

The methodology had it's drawbacks as a study of 'influence'. It became evident that a concentration on the influence of Augustine in the teaching of the mystics indicated it's ubiquity. However it did not explain the mystics' 'turning' as they experienced the divine presence in their lives. Moreover the methodology tended to obscure the personal contribution of individual mystics to the spirituality of the Christian community in their teaching and example. So the objectives which produced this book came to be defined:
- to explore how the mystics appropriated the reality of their own experience of the divine;
- how they interrogated the tradition of 'discernment of spirits', the instrument which had come into being as generations of Christians faced the problem of discerning the authentic spirit of the divine;
- how they extended tradition through their teaching in the language of their times;
- to place the seminal influence of Augustine within the tradition in some perspective.

The study I have undertaken is limited and thus suggestive rather than in any sense conclusive. It is confined to the classical texts of the mystics of late fourteenth-century England and sixteenth-century Spain and the cultural contexts in which they were created. These periods and locations were chosen because they were ones of heightened spiritual turmoil in which mystical experience itself was viewed with suspicion as the product of overwrought imaginations or, worse still, demonic intervention. As a consequence the mystics of the study, Julian of Norwich, the *Cloud* Author, and Walter Hilton in England and Ignatius of Loyola and John of the Cross in Spain, were very conscious of the need for discernment and the importance of traditional norms. By confining the study in this way, to lift the profile of the practice of 'discernment of spirits', it was not possible to do more than attempt to gauge the mood, the language in the broadest sense, of each period and location. So that the study is directed more to the process of discernment and the evolution of tradition and rather less to the lives of the mystics, their cultural milieus or the influence of Augustine, significant as all these factors are.

Despite the historical limitations of the book, I hope it will have some interest and value as an explanation of how a spiritual tradition lives, retaining continuity while continuously being adapted to new circumstances. It has had a long gestation period and the benefit of the interest of many people, too numerous to thank individually. However the responsibility for the outcome is entirely mine. This goes also for those whom I must thank by name for their generosity.

At the outset of the project, Rev. Dr. Austin Cooper omi. was very encouraging when I approached him with some preliminary ideas for the study of Augustinian influence and later, 'discernment of spirits'. Latterly, just when I was wondering about publication, he happened to invite me to conduct a seminar on Augustine at the Catholic Theological College in Melbourne. An unexpected benefit from the discussions with participants at the seminar was reassurance that the subjects of 'discernment of spirits' and 'mystical experience' were still of considerable interest and persuaded me to persevere with publication.

At this juncture, the Rev.Dr. Paul Chandler ocarm. came to my assistance about publication with an introduction to Dr. Hein Blommestijn at the Titus Brandsma Institute in the Netherlands. He, in turn, introduced me to Ineke Wackers who has expertly guided my book to press. I have to thank them all.

Ingrid Barker has cheerfully and expertly processed my barely decipherable handwritten pages over many years. Her help has been invaluable.

Professor Greg Dening has guided my studies in both their 'Augustinian' and 'Discernment' phases at the University of Melbourne. I thank him for his encouragement and advice which kept me 'on track' and especially for his generous friendship.

Finally I must thank my wife and family for their unfailing encouragement and for putting up with me on the many occasions they found me 'off the planet'. I can only hope the product will not turn out to be a disappointment.

Abbreviations

1. General

AHDLMA	*Archives d'histoire doctrinale et littéraire du moyen âge*, Paris 1926ff.
AHSJ	*Archivum Historicum Societatis Jesu* (Periodical of the Jesuit Historical Institute in Rome).
BIHR	*Bulletin of the Institute of Historical Research*, London.
BJRL	*Bulletin of the John Rylands Library*, Manchester.
CCSL	Corpus Christianorum Series Latina, Turnhout, Belgium 1953ff.
CSEL	Corpus Scriptorum Ecclesiasticorum Latinorum, Vienna, 1866ff.
Dict.Sp.	*Dictionnaire de Spiritualité*, ed. M. Viller, S.J. and others, 1937ff.
D.H.G.E.	*Dictionnaire d'Histoire et de Géographie Ecclésiastiques*, ed. A. Baudrillart and others, 1912ff.
D.T.C.	*Dictionnaire de Théologie Catholique*, ed. A. Vacant, E. Mangenot and É. Amann (15 vols), 1903-50.
Econ. HR	*Economic History Review*, London.
E.E.T.S.	Early English Text Society, London, 1864ff. (E.S. ≡ Extra Series; OS ≡ Original Series).
G.C.S.	Die griechischen christlichen Schriftsteller der ersten drei Jahrhunderte, Leipzig, 1897-1941; Berlin and Leipzig, 1953; Berlin, 1954ff.
JEH	*Journal of Ecclesiastical History*, London, 1950ff.
MHSJ	*Monumenta Historica Societatis Jesu*. For outline of this resource relevant to chapter 5 refer Bibliography,205.
M.M.T. in Eng.	*The Mediaeval Mystical Tradition in England*, ed. Marion Glasscoe, Exeter: D.S. Brewer, 1980ff.
N.C.E.	*New Catholic Encyclopedia* (14 vols and Index), New York, etc., 1967.
PG	Patrologia Graeca, ed. J.P. Migne (162 vols), Paris, 1857-66.
PL	Patrologia Latina, ed. J.P. Migne (221 vols), Paris, 1844-64.
R.A.M.	*Revue d'Ascétique et de Mystique*, Paris.
R.H.E.	*Revue d'Histoire Ecclésiastique*, Louvain, 1900ff.
S.C.	Sources Chrétiennes, Paris, 1940ff.
SCH	*Studies in Church History*, Leiden, Netherlands and since Vol. 10, 1973, Oxford: Blackwell.
S.P.C.K.	Society for Promoting Christian Knowledge.
ZAM	*Zeitschrift für Aszese und Mystik*, Würzburg (19 vols).

2. Specific

A number of abbreviations have been used for specific works for use in footnote references. They are explained in the footnotes, usually early, in the chapter concerned.

PROLOGUE

Two outstanding master story-tellers from the periods of history with which we will
be primarily concerned, Geoffrey Chaucer and Miguel de Cervantes, introduce their
most well-known stories, the *Canterbury Tales* and *Don Quixote de la Mancha*, with
Prologues. Their purpose is to mediate between the conventionalities of the real
world of their audience and those of their genre. Their stories and characters are
fictional creations but the audience should be able to recognise their own experiences of reality in the fictions which are presented to them. The fictions should seem
to become symbols of reality. Both Chaucer and Cervantes created for this purpose a
setting and a situation with which the audience would be immediately familiar. In
Chaucer's case the Prologue introduces and describes an entire nation, a real world[1].
The tales are to be anchored in a shared experience of 'reality'. By contrast,
Cervantes' Prologue is a parody of Prologues introducing, as it were, the parodic
genre, with a parody. His audience is left in no doubt about the nature of the story he
is about to tell. It really needs no Prologue because 'the chastest lover and most
valiant knight', Don Quixote, is already well known to them[2]. If there is any doubt,
it is revealed at the outset that he seems to be unbalanced and his world is an illusion. The readers are invited, as it were, to enjoy this parodic illusion as they would
a conjuring trick and the art of the conjuror[3]. For Cervantes it seems the relationship
between reality and illusion was the thematic issue.

The problematic of mediating between fact and fiction, reality and illusion, truth and
fantasy, is very much our concern with the mystics and their experiences. Discourse
about mystics tends to polarise opinion. It raises questions about the nature of their
experiences; whether what they tell us is what they actually experienced and a vari-

---

1 Geoffrey Chaucer, *Canterbury Tales*, trans. into modern English and with Introduction by
   Neville Coghill, London: Penguin Books, repr. 1977, 17 (referred to hereafter as Coghill ed.
   Canterbury Tales).
2 Miguel de Cervantes Saavedra, *Don Quixote de la Mancha*, trans. Charles Jarvis. Ed and Intro.
   E.C. Riley, Oxford: Oxford University Press, 1992. Author's Preface, 21 (referred to hereafter
   as Riley ed. *Don Quixote*).
3 *Ibid.*, x. See also E.C. Riley's, *Don Quixote*, London, 1986; J.J. Allen, *Don Quixote: Hero or
   Fool?*, Gainsville Fla. Pt. 1, 1969, Pt.2, 1979, and John Coulson, *Religion and Imagination*,
   Oxford, 1981, 87 on literary faith as 'suspension of disbelief'.

ety of questions of a similar kind which raise the issue whether the experiences were real or illusory. Not everyone will begin with the same view of mysticism and the mystics. In a Prologue we can begin by sharing their stories. Our purpose in this Prologue is to introduce the stories of the mystics we wish to discuss through accounts of their experiences and what is known of their lives. Then, hopefully, armed with a common understanding of who and what we are discussing, we are free to introduce the particular features of their mystical experiences we wish to understand.

Our particular interest is in how the mystics recognise that their experiences are 'real'. There are a number of aspects of the process. Our main interest is about how the process becomes a tradition of 'discernment of spirits' and how that tradition develops so that differences of spiritual style, personal genius and cultural ethos seem to be subsumed and the Christian community arrives at some consensus that the experiences of individuals are authentic and of prophetic significance.

In addition to introducing the mystics and their experiences, we wish also to introduce the cultural backgrounds which mediate their accounts of their experiences. Culture is a mediating expression of values, styles and mood which identifies a community's aspirations[4]. Its influence is pervasive but not easy to identify or describe in narrative form because it is not experienced as homogeneous. One way of approaching the problem of recognising cultural influence is through the artistic sensitivity of the literary masters of a period who were accepted as masters by their contemporaries and have seemed, through their genius, to symbolise the age in which they wrote. In the periods and places we are dealing with, fourteenth-century England and sixteenth-century Spain, Chaucer[5] and Cervantes[6] may perhaps be regarded as symbolising in a special way the mood of the period.

---

4   Bernard Lonergan, *Method in Theology*, London: Darton, Longman & Todd, repr., 1975 (first published 1972), 300-2, discusses the concept of 'culture' in a context relevant to this study. See also Rosemary Haughton, *Transformation of Man. A study of Conversion and Community*, London: Geoffrey Chapman, 1967, 220, on the function of 'language' within a 'culture'.

5   G.M. Trevelyan, *English Social History*, London, 1944, entitled the first two chapters 'Chaucer's England' [1340-1400]. However, Trevelyan begins 'In Chaucer's England we see for the first time the modern mingling with the mediaeval, and England herself beginning to emerge as a distinct nation, no longer a mere overseas extension of Franco-Latin Europe'. This is perhaps true but Chaucer's work also illustrates the close ties which continue to bind England to Europe in this period and the mood which R. Kieckhefer in *Unquiet Souls: Fourteenth Century Saints and their Religious Milieu*, University of Chicago, 1984, discerns among religious. Trevelyan is of course referring primarily to the emergence of an 'English tongue', which Chaucer perhaps sealed by the inspiration of his poetic imagination (as he himself had been inspired by his European contacts) and its importance in the development of a 'national' identity. See R.W. Chambers, *On the Continuity of English Prose*, London, 1932.

6   *The Oxford Companion to English Literature*, ed. Margaret Drabble, Oxford University Press, 5th edn, 1988, 284 and 1014, refers to Miguel de Unamuno y Jugo (1864-1936), *La Vida de Don Quixote y Sancho*, 1905, in which he perceives Don Quixote as 'the embodiment of the Spanish genius'. Unamuno's judgment of Don Quixote is perhaps interesting because of his

In our Prologue, therefore, we propose to preface our account of each pair of mystics, Julian of Norwich and the *Cloud* author from England in the fourteenth century and Ignatius of Loyola and John of the Cross from Spain in its 'Golden Age' by attempting to outline some relevant aspects of the mood of each period which Chaucer and Cervantes reflect in the *Canterbury Tales* and *Don Quixote de la Mancha* respectively.

The mystics and also Chaucer and Cervantes have individually been the subject of a great deal of scholarly investigation which is more far ranging and erudite than we can possibly hope to approach. In pursuing our particular interests in this study, we may perhaps be permitted to perch, to use a celebrated mediaeval metaphor[7], on the shoulders of these scholars the better to observe within the array of mystical paradigms the 'life' hidden in the tradition of 'discernment of spirits' as we range back and forth in time, unlike, hopefully, Don Quixote tilting at windmills perched on the back of the ill-used and long-suffering Rosinante.

1. A VIEW OF CHAUCER'S WORLD

The year of Geoffrey Chaucer's birth is not known with certainty. Coghill suggests 1342, the year in which Julian of Norwich was also born. Others suggest it may have been in 1343 or 1344[8]. He is thought to have started work on the *Canterbury Tales*

---

own philosophic position. In his *The Tragic Sense of Life* (1921) he suggests 'God is not the cause, but the consequence of man's longing for immortality' and concludes that all dogma, religious or anti-religious is false: 'the only tenable philosophical position is that of doubt and wonder'. In the last sentence we may perhaps recognise Cervantes' own early position but in his case it is perhaps the beginning of a search for meaning and faith since in 1613 he became a tertiary of the Franciscan Order (Riley ed. *Don Quixote*, xxii). On the other hand Don Quixote and 'Quixotism' have been adopted by many other countries. The book was translated into English as early as 1616 by Thomas Shelton. There may be something of the 'Don Quixote' in us all. As Lionel Trilling has said 'Don Quixote' contained within it 'the whole potentiality of the genre' (quoted by Riley ed. *Don Quixote*, xvi). Nevertheless, one is left to wonder whether the paradoxes of Don Quixote could have been inspired anywhere else other than where they were first embraced.

7 See Etienne Gilson, *The Spirit of Mediaeval Philosophy*, trans. A.H.C. Downes, New York, 1940, 425/6. The metaphor is attributed to Bernard of Chartres (d.c. 1130). It is also used in John of Salisbury's (1115-80) *Metalogicon*, ed. C.C.J. Webb, 136 (P.L. vol. 199.900) who studied under William of Conches and Gilbert de la Porrée both of whom in turn carried on the work of Bernard. See R.W. Southern, *The Making of the Middle Ages*, London, Hutchinson, repr. 1967 (first published 1953), 194.

N.B. To avoid confusion I have referred to a note in another author's work by the abbreviation(s) n(n) and the cross-reference to a note(s) in my own work as N(N). In the footnotes a line in a work is cited as L and LL in the plural unless otherwise indicated to distinguish them from the Roman numeral 'l' (50).

8 *Oxford Companion to English Literature*, ed. Margaret Drabble, *op.cit.*, suggests a range 1339-46.

in 1386 or 1387[9]; perhaps a decade or so later than the *Cloud* Author's, *Cloud of Unknowing* was completed[10] and about the same time as Walter Hilton is thought to have been working on the *Scale of Perfection* and a few years before Julian of Norwich completed the long version of her *Showings* in 1393. The world of Geoffrey Chaucer as well as being that of the fourteenth-century English mystics, was also the world in which miracle and morality plays were flourishing and also the great Corpus Christi cycles[11]. The cult of the Saints whose development in Late Antiquity has been so well described by Peter Brown[12], was very much alive in England. It has been suggested that Chaucer himself during his wife's last illness may have undertaken the pilgrimage to Becket's tomb at Canterbury[13]. Secular authors of the period, like Chaucer, reflect both its religious ethos and its mirror image, if somewhat flawed in the secular imagination, the 'Amour Courtois'[14]. Chaucer stands out among them because of his extraordinary gifts and interests, the range of which explains how he has come to symbolise the period in which he lived.

The range of Chaucer's secular experience may perhaps in part explain the quality of his writings which Roland Barthes might have called 'serieux'[15]; while the range of his literary interest also testifies to the vitality of his ironic curiosity. Apart from the *Canterbury Tales*, he wrote several long and distinguished poems; the *Book of the Duchess*, the *House of Fame*, the *Parliament of Fowles*, *Troilus and Criseyde*, which it has been suggested was the first English novel in the *Amour Courtois* genre, and

---

9   Coghill ed. *Canterbury Tales*, Intro, 16.
10 The date of the *Cloud of Unknowing* is uncertain. The extant manuscripts are of later date; the earliest HAR[1] was written in the early fifteenth century. The suggestion has been made that Hilton might have been acquainted with the *Cloud of Unknowing* and on this basis a tentative date has been postulated. However we can be reasonably sure it was produced in the last quarter of the fourteenth century and earlier rather than later in the quarter.
11 Anderson, M.D., *Drama and Imagery in English Mediaeval Churches*, Cambridge, 1963, 3: 'The way in which the great cycles of mystery plays were written and produced in the fourteenth and fifteenth centuries is an important aspect of literary history, not only because the plays themselves have a natural reverence and warm humanity which can still capture the imagination of a modern audience, but because they prepared the way for some of the great masterpieces of our language ... by the creation of a public'.
    See also, G. Bourquin, 'The Dynamics of the Signans in the Spiritual Quest' (*Piers Plowman, the Mystics and Religious Drama*), in *M.M.T. in Eng.*, 1982, 182-98.
12 Peter Brown, *Cult of the Saints. Its Rise and Function in Latin Christianity*, London: S.C.M. Press, 1981.
13 A.C. Cawley, middle English ed. G. Chaucer, *Canterbury Tales*, London: J.M. Dent & Sons Ltd., 1958, repr. 1991, ix (hereafter referred to as Cawley ed. *Canterbury Tales*).
14 C.S. Lewis, *The Allegory of Love*, Oxford University Press, 1936. For the religious ethos of the period, see for example A.P. Baldwin, The Tripartite Reformation of the Soul in 'The Scale of Perfection', 'Pearl' and 'Piers Plowman', in *M.M.T. in Eng.* 1984, 136-149 and particularly the conclusion at page 147.
15 Roland Barthes, *Sade, Fourier, Loyola*, Paris: Editions du Seuil, 1971, 46: 'seule compte l'assertion de son être [l'écriture] c'est-à-dire en somme son sérieux ...'.

the *Legend of Good Women.* In addition he made a prose translation of Boethius' *Consolation of Philosophy* and of a treatise on the Astrolabe.

Chaucer's writing was a spare time activity in his busy life. He was successively a member of the Kings Household, a soldier, captured near Rheims and ransomed - a ransom to which the King contributed, a diplomatic envoy to France and Italy, a high customs official as, may be, befits a vintner's son and grandson, a justice of the peace for the Shire of Kent, a member of parliament and a Clerk of the King's Works where among other activities he had the task in 1390 of supervising repairs to St George's Chapel, Windsor. In 1391 he perhaps received a sinecure in the appointment as deputy forester of the royal forest of North Petherton in Somerset. In one sense the *Canterbury Tales* may be regarded as a reflection on his own life and of the world in which he lived. It was a reflection perhaps undertaken in the aftermath of his wife's death.

But it was certainly no morbid reflection. It was written after the manner of the French and Italian poets whose work he had encountered, especially Deschamps, Dante, Petrarch and Boccaccio, in his diplomatic missions to France and Italy[16]. Yet his setting and the source of his inspiration seem to have been particularly English. As Neville Coghill has said of the Prologue:

> it is a concise portrait of an entire nation, high and low, old and young, male and female, lay and clerical, learned and ignorant, rogue and righteous, land and sea, town and country, but without extremes[17].

In it we recognise real people:

> They are the perennial progeny of men and women, sharply individual, together they make a party[18].

The party to which Coghill refers is the group of pilgrims which Chaucer assembles in the Prologue of the *Canterbury Tales* at the Tabard Inn at Southwark:

> to Caunterbury they wende the hooly blisful
> martir for to seke that hem hath
> holpen whan that they were seeke[19].

---

16 Cawley ed. *Canterbury Tales*, vii. See also Ralph Elliott, 'Chaucer's Clerical Voices', in *Mediaeval English Religious Literature*, eds G. Kratzmann and J. Simpson, Cambridge: D.S. Brewer, 1986, 149, in relation to Dante's influence in 'Chaucer's linguistic register'.

17 Coghill ed. *Canterbury Tales*, 17.

18 *Ibid.*

19 Cawley ed. *Canterbury Tales*, 1, LL.16-18.

There has been a great deal of scholarly speculation about why Chaucer chose the pilgrimage in which to frame the *Canterbury Tales*. There are literary precedents of which he may have been aware[20]. It seems however that there may be a simpler more natural explanation, apart from the possibility that he had recently been a pilgrim himself. From his house at Greenwich he would probably have seen numerous groups of pilgrims setting out for Canterbury[21].

The occasion which provided the leisure on which to make a start on the *Canterbury Tales*, was his temporary loss of favour at court during the absence of John of Gaunt, who was both his patron and kinsman by marriage. The connection between the pilgrim journey and life might easily have been made in these circumstances. The pilgrimage was a common place allegory for life used in literature of the period[22]. The goal of the journey to Canterbury reflects the ultimate mystery of life and death. The murder of Becket and the reputation he subsequently acquired as a powerful intercessor point, on the one hand, to the vagaries of life particularly his own eclipse; on the other to a spiritual existence beyond the material realm which seemed real enough in Becket's case, but remained always mysterious, even privileged, if sometimes accessible through the patronage of the Saint.

Whatever Chaucer's motives for the choice of the pilgrimage to frame his stories, it was a happy one. The tales and the characters who tell them seem to grow naturally out of such an undertaking and it enables him to display a range of stories drawn from all over Europe and further afield, which exemplify 'the whole range of contemporary European imagination, then particularly addicted to stories, especially to stories that had some sharp point and deducible maxim, moral or idea'.

If the evidence of the Prologue may be relied upon, Chaucer's original intention was that each pilgrim should tell a tale on the way to Canterbury and another during the return journey[23]. There were some thirty pilgrims, so the plan was very ambitious. It was never completed. At his death in 1400 ten fragments had been completed, though not all of them had been edited. Not all the pilgrims had told their first story. However the Parson's tale which most scholars believe Chaucer intended to be the final piece to be told as the group reached the outskirts of Canterbury, was completed. We are left to speculate about the nature of the stories which might have

---

20 *Ibid.*, viii.
21 *Ibid.*, ix.
22 See for example Walter Hilton's use of the theme. *Scale of Perfection*, ed. John P.H. Clark and Rosemary Dorward, New York, Mahwah: Paulist Press, 1991, 227-33 and n.102, 309. There was a very considerable 'spiritual' literary output in mediaeval England. See both G.R. Owst, *Literature and Pulpit in Mediaeval England*, Cambridge, 1933 and Peter S. Joliffe, *A Check-List of Middle English Prose Writings of Spiritual Guidance*, Toronto: Pontifical Institute of Mediaeval Studies, 1974.
23 Coghill ed., *Canterbury Tales*, 16.

been told on the return journey to London and how the pilgrims would have reacted to their encounter with the mystical world of Becket's cult[24].

The sympathetic sketch of the Parson which Chaucer provides in the Prologue together with the sermon he preaches as the group approached its goal, suggests that Chaucer's intention was not to parody the Christian practice of pilgrimage but rather perhaps to suggest that it was only efficacious with the aid of divine grace mediated by a saint's recognition of true contrition. The portraits of the Pardonner and the Friar, for example, certainly parody some of the clerical abuses of the time. However the impression created by the group as a whole suggests that Chaucer neither expected nor had encountered in his life a society of saints. As Coghill suggests the group were 'without extremes', neither wholly good nor bad, just a reflection of the 'human progeny'[25].

Chaucer it appears, holds up 'pilgrimage' as a symbol of the Christian aspiration, as something for which it is worth suffering the trials of life. It is the abuses of the ideal for which he reserves his venom. Unlike his contemporary Wycliffe, who was ten years his senior and had also received the patronage of John of Gaunt, he does not seek to attack the doctrines which underlie the practices which provide the opportunity for the abuses he pillories. He rather exposes the abuses for what they are, the evidence of human weakness and of the sins endemic to flawed humanity which the parson inveighs against and dissects in his sermon. While Wycliffe is sometimes considered to symbolise the age as the farsighted precursor of the Reformation[26], Chaucer seems to provide an alternative symbol for it, that of the Christian humanist, a precursor of the full flowering of the Renaissance in England, a Thomas More rather than a Cranmer who is the ironic and gifted but balanced observer of all aspects of life, material and spiritual, and one of the channels through which its artistic ideals were transmitted.

The secular viewpoint of the age which Chaucer provides seems to emphasise a clear-sighted, unsentimental acceptance of the nature of the human predicament. It seems to be a perennial predicament in which he believes the church is integral with society. But the Christian element of his understanding seems to provide hope that the finer aspirations of human beings are worthwhile and have an autonomous nobil-

---

24 Stephen Knight, 'Chaucer's Religious Canterbury Tales', in *Mediaeval English Religious Literature, op.cit.*, 165. Discussing the arrival of the pilgrims on the outskirts of Canterbury: 'As Chaucer sets the scene, the Caen stone [of the Cathedral] catches the late afternoon spring sunshine, and as it still does, it would shimmer with pale golden light. Regular travellers to Dover and Sandwich like Chaucer and his friends could hardly have missed the sight or its anagogical implication; here is the imagistic setting for the words that redirect this pilgrimage to celestial Jerusalem'. (Parson's Prologue, x 49-51. Cawley ed. *Canterbury Tales*, 531.)

25 Coghill ed., *Canterbury Tales*, 17.

26 See K.B. McFarlane, *John Wycliffe and the Beginnings of English Non-Conformity*, London: English Universities Press Ltd., 1952, Prologue 10-11 and Epilogue 187-88.

ity which human weakness may mask but not destroy. Despite the shortcomings of some of those in positions of trust in the church of the day he seems to recognise in the object of pilgrimage the compelling power of the Christian dream for which in their different milieu the mystics also provide tangible evidence in their lives and writings that the Christian ideal may not be a Quixotic fantasy.

2. JULIAN OF NORWICH

Julian of Norwich is one of those shadowy mediaeval figures who in psychological terms seems so real yet about whose life very little is positively known. The evidence of bequests made to Julian in wills of the period[27] and the testimony of Margery Kempe whose life story is more fully documented, that she visited Julian in her cell at Norwich in search of spiritual guidance[28], are the most concrete corroborative evidence we have that she lived in the period which her writings suggest. Even this evidence, particularly about the age to which she lived, is uncertain, for the wills may have been referring to a successor in the anchorhold at St Julian's Church, which gave Julian her name.

Her writings, through which her psychological profile emerges, consist of two accounts of a series of sixteen 'showings', visions and locutions, which she received on 13th May 1373[29]. The shorter version is believed to have been written soon after the revelations took place; the longer one, some twenty years later. The Long text incorporates her reflections on the original showings and on the 'illuminations' she subsequently received in meditating their meaning.

---

27   There are four bequests in wills of the late 14th and early 15th centuries that probably were made to her. The last is dated 1416 and, if our Julian was that beneficiary, extends her life-span beyond the three score years and ten. The scribe who copied the short text noted in the introductory chapter that she was still alive in 1413. See N.P. Tanner, *Popular Religion in Norfolk with Special Reference to the Evidence of Wills 1370-1532*, unpublished D. phil thesis, Oxford 1973.

28   Clifton Wolters ed., *Julian of Norwich. Revelations of Divine Love*, Penguin Books, repr. 1984, 16-17, cites the *Book of Margery Kempe*, ed. W. Butler-Bowden, Oxford: The World Classics, 1954, 54-56 in a modernised translation.

29   *A Book of Showings to the Anchoress Julian of Norwich*, ed. Edmund Colledge OSA and James Walsh SJ. Toronto: Pontifical Institute of Mediaeval Studies, 2 vols, 1978, has been used for quotations in Middle English and a translation of this critical text by the editors in the Classics of Western Spirituality series entitled *Julian of Norwich, Showings*, New York: Paulist Press, 1978, has been used for quotations in modern English, referred to hereafter as *Showings, Crit. Ed.*, *S.T.* and *L.T.* (Short and Long texts) and *Showings trans.*, *S.T.* and *L.T.*, respectively. The date of the Showings is recorded in the Crit. Ed. *L.T.*, 285 L.3 (e.g.285.3 hereafter). There is another edition of the Long text (only) by Marion Glasscoe, Exeter, 1976, which follows the Sloane MSS whereas Colledge and Walsh follow the Paris MS (see below N.31).

The provenance of the texts on which we rely for the knowledge we have of Julian and her experiences, illustrate the extent to which historians are hostage to fortune in their attempts to reconstruct a past for which the evidence is often oblique and uneven[30]. There is only one manuscript copy of the Short text in existence, the so-called 'Amherst MS', named after its last private owner, MS British Library Additional 37790. This is a considerable anthology of shorter spiritual classics and it is thought to have been in the hands of James Greenhalgh of Sheen Charterhouse in about 1500. The writing suggests it was made about 1450.

There is only one MS text for the longer version which predates the Dissolution - Westminster (Diocesan Archives), an anthology which contains only extracts from the Long text written by a professional scribe about 1500. The 'full' MS version of the Long text is described in the Bibliothèque Nationale Catalogue, MS Fonds anglais 40, as 'early 16th century'. However it is now suggested that it is an attempt made about 1650 to imitate an early 16th-century hand. This, however, remains the most important long-text manuscript. Cressy's printed text was most probably made from it during the brief period when he served as chaplain in Paris to the English Benedictine nuns whose house had recently been founded from Cambrai. The other versions of the Long text in existence, the two Sloane Manuscripts and the 'Upholland Anthology' are believed to have originated from Cambrai also. The suggestion has been made on this evidence that the preservation of these texts was the work of Augustine Baker and his spiritual school among the exiled Benedictine monks and nuns in the Low Countries and France[31].

From all these uncertainties of text and circumstance there emerges a story which reveals a person of a learning and devotion expressing ideas about the Christian faith which seem very relevant to the problematic of our own age.

The story is set in the bedroom of a sick woman, about thirty and a half years of age, who is thought to be on the point of death. The curate has been called and stands with Julian's mother and some others watching. Last rites have been administered and a crucifix set at the foot of the bed where Julian can gaze upon it. The crucifix is the focal point for the *Showings*, which unbeknown to those gathered around the

---

30 Andrew Louth, *The Wilderness of God*, London: Darton, Longman and Todd, 1991, in his Chapter on 'Mediaeval Anchorism and Julian of Norwich', 63, suggests 'Julian hid herself from the interest of her age' and 65/66, 'Julian's 'desert', ... provided a very effective retreat from the world of her day' but 'has a message that has spoken to the hearts of many in this century'.

31 *Showings trans.*, 21/22, for a discussion of the Long text provenance. Details of the manuscripts are included in the Introduction to the Crit. Ed. *op.cit.*, 1-18. Augustine Baker (1575-1641) was a Benedictine monk and author of the mystical classic *Holy Wisdom*, ed. G. Stiwell, London, 1964. See *Oxford Dictionary of the Christian Church*, 122, for brief outline of his life and work with bibliography. See also Marion Glasscoe, 'Visions and Revisions: A Further Look at the Manuscripts of Julian of Norwich', in *Studies in Bibliography* 42 (1989), 103-20.

bed, have begun and will continue with apparently only one intermission which occurs after the fifteenth 'showing' when Julian becomes aware of the presence of bystanders and speaks about what has happened to her. Two references are made in her story which provide some perspective to her life. The first is about an event which preceded the showings; the second is to her complete recovery of health which followed their cessation[32].

The first relates to three wishes Julian had made when she was young - how young we are not told. She had apparently on some occasion sought three graces from God; first, a recollection of the Passion so that she might understand Christ's sufferings more vividly; second, a bodily sickness through which she might experience the approach of death but not actually die; and the last was three wounds, of contrition, compassion and longing. In the case of the bodily sickness she had further asked that it might be experienced when she was about thirty years old. Apparently, while the third of these wishes had been constantly in her mind, the other two had been forgotten until the 'showings' began. The recollection of these wishes at the moment of the showings seem to have predisposed her to take them seriously. As they unfolded she apparently became convinced that the visions, locutions and spiritual insights she received in the process of the showings, were the graces she had sought on that earlier occasion[33].

The other factor which must have influenced Julian's evaluation of the showings and almost certainly would have influenced those who were present at her bedside, was her almost instantaneous restoration to full health when they ceased[34]. She is believed to have lived into the second decade of the next century, on the fallible evidence of the bequests it is true, which would have made her something over three score and ten years, a good age for that era.

---

32 The recovery is of course verified by her subsequent life. For example see *Showings trans., L.T.* chap. 86, 342, where she refers to the interval of fifteen years which elapsed before she understood 'our Lord's meaning'. As suggested she seems to have lived at least until 1413 and perhaps beyond 1416. There are graphic descriptions of the progress of her sickness in *ibid., L.T.* chap. 3, 179/180 and *S.T.* chap. 2, 128/9. In both texts she records that quite suddenly after believing she was on the point of death, all her pain left her and she was as sound in the upper part of her body as she had ever been before or since. She was astonished by the change for it seemed 'God's secret doing' and not natural. In *L.T.* chap. 3, 162, she records how the pains returned but she understood she was going to live. Likewise in chap. 64 of the Long text.

33 *Showings trans., S.T.* chap. 1, 125/7 and *L.T.* chap. 2, 177/79. For the context of the wishes in the spiritual tradition see Sandra McEntire, 'The Doctrine of Compunction from Bede to Margery Kempe', in *M.M.T. in Eng.*, Exeter 1987, which particularly refers to Julian's reactions to the 'reality' of Christ's sufferings to which she was exposed in the *Showings*.

34 See discussion in *Showings*, Crit. Ed., 67-70, of Paul Molinari's analysis in *Julian of Norwich; The Teaching of a 14th Century English Mystic*, London, 1958, 22-31.

We may ask ourselves what circumstance prompted the young Julian to seek the three graces she mentions. It suggests she was a devout and impressionable young- ster at the time. It also suggests that some events perhaps occasioned her personal identification with, and responses to, the 'scenes' of the Crucifixion. It is possible that she had just witnessed the performance of a mystery play. Although only a fragment remains, it is known that in the latter part of the fourteenth century, a cycle of mystery plays were performed regularly at Norwich[35]. The Craft Guilds of the city were responsible for the production, each guild being responsible for a particu- lar scene. The plays had a great deal of impact upon the visual imagery of the time. For example, it has been suggested that the bosses in Norwich Cathedral may have been influenced by the scenes from the plays which the craftsmen witnessed. They depict in serial form what Mary Anderson in her *Drama and Imagery in English Medieval Churches* concludes are symbolic representations of the scenes of the plays[36]. There is abundant evidence, in any event, that there was a good deal of in- terconnection, by way of reciprocal influence, between drama, in the form of plays and liturgical representations, and church imagery of various kinds. It does not therefore seem to be too wild a speculation to wonder whether Julian, as an impres- sionable young woman, may not have been prompted to make her wishes after being deeply impressed by scenes from a mystery play.

The three wishes, although they may not be directly linked to the images which originally evoked them, came to the forefront of Julian's mind as she experienced the visions. The relationship between a divine communication and the image content by which it is mediated is one of the more difficult problems of discussing mystical experience. There is a school of mystical thought, the apophatic or negative school, which believes that visions and locutions are suspect for the very reason that they depend on symbols in the form of images or sounds[37]. This school believes that

---

35 Richard Beadle on 'Mystery Plays' in *Dictionary of the Middle Ages*, ed. Strayer J.R., New York: Charles Scribner & Sons, 1987, vol. 8, 657-663. See also Rosemary Woolf, *The English Mystery Plays*, London: Routledge Kegan Paul, 1972.

36 Mary Anderson, *Drama and Imagery in English Mediaeval Churches*, 143-177 and plates e.g. 12b and also page 208, refers to the windows in the churches at Ludlow, Ashton-under-Lyne and Greystoke which she suggests 'may serve to illustrate the essential unity of mediaeval life: the way in which education and work, imagery and drama were drawn together by the all- pervading direction of the Church'. See also Emile Mâle, *L'Art Religieux de la Fin du Moyen- Age en France*, Paris, 1931.

37 Three articles included in *Mysticism and Philosophical Analysis*, ed. Stephen Katz, New York: Oxford University Press, 1978, suggest this is so. Ninian Smart, Understanding Religious Ex- perience, 10-21; Nelson Pike, On Mystic Visions as Sources of Knowledge, 214-234; and George Mavrodis, Real v Deceptive Mystical Experiences, 235-58. In drawing the distinction between apophatic and kataphatic prayer phenomenologies in what follows, I am not suggest- ing that either one or the other is valid or more valid. Simply that there seem to be two tenden- cies depending on whether the mystic is in a receptive mode of consciousness, being drawn to- wards union with God or in an active mode being drawn towards serving in some divinely sug- gested specific activity.

divine communications may be felt but not seen or heard. The devil in this view is able to penetrate the psyche at the image or audio level, but is unable to penetrate to the fine point of consciousness where the divinity dwells all alone and makes his presence felt by impulses which reverberate in the affections. In Julian's day concern was expressed by other English mystics, the *Cloud* author and Walter Hilton in particular, about the kind of physical confirmation of divine presence which Richard Rolle's admirers appear to have been seeking in their devotional life[38]. Julian would probably have been aware of these misgivings.

On the other hand, there is another school of mystical thought, the kataphatic, which regards images as a necessary focus for a spiritual world, so that it can be recognised and become the object of discourse, providing always the image is not mistaken for the substance. They point out that Christ himself took on the image and substance of man while remaining the Divine Being.

In either case, whether it is the apophatic or kataphatic school in question, it seems to be recognised that a genuinely divine communication will be accompanied by a complete transformation of the individual. Ultimately it is upon a judgement based on this criterion that the authenticity of Julian's experiences as divinely instigated may rest. Julian herself recognises this criterion as we shall see.

However, at the time the crucifix had been placed at the foot of her bed, she really believed she was about to die. She fixed her eyes on the cross and everything else around it seemed dark, as she says, as if full of demons. The cross remains the focus of her attention and the suffering which is revealed to her in such graphic form makes her feel appalled that she could have ever wished for such an insight. She becomes conscious of the battle between divine love and the powers of destruction; the suffering is to bring about the victory of divine love. The cross becomes the symbol of divine love in this elemental struggle between good and evil. The mystery of evil is initially symbolised by the darkness which surrounds the cross; a mystery which vanishes in the light shed by the cross[39].

---

38   Richard Rolle (c. 1300-1349), *Fire of Love* (*Incendium Amoris*), trans. Clifton Wolters, Penguin Books, 1972, 23. Rolle speaks of the warmth (physical as well as spiritual), sweetness and melody (both spiritual) he experienced in contemplation. His influence was widespread as the manuscript tradition indicates. Some of his disciples thought he meant that physical experiences should be sought after as confirmation of God's love and were indicative of it. Taken out of context such suggestions as 'It is clear that those who love Christ with such fervour as never to want to sin again, not only will be free from punishment, but will rejoice for ever with the angel hosts' (66) might be misleading. He might give the impression that purgative discipline may be bypassed. Both the *Cloud* Author and Walter Hilton emphasise that purgative discipline is the foundation, the *sine qua non*, of contemplative prayer. See also J.P.H. Clark, 'Walter Hilton and 'Liberty of Spirit'', in *The Downside Review*, Vol. 96, 1978, 61 and n.1.

39   *Showings trans.*, *S.T.* chap. 2, 127/8 and *L.T.* chap. 3, 179/80.

However she becomes aware of the power of evil attempting by subterfuge to distract her attention from the cross which she has come to recognise as her life-line. She is tempted to lift up her eyes to the Father in heaven. She tells us she was eternally grateful that in the moment of temptation she deliberately chose Christ as her 'heaven'[40].

There is a moment at the conclusion of the first fifteen showings when Julian seemed to emerge from the semi-comatose condition of concentration and became aware of her pain which seems to have disappeared during the showings. At this moment the curate, who had been called in to be present at the moment of her death, must have become aware of some relaxation in her demeanour. He asks her how she is. She responds that she had been 'raving' and that she imagined blood had flowed from the crucifix at the foot of her bed. Julian is shocked by her own reflex denial of the 'reality' of the showings but notices that the curate is impressed by her reference to the bleeding Christ. She is perplexed and distressed. On the one hand she was fully convinced that they were not hallucinations. On the other how could she possibly convince the bystanders, let alone the curate, that the showings were 'real' and not just the product of a feverish nightmare, particularly as she had already admitted they were 'ravings'? She is conscious of the privilege she has been granted in being made as if present at Christ's crucifixion and the graces conferred on her. She wants to confess the sin she recognises in doubting the reality of such a grace. At this point she falls asleep and the final revelation begins[41].

This revelation opens with a physical attack by the fiend:

> As soon as I fell asleep, it seemed to me that the devil set himself at my throat, thrusting his face, like that of a young man, long and strangely lean, close to mine. I never saw anything like him; his colour was red, like a newly baked tile, with black spots like freckles, uglier than a tile. His hair was red as rust, not cut short in front, with side locks hanging at his temples. He grinned at me with a vicious look, showing me white teeth so big that it all seemed the uglier to me. His body and his hands were misshapen, but he held me by the throat with his paws, and wanted to stop my breath and kill me, but he could not[42].

Julian is not immediately sure the apparition is the devil. She is conscious only of her sense of guilt in denying Christ, of her fear and of the need to concentrate on the cross as a means of survival. It is only when she wakes from the dream and finds

---

40 *Showings trans.*, *S.T.* chap. 10 and 11, 143 and *L.T.* chap. 19, 211/12.

41 *Showings trans.*, *L.T.* chap. 66, 310/11 and *S.T.* chap. 21, 162/3. The annotations indicate the differences between the accounts in the Short and Long texts and cross-reference the Crit. Ed. ii, 631. The Long text account clarifies the earlier account.

42 *Showings trans.*, *L.T.* chap. 67, 311/2. The details of the 'showing' do not appear in the Short text account. See *ibid.*, *S.T.* chap. 21, 163.

that none of the bystanders had seen the smoke or been conscious of the stench, which for her had accompanied the apparition, that she recognises with certainty demonic activity and intervention[43].

Her description of the fiend, though she denies having seen the image before, may have been absorbed subconsciously from the iconography of the period. No specific connection has been established so that the source of the icon must remain conjectural. The mystery play which, as Mary Anderson demonstrated, influenced the transmission of images by the use of lively symbolic representations, seems to be a likely source. As J.B. Russell has suggested in his *Lucifer: The Devil in the Middle Ages*:

> The desire to impress audiences with grotesque costumes may have encouraged the development of the grotesque in art, for there were animal costumes with horns, tails, fangs, cloven hooves and wings; monster costumes with faces on buttocks, belly or knees. Masks, clawed gloves and devices to project smoke through human demon faces were also used[44].

The presence of smoke and its stench in the vision reinforces the possible connection with a dramatic production.

The use of effects was apparently quite common, as Mary Anderson's research demonstrates:

> On the stage plan of the Castle of Perseverance [a fifteenth-century morality play] it is specified that he who plays Belial shall have powder burning in pipes in his hands and ears when he goes to battle[45].

For Julian it was the presence of these effects in her vision which convinced her of the devil's identity.

---

43 *Showings trans.*, *L.T.* chap. 67, 312, corresponds with *S.T.* chap. 21, 163. In both accounts she is conscious of her temples being bathed after the devil's attack but before she becomes conscious of the smoke and the stench.

44 J.B. Russell, *Lucifer: The Devil in the Middle Ages*, Ithaca and London: Cornell University Press, 1984, 254, in a chapter on 'Lucifer on the Stage', 245-273. See also chapter 8, 'Lucifer in High Mediaeval Art and Literature', 208-244. The companion volumes are *The Devil: Perceptions of Evil from Antiquity to Primitive Christianity*, 1977, and *Satan: The Early Christian Tradition*, 1981, both by the same publisher. See also Neil Forsyth, *The Old Enemy: Satan and the Combat Myth*, Princeton University Press, 1987.

45 Mary Anderson, *Drama and Imagery in English Mediaeval Churches*, 172. See also R. Southern, *The Mediaeval Theatre in the Round. A Study of the Staging of the Castle of Perseverance and Related Matters*, London: Faber, 1957.

The recognition that her assailant was the devil is almost a moment of relief. The earlier vision had taught her that the purpose of the Passion had been to defeat the devil and demonstrate the devil's ultimate impotence in the face of love in the form of Christ's willing self-sacrifice. She actually laughed in an earlier showing, at the devil's frustration and impotence:

> But I did not see Christ laughing, but I know well that it was the vision he showed me that made me laugh, for I understood that we may laugh, to comfort ourselves and rejoice in God, because the devil is overcome[46].

The appearance of the devil in mystery plays provided an opportunity for a certain amount of burlesque. The burlesque is also reflected in the literature and iconography of the period[47]. The fourteenth-century *A Book for Daughters* of the Knight de la Tour-Laudry tells how St Brice saw a fiend writing down 'all the laughings that there were between the women at mass, and it happened that the parchment he wrote in was short, and he plucked hard to have it made longer with his teeth, and it scaped out of his mouth and his head had a great stroke against the wall', which made the saint laugh. Moreover, there is a full illustration of his story on a misericord in Ely Cathedral[48]. We may wonder perhaps whether Julian was familiar with the story.

Julian's mood of jollity was short-lived. The sixth and seventh revelations had already prepared her to experience the joy and sorrow which the single-minded service of Christ would bring. The sixth revelation had begun with Christ thanking her 'for your service and your labour in your youth' and then she had been given an idea of the bliss with which Christ rewarded service with the image of a splendid feast[49]. This image of bliss was followed in the seventh revelation by the experiencing of 'supreme spiritual delight' which then alternated some 'twenty times' with a sense of abandonment when left to herself. She describes the sense of abandonment:

> I felt that there was no ease or comfort for me except faith, hope and love, and truly I felt very little of this[50].

And she concluded that the purpose of this teaching was:

---

46 *Showings trans.*, *L.T.* chap. 12, 202 and *S.T.* chap. 8, 138.
47 Mary Anderson, *Drama and Imagery in English Mediaeval Churches*, 172.
48 *The Knight de la Tour-Laudry; A Book for Daughters*, ed. T. Wright, E.E.T.S. (O.S.) xxxiii, 1968, 41, quoted by Mary Anderson, *op.cit.*, 173, n.9. Stephen Knight in 'Chaucer's Religious Canterbury Tales' in *Mediaeval English Religious Literature*, 161, discussing the Physician's Tale as a 'strained harangue urging the control of daughters' suggests that this was a central anxiety of patriarchal families found in ballad, folk-tale, romance and novel because a father with only one daughter had reason to fear the loss of his familial property as well as his name.
49 *Showings trans.*, *L.T.* chap. 14, 201 and *S.T.* chap. 8, 138. The image of the feast only appears in the Long text account.
50 *Ibid.*, *L.T.* chap. 15, 204/5 and *S.T.* chap. 9, 139/40.

Some souls profit by experiencing this, to be comforted at one time, and at another to fail and to be left to themselves. God wishes us to know that he keeps us safe all the time, in sorrow and in joy; and sometimes a person is left to himself for the profit of his soul, although his sin is not always the cause[51].

The message is repeated and reinforced at the conclusion of the devil's nightmarish attack in the final revelation. She sees a vision of Christ residing in her soul which is set in the middle of her heart[52]. The knowledge of Christ's presence enables her to withstand the continued attacks of the demons whose 'mutterings', she thinks, are designed to drive her to despair. In the revelation she is reassured that what she has experienced is no hallucination[53] and she is provided with the opportunity to put the teaching into practice and see for herself that it is effective:

And our good Lord God gave me grace to trust greatly in him, and to comfort my soul by speaking words aloud, as I should have done to another person who was so belaboured. It seemed to me that this commotion [the devil's return with 'his heat and his stench' and 'all low muttering'] could not be compared with any natural event ... so that I thought privately to myself: Now you have plenty to do to keep yourself in the faith, so that you may not be caught by your enemies ... For it is so [setting my eyes on the ... Cross] that the fiend is overcome, as our Lord Jesus Christ said before[54].

It is unlikely that Julian will succeed in convincing all people that her experiences were not hallucinations induced by fever. Mediaeval imagery moreover may seem unsubtle to the modern mind. If however the limited resources of the fourteenth century to provide religious education to a largely illiterate community is taken into account, we may be more sympathetic to the use of dramatic symbolism and its encouragement by some Church authorities in order to educate their communities to recognise the difference between good and evil and the nature of evil.

In whatever ways modern readers may react to Julian's experiences, she herself is well aware that in her own time she will find it difficult to convince her fellow Christians not only that the experiences are not hallucinations but also that she is the vehicle chosen by God to convey a message of hope and encouragement[55]. She is conscious that she is a woman and 'unlettered'[56]; the latter claim is perhaps prudent

---

51 *Ibid.*, *L.T.* chap. 15, 205. The account is similar in *S.T.* chap. 9, 140.
52 *Ibid.*, *L.T.* chap. 68, 312/313 and *S.T.* chap. 22, 163/4.
53 *Ibid.*, *L.T.* chap. 69, 314/16 and *S.T.* chap. 23, 164.
54 *Ibid.*, *L.T.* chap. 69, 316 and chap. 70, 316 and *S.T.* chap. 23, 165 and 166 in modified form.
55 Julian is herself assured in the last showing by 'our Lord without voice and without opening of lips', 'know it well, it was no hallucination which you saw today'. *Showings trans.*, *L.T.* chap. 68, 314 and *S.T.* chap. 22, 164 and n.29. Modern sceptics are cited in the *Showings, Crit. Ed.*, 67, ns 166 and 167.
56 *Showings trans.*, *L.T.* chap. 2, 177, n.1.

modesty since her texts reveal her to be both theologically highly literate and also of the highest intelligence. Nevertheless, mystery continues to shroud Julian's early life and the source of her learning is still a matter of speculation. As a woman, in her day, she was not expected to be literate, despite the evidence that some were[57].

The care with which Julian unravels the mysteries surrounding her experiences, tends to confirm her *bona fides*. Despite her conviction that she has received singular graces, her reaction to them is one of genuine humility. The graces have been given to her not for herself alone but to share with her 'even-Christians'[58]. Her problematic is not conviction so much as understanding. She is conscious of the need for interpretation and of sure understanding before proceeding to disseminate the message.

In the Long text she provides an insight into the difficulty she experienced in understanding the meaning of one of the visions. It turns out to be of key importance and there is no mention of it in the Short text. She recalls it in the fifty-first chapter of the Long text as a 'wonderful example', the 'Lord and Servant' parable:

> And in this an inward spiritual revelation of the Lord's meaning descended into my soul, in which I saw that this must necessarily be the case, that his great goodness and his own honour require that his beloved servant, who he loved so much, should be highly and blessedly rewarded forever, above what he would have been if he had not fallen, yes, and so much that his falling and all the woe that he received from it will be turned into high, surpassing honour and endless bliss[59].

As Julian points out there is a double meaning in the role of the servant who is both Christ and Adam. However, on one level the theological meaning implied in her interpretation of the parable is that the Fall is not so much the result of deliberate disobedience as of the exercise of human-kind's God-given desire to serve spontaneously with impetuosity and without careful thought. Obedience is not, it seems, the virtue of 'not-doing'. It is rather the virtue of the prompt reaction of a nature created virtuous to the promptings of the Creator. The virtue does not prevent a person from losing sight of the Lord as the servant did when his impetuosity or reck-

---

57 *Showings*, Crit. Ed., 152, quotes John Gerson, *De Examinatio doctrinarum*, Pars 1 Consideratio 2a, 3a; *Omnia opera*, ed. L.E. Dupin, Antwerp, 1706, I. 14-16, writing a few years after the Long text was completed and probably with Catherine of Siena in mind:
'All women's teaching, particularly formal teaching by word and by writing, is to be held suspect unless it has been diligently examined, and much more fully than men's ... Because they are easily seduced, and determined seducers'.

58 *Showings trans.*, *L.T.* chap. 86, 342. See N.61 below, she begins the concluding quotation: 'I [God] am the foundation of your beseeching'. See also *S.T.* chap. 19, 157 as she discusses 'prayer'.

59 *Showings, trans.*, *L.T.* chap. 51, 269.

lessness led him to fall into a deep hole. In the parable she describes the circumstances in which the mishap occurred. He was about his master's business. The business was not apparently clearly defined as the servant is not expected to be privy to his master's intentions. As Julian points out the mishap makes the Lord more eager to reward the servant than if it had not occurred.

The point of the foregoing limited exegesis of the several layers of meaning in the parable is to illustrate the cogency of the insights which arise from Julian's mystical experience. As she says:

> The secrets of the revelation were deeply hidden in this mysterious example; and despite this I saw and understood that every showing is full of secrets[60].

The impact of her experience began a transformation which led Julian to retire to her anchorhold. The transformation developed as her meditations and further spiritual insights led to a fuller appreciation and understanding of their meaning. She was finally led to develop her Long text as a manifestation, the fruition, of her transformation:

> For truly I saw and understood in our Lord's meaning that he revealed it because he wants to have it better known than it is[61].

3. THE *CLOUD* AUTHOR AND WALTER HILTON

The anonymous author of the late fourteenth-century English spiritual classic, *The Cloud of Unknowing*, has not been unmasked despite a great deal of scholarly effort. One of the crosses mediaeval historians frequently have to bear, is the absence of surviving contemporary evidence to enable them to locate historical characters in their environments without a good deal of conjecture and exercise of imagination. Almost all that is known about this author is derived from his work which we can be reasonably sure dates from the late century[62]. The character of the man and his style suggests that in addition to the *Cloud of Unknowing*, he is also the author of what has become known as the *Cloud* canon[63]. It consists of two sorts of material; transla-

---

60 *Showings trans.*, *L.T.* chap. 51, 269.
61 *Showings trans.*, *L.T.* chap. 86, 342. Oliver Davies in 'Transformational Processes in the Work of Julian of Norwich and Mechtild of Magdeburg' in *M.M.T. in Eng.* 1992, 39-52, uses an apt expression about Julian's and Mechtild's experiences. They both engender a 'transformative textuality'.
62 See N.10 above.
63 Phyllis Hodgson, ed. *The Cloud of Unknowing and related treatises*, Salzburg: Institut für Anglistik und Amerikanistik, Universität Salzburg, 1982. The *Cloud* canon is discussed xii-xiv and the manuscripts xiv-xix. The manuscripts ascribe various Middle English titles to the works which are noted in Hodgson's work. She also records various conventionally used mod-

tions such as the influential *Mystical Theology* of Dionysius the Areopagite (alias the Pseudo-Dionysius and thought to be a Syrian monk writing in the late fifth century), 'Denis Hid Divinity' and *The Study of Wisdom*, which is a free translation of the twelfth-century mystic, Richard of St Victor's *Benjamin Minor*; in this class is also the adaptation of two of St Bernard of Clairvaux's sermons, as a *Treatise of Discernment of Spirits*, which also contains some original material which draws the borrowed matter together. In the other class are discussions of spiritual, contemplative practice based on traditional teaching but evidently illuminated by an extensive experience of spiritual direction[64]. The presentation of this latter material is sufficiently original for the author to be referred to by David Knowles as

> the most subtle and incisive, as well as the most original, spiritual writer in the English language[65].

The major work, the *Cloud of Unknowing*, purports to be addressed to a twenty-four-year old who is perhaps well known to the author[66]. We are not sure whether the person addressed is a fictional character invented to make the presentation of the material more vivid or a real person, perhaps someone within a religious order for whom our author had been made responsible[67]. We are told that there are four states or kinds of vocation in Christian life, Common, Special, Solitary and Perfect, and that the person addressed has been drawn through the earlier stages to the third stage, that of Solitary[68], and he is advised:

---

ern titles. I have used modern titles in the Prologue and Middle English titles (and shortened forms) in chapter 3 below which I have set out in N.1 of that chapter. The modern titles used in the Prologue and the abbreviations which are also used in the notes in chapter 3 below are as follows:
> The Cloud of Unknowing (CL)
> The Book of Privy Counselling (P.C.)
> An Epistle of Prayer (P)
> An Epistle of Discretion of Stirrings (ST)
> Denis Hid Divinity (HD)
> The Study of Wisdom (B.M.W.)
> The Treatise of Discerning of Spirits (S)

In the notes I have referred to Hodgson's Critical Edition in Middle English (H) by page and line number, and Abbot Justin McCann's (M) modernised translation, from which I have quoted, by chapter and page number. In relation to *The Study of Wisdom* see Roger Ellis, 'Author(s) Compilers, Scribes and Bible Texts: Did the Cloud-Author translate The Twelve Patriarchs?', in *M.M.T. in Eng.*, 1992, 193-221, in which he suggests *The Study of Wisdom* may not be the work of the *Cloud* Author.

64 In this class I have grouped the first four works listed in N.63 above.
65 M.D. Knowles, *The English Mystical Tradition*, London, 1961, 67, quoted by H. Intro., lvii.
66 *CL* H. 11.32.
67 H., l-li.
68 *CL* M. chap. 1, 5; H. 7.31-38.

In the which solitary form and manner of living thou mayest learn to lift up the
foot of thy love, and to step towards the state and degree of living that is perfect,
and the last state of all[69].

This stage may, 'by the grace of God', be begun here but 'it goes on for ever in the
bliss of Heaven!' The addressee is located in the general context of Christian life, a
series of stages through which every Christian will pass. In this series, real or not,
the twenty-four-year old 'solitary' is a mediaeval Everyman.

On the other hand, the style of address might suggest the author had a real individual
in mind. His discourse is composed of urging, encouraging, instructing, begging and
even cajoling the young man to fulfil his vocation. Cajoling too! The second chapter
of the *Cloud of Unknowing* begins

Look up now, thou weak wretch, and see what thou art. What are thou, and what
hast thou deserved, thus to be called by our Lord? What weary wretched heart
and sleeping in sloth is that, the which is not wakened with the drawing of this
love and the voice of this calling?[70].

and he goes on to urge the young man to 'Beware now, wretch, in this while of thine
enemy'[71], presumably 'the world, the flesh and the devil', at this stage of his development. Let him remember the graces that have been bestowed upon him and feel
'more wretched and cursed'[72] unless he is doing his very best to live up to his calling:

Do on then fast, I pray thee. Look forwards and let the backwards be. And see
what thou lackest and not what thou hast[73].

We shall probably never know whether this young man is fictional or not. A similar
character is addressed in the author's other major instructional work, *The Book of
Privy Counselling*[74]. Except as a historical puzzle it probably does not matter. Readers who have appropriated the *Cloud* author's teaching have identified themselves
with the young man and sympathised with him in his task of seeking 'perfection'.

The key phrase, which illuminates the young man's task in pursuing his calling to a
life of perfection, and which is also characteristic of the author's teaching, is the

---

69 *CL* M. chap. 1, 6; H. 8.15-17.
70 *CL* M. chap. 2, 6; H. 8.19-22.
71 *CL* M. chap. 2, 6; H. 8.23.
72 *CL* M. chap. 2, 6; H. 8.25.
73 *CL* M. chap. 2, 7; H. 8.34-35.
74 See H. 'Commentary', 175, linking the person addressed with the promise in *The Cloud* chap.
    74 (73.9-11), for which *Privy Counselling* might have been the fulfilment.

'look forward, not backward' injunction. There are several aspects of the *Cloud* author's teaching which might account for the tradition which identifies him as Walter Hilton, another late fourteenth-century English mystic who ended his days as an Augustinian canon in the community based at Thurgaton in Nottinghamshire[75]. However, apart from differences in the style and language of Hilton's major work, the *Scale of Perfection*, compared with those of the *Cloud* author's canon, it is the outlook, particularly the 'look forward, not backwards' theme of the *Cloud* author which distinguishes his teaching as different in perspective from Hilton's.

The trail which ascribes the *Cloud* canon to Hilton leads back to the ascription of James Greenhalgh, a Carthusian of Sheen (the same who annotated the Amherst MS in which the short version of Julian's *Showings* appears), in the fifteenth century, who annotated the *Cloud* MSS, Harleian 2373 and Pembroke 221[76]. He was possibly impressed by some characteristics of the *Cloud* author's teaching which suggest he was influenced by the Augustinian tradition which is also evident in Hilton's work. On the other hand, he may have been repeating an already well established Carthusian tradition of ascription. This explanation seems less likely because another Carthusian Richard Methley of Mount Grace who translated the Pembroke text, probably thought the *Cloud* was a Carthusian work, as a note at the end of the first chapter of this late fifteenth-century Latin translation suggests[77]. Whatever the origin of Greenhalgh's ascription, the comparison between the *Cloud* canon and Hilton is instructive because it throws into relief a significant difference in approach to the achievement of Christian perfection which was seen to be characterised by some change in consciousness which the ultimate mystical experience of unitive prayer precipitated. We shall return to the comparison with Walter Hilton in a moment.

The *Cloud* author anticipates the young man's question about the meaning of 'looking forward rather than backwards' and how he might 'lay hold' of the teaching[78]. The approach the *Cloud* author recommends is consciously paradoxical. The young man is to trample the imagination under foot and immerse himself in the darkness of the Cloud of Forgetting. He explains his meaning precisely:

---

[75] See H. Intro, ix-xii in which she discusses the problem of the *Cloud* Author's anonymity and the attribution of the *Cloud* canon to Walter Hilton by the Carthusian James Greenhalgh in the late fifteenth century. See John P.H. Clark's Introduction to Hilton's *The Scale of Perfection*, trans. and ed. by J.P.H. Clark and Rosemary Dorward, New York, Mahwah: Paulist Press, 1991, for a discussion of Hilton's life and work particularly 13-19 (hereafter this work is referred to in the notes as Clark/Dorward ed *Scale*; Book 1 as *Scale* 1 and Book 2 as *Scale* 2). See also Helen Gardner, 'Walter Hilton and the Authorship of *The Cloud of Unknowing*', in *Review of English Studies* 9, 1933, 129-47 and her 'The Text of the Scale of Perfection' in *Medium Aevum* 5, 1936, 11-30.

[76] H. Intro, xi. James Greenhalgh's (Grenehalgh) monogram appears on the Amherst MS also.

[77] *Ibid.*

[78] *CL* M. chap. 4, 11; H. 11.30-31.

And ween not, because I call it a darkness or a cloud, that it is any cloud congealed of the vapours that fly in the air, or any darkness such as is in thine house on nights, when thy candle is out ... [These can be pictured in the mind's eye] ... For when I say darkness, I mean a lack of knowing: as all thing that thou knowest not, or hast forgotten, is dark to thee; for thou seest it not with thy ghostly eye. And for this reason it is called, not a cloud of the air, but a cloud of unknowing; which is betwixt thee and thy God[79].

And in his customary style he goes on:

But now thou askest me and sayest: 'How shall I think on himself, and what is he?'. Unto this I cannot answer thee, except to say: 'I know not'. For thou hast brought me with thy question into that same darkness, and into that same cloud of unknowing, that I would thou wert in thyself. For of all other creatures and their works - yea and of the works of God himself - may a man through grace have fulness of knowing, and well can he think of them; but of God himself can no man think. And therefore I would leave all that thing that I can think, and choose to my love that thing that I cannot think. For why, he may well be loved, but not thought. By love may he be gotten and holden; but by thought neither[80].

Now there are a number of features of this teaching which bear similarity to the dichotomy which Walter Hilton draws in the second book of his *Scale of Perfection* between 'Reformation in faith' and 'Reformation in faith and feeling' as successive stages in spiritual development which are separated by a 'darkness'[81]. The 'Reformation in faith' stage is characterised by Hilton as concerned with Christ's life as man; with meditation about it and imitation of it. The result of this stage is to induce 'darkness' as a recognition of the gulf which separates the creature from the creator by virtue of human sinfulness. The 'darkness' is a state of sorrow and contrition for personal sinfulness which the desire and attempt to reform has brought to the forefront of consciousness. The grace which the darkness of remorse, sorrow and contrition may draw upon as a response in the divine mercy may enable the creature to change its perspective and recognise God not so much as the crucified Christ but as the triune God, with absolute power as the Creator of human kind out of a continuing love which sin cannot destroy. From the darkness of sorrow and contrition, the contemplative emerges into the light of love and forgiveness which is

---

79 *CL* M. chap. 4, 12; H. 13.11-22.
80 *CL* M. chap. 6, 14; H. 14.14-23.
81 Clark/Dorward ed *Scale* 2, chaps 5 and 24. The 'darkness' is like that of the 'night' which separates two days.

what Hilton characterises as a change of consciousness, 'reformation in faith and feeling'[82].

There are subtle differences here between the *Cloud* author and Hilton, both on the role of imagination and reason and on the way in which sin should be regarded. They are at one on the change of consciousness induced by the powerful experience of divine love in the 'darkness'. Hilton, like the *Cloud* author, is unable to describe what happens; only to recognise that something has happened. Indeed, Hilton goes so far as to say he has not himself experienced this second stage of spiritual development[83]. However it would seem this is the natural deprecation of the truly humble person who understands that though they may have made a beginning in the reformation in feeling, they still have far to go to resemble the perfect love of God, the depth of which they are only in part aware.

For Hilton the consciousness of sin and the sorrow and remorse which this induces seems to be the trigger mechanism which leads ultimately to the 'reformation in feeling' induced by a gratuitous revelation and experience of God's love. The *Cloud* author also acknowledges that the young man will 'feel sin a lump'[84]. The idea is similar to the *'pondus'* metaphor, originally a neoplatonic concept, which St Augustine of Hippo uses[85]. The gravitational force which holds body and soul on earth and entraps the spirit which cannot escape, is likened to the hold of sin. In the *Cloud* author's concept, this is what has to be left behind. In order to escape the pull of sin, everything must be forgotten, a state of detachment induced, so that the divine action can draw the spirit into the cloud of unknowing. Indeed sorrow and contrition, although good in themselves, must be deliberately forgotten. In both cases

---

82 Clark/Dorward ed *Scale* 2, chap. 24. Thus it is referred to as the 'good night' and a 'luminous darkness'. See J.P.H. Clark, 'The Lightsome Darkness' in *Downside Review*, Vol. 95, 1977 and G. Sitwell, 'Contemplation in *The Scale of Perfection*' in *Downside Review*, Vol. 67, 1949, 276-90 and Vol. 68, 1950, 21-34 and 271-89.

83 Clark/Dorward ed *Scale* 2, chap. 40, 280. Hilton expresses both a lack of experience and a degree of unfitness. The series of articles by J.P.H. Clark which appeared in the *Downside Review*, which are noted in the bibliography, illustrate Hilton's theological perceptiveness which belie his protestations.

84 *CL* M. chap. 40, 57; H. 43.29 and M. chap. 43, 60 and H. 45.33-35.

85 Augustine of Hippo, *Confessions*, trans. E.B. Pusey, London: J.M. Dent & Sons Ltd. Everyman ed., repr. 1953, Bk xiii.10, 315. See E.J. Stormon, 'The Spirituality of St Augustine' in *Christian Spiritual Theology. An Ecumenical Reflection*, ed. Noel J. Ryan, Melbourne: Dove Communications, 1976, 135/6. He points out that the Greek physical system Augustine inherited, useful as the imagery it provided was, did not meet all his needs. 'There was no room for a conversion of weights with a reverse of movement from downward to upward or vice versa'. Augustine believed that by God's grace there could be a change in direction from selfish love to love of God, from 'cupiditas' to 'caritas' so he resorted to the imagery of the two cities and two loves in the *City of God*, an earthly one and a heavenly one. See Augustine, *City of God*, trans. John Healy, ed. R.V.G. Tasker 2 vols, London: J.M. Dent & Sons Ltd., Everyman ed., repr. 1950, vol. 2, Bk xiv, chap. xxviii, 58.

the cleansing and peace producing effects of divine love are similar but the recommended paths to achieve these effects are different.

In the *Cloud* author's teaching there is some distrust of the 'purity' of sorrow and contrition as a sufficient remedy for sin. He is no less aware of the destructive effects of sin than Hilton. It is this very consciousness of its riveting effects that lead him to recommend his young charge to concentrate all his attention on a longing for God and to do so by uttering short, single word ejaculatory prayers such as 'God' or 'synne'[86]. The young man is to hurl himself across the no-mans land of detachment which lies between the cloud of forgetting and the cloud of unknowing, and batter the cloud of unknowing with longing darts of love[87]. He is to persist in hurling the longing darts of love until the cloud of unknowing is pierced. He suggests that the method he recommends will work quickly. God will not be slow to respond to the loving intention and pricks of the darts and admit the young man to the cloud of unknowing.

Despite this 'forward looking' method of contemplative prayer which the *Cloud* author suggests, he does not flinch from reminding the young man of the horrors of sin and the importunities of the world, the flesh and the devil[88]. He uses all the powers of reason and imagination to remind the young man of the world of sin he is to leave behind:

> The devil is a spirit, and of his own nature he hath no body, no more than hath an angel. But nevertheless, what time he or an angel shall take any body by leave of God, to make any ministration to any man in this life, according as the work is that he shall minister, thereafter in likeness is the quality of his body in some part... For when he appeareth in body, he figureth in some quality of his body what his servants be in spirit[89].

> Ensample of this may be seen in one case instead of all others ... in what bodily likeness the fiend appeareth, ever-more he hath but one nostril, and that is great and wide; and he will gladly cast it up so that a man may see in thereat to his brain up in his head. The which brain is nought else but the fire of hell[90].

---

86 *CL* M. chap. 36, 52; H. 40.25 and M. chap. 38, 54; H. 41.30-33 and M. chap. 7, 16; H. 15.30-35.

87 *CL* M. chap. 6, 14; H. 14.26-30 and M. chap. 7, 15; H. 15.38-16.1.

88 In the comparison between the *Cloud* Author and Hilton and in emphasising on the one hand the 'forward looking' approach of the *Cloud* Author, it must of course be remembered that the *Cloud* Author is addressing a person who is trying to move from the contemplative state of 'solitary' to 'perfect'. Hilton by contrast is perhaps addressing a much more general audience of both 'actives' and 'contemplatives'.

89 *CL* M. chap. 55, 75; H. 57.5-10 and 14-16.

90 *CL* M. chap. 55, 75; H. 57.17 and 20-24.

An Allegory of Human 'Animality'

The traditional symbol of the whale as the image of Hell, a recurrent nightmare in the mediaeval psyche. It seems to capture the notion of the self-consuming fate of those who do not rise above their own instinctive 'animality',

El Greco, Detail of the Adoration of the Name of Jesus, ca. 1580 (See Figure 3).

The allusion of the single nostril as characteristic of the devil has a long history. From St Gregory the Great's exegesis of Job in the *Morals on Job* onwards, the 'whale' has been treated as a figure of Satan[91]. From this developed the whale image as it appears in manuscript illuminations and other iconographical representations of *The Last Judgement*. Through a whale's gaping jaws the damned are thrust into a hell belching forth flames. The one nostril has some affinity with the whale's spout-hole, or spiracle. The *Golden Legend*, a popular manual, also known as the *Lombardica Historia*, mainly about the lives of Saints and thought to have been composed between 1255 and 1266, provides an example of the linking of the 'nose' with the idea of 'discretion'. The name of St Apollinaris, thought to be the martyred first bishop of Ravenna, is derived from 'apollo', meaning 'admirable' and 'naris', nostril, signifying discretion, and thus indicating a man of amazing discretion and prudence. The same idea occurs in St Bridget's *Revelations*:

> His nose is cutt awai for all discrecion is taken fro him, bi þe whicke he saild deme bitwene sin and vertue[92].

The *Cloud* author's young man may not have been familiar with the symbolism of the nostril reference for he goes on to explain:

> For that division that is in a man's nose bodily, and the which separateth the one nostril from the other, betokeneth that a man should have discretion ghostly, and know how to dissever the good from the evil, and the evil from the worse, and the good from the better, ere that he gave any full judgement of anything that he heard or saw done or spoken about him. And by a man's brain is ghostly under-stood imagination; for by nature it dwelleth and worketh in the head[93].

Though the *Cloud* author's teaching is about divine love, the symbolism of Christ's Passion as evidence of it is always in the background. The pain and horror of the Crucifixion are projected into the punishment which is the penalty for sin, a cruel and lingering death which is without end. The fear of hell is rarely absent from the mediaeval imagination and one can conceive the young man who receives the *Cloud* author's teaching, contemplating the fires of hell which he wants to forget as he

---

91   See for example Fig. 1, El Greco, Hell. (Detail from Fig. 3: The Adoration of the Name of Jesus, c.1580) which I have named 'The Allegory of Animality', graphically reflects this ico-nography still current in the sixteenth century. The whale, as the symbol for Hell is also present in Fig. 2.

92   *CL* H., Commentary, 171. 57/21 also quotes *St Bridget's Revelations* (I, 23, MS Cotton Claudius B I, f.25vᵃ). For the *Golden Legend* see *Oxford Dictionary of the Christian Church*, 579. See page 31 below for Ignatius of Loyola's acquaintance with the same work. There is an interesting discussion of Bridget of Sweden (1303-1373) by M. Manion in the article 'Women in the Catholic Tradition' in *Christian Spiritual Theology*, *op.cit.*, 250-56 and n.1, 262, for works on St Bridget. See Bibliography for editions of her *Revelations*.

93   *CL* M. chap. 55, 76; H. 57.35-41.

attempts to precipitate his spirit across the weightless space between the cloud of forgetting and the cloud of unknowing attached to those longing darts of love.

4. A VIEW OF CERVANTES' WORLD

There is a note of sadness about Don Quixote de la Mancha which belies the good-humoured and comic parody with which Cervantes mocks the chivalric ideal of a world like Chaucer's which has passed but to which some of his countrymen still clung. Is it a passing which Cervantes regretted or was it a fantasy which never ex-isted in fact? These are questions which Cervantes leaves open for his readers.

Cervantes published the first part of *Don Quixote* in 1605 and the second part ten years later. The idea had apparently come to him in prison. In this respect it is simi-lar to the *Spiritual Canticle* of John of the Cross, which was also conceived in prison. However, in Cervantes' case, the idea might have arisen as a reflection about the line which distinguishes guilt from innocence. The first part of *Don Quixote* was published when Cervantes was fifty-seven. It was an achievement which came late and crowned his life, and perhaps it may be regarded as a reflection on the passing of Spain's 'Golden Age' and his own youthful hopes. The ideals which envigoured Spanish achievements in that century also, like the Armada, ultimately foundered when confronted by reality[94]. Don Quixote's final return to sanity coincides with the approach of death. It is precipitated by his eventual disillusionment in part two[95]. The symbolism of the tragi-comedy gives the story its quality of being 'serieux'.

The chivalric ideal survived in Spain longer than in other parts of Europe. It had perhaps been kept alive by the long crusade against the Moors which had been con-tinuous from the eighth century until 1492 when the last Moorish stronghold at Gra-nada fell. In literature the picaresque novel with the theme of the anti-hero had chal-lenged the ideal[96] which, for example, two centuries earlier had charmed Chaucer when he encountered and translated *Roman de la Rose* while in France[97]; but still at the turn of the century the chivalric ideal captivated Ignatius of Loyola until his encounter with the lives of the Saints changed the focus of his aspirations[98].

---

94 Riley ed. *Don Quixote*, xiii. It was being unseated and defeated in combat which consolidated Don Quixote's 'disillusionment' (Part II, chap. 64).

95 *Ibid.*, Part II, chap. 74. There is a certain irony in the closing scene when Don Quixote (now Alfonso Quixano, the Good) has to say to his friends, 'I feel, gentlemen, the quick approach of death: let us be serious, and bring me a confessor, and a notary to draw my will', 1047.

96 *Ibid.*, viii/ix.

97 Coghill ed., *Canterbury Tales*, 12, a thirteenth century French poem begun by Guillaume de Lorris and later completed by Jean de Meun. See *The Oxford Companion to English Literature*, page 842.

98 Joseph Tylenda, trans. and commentary, *A Pilgrim's Journey: The Autobiography of Ignatius of Loyola*, Wilmington, Delaware: Michael Glazier, 1985, 12 (hereafter referred to as Ignatius

Don Quixote, though represented by Cervantes as driven insane by his addiction to chivalric literature which led him to believe it was literally true, nevertheless reflects the grandeur and self-sacrificing innocence of the chivalric ideal. The folly lies in attempting the practical application of the ideal and believing that it could be attained. Cervantes may well have intended to parody with some savagery the chivalric literature which had been and remained so popular in Spain and elsewhere in Europe but the parody was not so much aimed at the ideal as at its literal application and the flight from reality which that entailed. He raises the question, however, whether an ideal which is ultimately unattainable in the real world is worth pursuing for its own sake. In contrast to the mystics, he might ultimately not have thought so, though he leaves it as an open question.

The delight which Cervantes, by his art, gave to his contemporaries[99] and to many generations since is evidence not only of Don Quixote's ingenuous and delightfully imaginative world but also the serious question about the world which fantasy poses. In the kind of world which Cervantes recognised it is not really surprising that some of the greatest Christian mystics found their inspiration. The possibility of glory and outstanding achievement by pursuing ideals to their ultimate end was perhaps inherent in Spanish history and realised in that Golden Age which Cervantes saw passing away. The question which both Cervantes and the mystics pose is about the nature of the ideal and the relationship between ideals and fantasy.

In its mediaeval form the chivalric ideal was never realisable. The object of the knight's adoration is remote and unattainable; a smile is the only reward the knight can hope for in all his deeds of valour. The pursuit, even if unrecognised, is sufficient reward. The code of behaviour is strict. The dreams which the hidalgo, Ignatius of Loyola, entertained during his convalescence from the wounds he received at Pamplona were of this kind[100]. Unlike Don Quixote he found his dreams of chivalry unsatisfying. Don Quixote eventually arrived at the same conclusion but too late to do other than accept it.

---

of Loyola, *Autobiography* ed. Tylenda). Ignatius recalls he was an 'avid reader of books of worldly fiction, commonly called chivalrous romances'. He tells us (23/24) that while on his way to Montserrat his thoughts were full of exploits he might perform such as those he read of 'in Amadis de Gaule and other like books'. Cervantes writes in chap. 74 of Riley ed. *Don Quixote*, 1046: 'I am now an utter enemy of Amadis of Gaul, and the innumerable rabble of his descendants: now all the histories of knight-errantry are to me odious and profane'. As of course they seem to have become to Ignatius of Loyola following his conversion. See N.100 below.

99 Riley ed. *Don Quixote*, vii. There were five or six editions (two of them unauthorised) by the end of the year 1605. As early as June 1605 the figure of Don Quixote was well enough known to appear in a festival masquerade in Valladolid and then in numerous other places as far afield as Cuzco in Peru and Heidelberg. *The Oxford Companion to English Literature* records that it was translated into English as early as 1617.

100 Ignatius of Loyola, *Autobiography* ed. Tylenda, 8, 9 and 10, 14-16.

In part two of the book Don Quixote enjoys the recognition which his fantastic exploits in part one had brought[101]. Fantasy, as it were, feeds upon fantasy. The world he inhabits enjoys the fantasy and encourages its pursuit. We may ask whether in this development there is some veiled questioning of the relationship between faith and fantasy and the nexus which links the two. It is perhaps doubtful whether Cervantes' admiring readers in his own day would have recognised the question in this form. It is the skill of great artists to present a multi-layered reality which enables so many various interpretations to be placed upon their work. The story remains always enjoyable and each individual's imagination is free to enter into it and ask what it means or simply enjoy it as a good tale.

In Cervantes' creation of Don Quixote we may see the confrontation of the mediaeval chivalric ideal with the Renaissance spirit which questions a received view of material reality as ephemeral, in which humanity and the world are 'nothing' and God is 'everything'. The idea which Chaucer subscribed to, of life as a pilgrimage, is certainly different from Don Quixote's notion of life's pilgrimage. What seems to be new is the note of disillusionment and the search for some other ideal towards which to aspire and to provide life's inspiration. It is a new world in which the mystics are also seeking to reinterpret the mediaeval inheritance in the light of their own mystical experiences. Chaucer's world despite its incongruities was a world of hope, Cervantes' despite its courage, of disillusion; they perhaps mark the beginning and the end of a 'Renaissance' pilgrimage whose artistic achievement alone remains unquestionable.

5. IGNATIUS OF LOYOLA

Ignatius of Loyola, as he is known to history, was born in 1491[102] in the Basque province of Guipúzcoa, the year before Columbus set sail on the voyage on which he discovered the New World, and in which the last Moorish stronghold in Spain capitulated.

Basque families take their names from their estates and Ignatius was born into one of the great families of ancient lineage of the province which were yet small landholders. The Loyola (Õnaz) escutcheon incorporates seven bars which reflect the chivalric tradition into which Ignatius was born. It commemorates a famous victory

---

101 Riley ed. *Don Quixote*, xiii, remarks of Part II: 'Others have taken charge of his game and he is no longer in control'.

102 There is some uncertainty about the date of Ignatius' birth (see Tylenda's commentary to the *Autobiography* I, 7) since the records were destroyed in a fire (*ibid.*, intro. xv). He received the name Inigo by which he was known until he adopted Ignatius while studying in Paris (*ibid.*, intro. xiv).

at the battle of Beotibar in 1321 in which seven grandchildren of the Loyola and Õnaz connection distinguished themselves[103].

Ignatius' Loyolan pedigree was fired in the household of the Royal Treasurer at Arévalo in the heart of Castile where his father was invited to send one of his sons to be educated[104]. He emerged with all the refinement of a Spanish hidalgo. Ignatius' conduct at the siege of Pamplona illustrated his proficiency as a soldier as well as his strength of character and leadership. In a memoir which he reluctantly dictated in 1553, some thirty-two years after he was wounded at the siege, he recalls how he was able to persuade the garrison commander to fight on in the Citadel in the hope that reinforcements would arrive after the city had already opened its gates without a fight to admit the French invading force[105].

The wounds he received were serious. He was struck by a shot that passed between his legs shattering the right one and leaving gaping flesh wounds in the left. The period of recovery and convalescence which followed proved a turning point in his life[106].

We take up his story on the road between Montserrat and Manresa in March 1522. Dressed as a beggar, he was overtaken by a constable in the service of the procurator of the monastery from which he had only recently departed. The official had come to investigate the story of a beggar who had been found wearing Ignatius' fine clothes. Ignatius had arrived at Montserrat as a pilgrim-hidalgo. He departed as a beggar-pilgrim having hung up his sword at the monastery[107].

The change of clothes was symbolic of a spiritual transformation which had overtaken him during his convalescence and his brief, three-day sojourn at the Monastery of Montserrat[108]. There he had unburdened himself with a detailed written con-

---

103 P. Leturia, *Inigo de Loyola*, trans. A.J. Owen S.J. Reissued, Chicago: Loyola University Press, 1965, 27-29. Philip Caraman S.J. *Ignatius Loyola. A biography of the Founder of the Jesuits*, San Francisco: Harper & Row, 1990, 3. There is a discrepancy about the date. Leturia puts the year as 1321 (following G. Henao-Villalta, *Averiguaciones de las antigüedades de cantabria ... a honor y gloria de San Ignacio de Loyola, cantebro de padre y madre*. New ed. corrected by Fr. Miguel Villalta of Las Escuelas Pias. Tolosa, 1894, 7 vols, vi, 274ff.). Caraman suggests 1324. Leturia records: 'The paladins in the fray were Gil Lopez de Õnaz and Juan Perez de Loyola along with his five brothers'. They were grandchildren of the marriage (1261) between Inés de Loyola and Lope Garcia de Õnaz. Caraman (3) suggests this union of the houses of Loyola and Õnaz marks the emergence of the Loyola family. He further suggests that since Basque families took their name from their estates the names of Õnaz and Loyola alternate among the children of the same parents from the time the two houses were united by marriage.
104 Caraman, *Ignatius Loyola*, 10-16.
105 Ignatius of Loyola, *Autobiography* ed. Tylenda 1 and 2, 7-10 and commentary.
106 *Ibid.*, 2-5, 9-12 with accompanying commentary.
107 *Ibid.*, 18, 27 and commentary.
108 *Ibid.*, 5-12 and commentary for Ignatius' 'conversion'.

fession of his former sins and was given a copy of the *Exercitatorio de la Vida Espiritual* by his confessor, Jean Chanon. It was written by a former and most distinguished abbot of the Benedictine Monastery Garcia Jiménez de Cisneros, of whom Ignatius may have heard during his time in the household of the Royal Treasurer. The idea for Ignatius' own *Spiritual Exercises* may well have germinated from this influence, which he no doubt absorbed during his stay at Manresa[109].

The town of Manresa is located below Montserrat. We are not sure why Ignatius stayed there. Evidently he wished to find a quiet place to prepare spiritually for the pilgrimage to Jerusalem he had decided to undertake. In any event his experiences at Manresa shaped the course of his spiritual development and became the source for the direction of his future teaching[110].

His manner of life there may have been influenced by his reading about Saint Honofrio[111]. One of the books which Ignatius had had at his disposal during his convalescence at Loyola was a Spanish translation of that same *Lives of the Saints or Legenda Aurea* with which the *Cloud* Author may have been familiar. It had appeared in Spanish as late as 1480. Among the Saints whose lives were attractively portrayed in that book was Honofrio. He is said to have lived in such a narrow cave that he had to crawl in and out on all fours. Ignatius did not emulate, as has been suggested, Honofrio's example in this respect. Apparently he sometimes withdrew to a rock which overhung the river Cardoner to pray and make notes. On the other hand, he may well have emulated the Saint's appearance. Apparently when Abbot Paphnutius visited Honofrio in the Thebaid, he thought he had met some unknown species of wild beast and fled. Such was Ignatius' state of dishevelment that the former courtier was unrecognisable in appearance. However, his manners gave him away and fantastic stories began to circulate about him[112].

Ignatius' dishevelled appearance matched the spiritual traumas he began to experience once the period of initial exhilaration and peace faded. All his life he was to remember the prayer he then made:

> Help me, Lord, for I find no remedy among men nor in any creature. If I thought I could find help, no trial would be too hard for me to endure. Show me, Lord, where I can obtain help: and if I have to follow a little dog to obtain the cure I need, I am ready to do just that.

---

109 *Ibid.*, 17, 25-26. See Tylenda's commentary page 25. See also Caraman, *Ignatius Loyola*, 34-36.

110 Caraman, *Ignatius Loyola*, 33-42.

111 Ignatius of Loyola, *Autobiography* ed. Tylenda 19, 28/29 merely mentions that he deliberately allowed his hair and nails to grow because he had previously been meticulous about his appearance. Tylenda, page 28, in his commentary refers to 'Saint Onuphorius or Humphrey'. See also Caraman, *Ignatius Loyola*, 37.

112 Caraman, *Ignatius Loyola*, 38.

His extremity was reflected in thoughts of suicide[113].

In the autumn of 1522 he was found unconscious at a shrine of Our Lady[114]. He had contracted a severe fever and had he not been found would almost certainly have died. The breakdown in his health reflects the austerity of his life rather than his state of mind. Prior to the illness he had managed to shake off his scruples quite suddenly and was never troubled by them again[115]. He also received another sudden illumination when at prayer on the banks of the Cardoner. In his own words

> the eyes of his understanding were opened and though he saw no vision he understood and perceived many things, numerous spiritual things as well as matters touching on faith and learning[116].

He understood God was making his presence felt in his life, acting, as he explained later, 'like a schoolmaster with a child'[117]. He seems to have been given a total mystical view of the world with a perception that all things proceed from God and returned to their Trinitarian origin[118]. He perceived that all the mysteries of the Christian faith interlocked. He could not put into words all that he had been given to understand, but he was possessed of a new understanding and a desire to share his insights[119].

By the time Ignatius died in 1556, he had worked out his vocation over the 34 years remaining to him, and his spiritual experiences developed out of those initial inspirations. The directional thrust of *Spiritual Exercises* in particular were founded upon the recognition of his insights during the convalescence at Loyola and subsequently confirmed by the traumas of Manresa. As Philip Caraman has suggested:

> It was through his Spiritual Exercises, a small book which condensed his ideas on the spiritual life, that he influenced the course of European education and cul-

---

113 Ignatius of Loyola, *Autobiography* ed. Tylenda 23 and 24, 32/33.

114 *Ibid.*, 32, 39. He fell ill again in the winter of 1522 which he refers to in 34, 41/42. His penances at Manresa seem to have permanently affected his health.

115 *Ibid.*, 25, 34.

116 *Ibid.*, 30, 38/39.

117 *Ibid.*, 27, 35/36.

118 *Ibid.*, 28, 36, 'his understanding was raised on high, so as to see the Most Holy Trinity under the aspect of three keys on a musical instrument'. As Tylenda remarks in his commentary (36) 'Ignatius was given to understand how the three distinct persons in the Godhead could form a single unity. Each key has its own individual sound, but when the three keys are played together, each key without losing its own distinctiveness, contributes itself and together the three form a unified harmonic chord'. The vision seems to have stayed with Ignatius for the rest of his life (*Ibid.*, 28, 36/37).

119 *Ibid.*, 29, 37/38. Ignatius records a number of other divine insights he received during this period.

ture for two centuries and brought about a revolution in the Catholic world that is not a spent force today. The impact of the manual made it possible not only for his first followers but for future generations of men and women to live as he had done, by the same personal experience of life[120].

As Roland Barthes has suggested Ignatius was a logothete[121], the inventor of a new language of prayer, which paradoxically enabled the skilled and less skilled practitioners to understand the wordless cadences of their being. It is a suggestion we must perhaps qualify; the mystery of this 'small book' in which the 'logothete' reveals 'his invention' is also the mystery of the echoes and cadences of historical process and tradition.

6. JOHN OF THE CROSS

The occasion for the composition of perhaps the greatest of all mystical works, the *Spiritual Canticle* of St John of the Cross, was paradoxically one of the least impressive episodes in the history of the deeply spiritual and visionary Carmelite order. John was thirty-five when on the night of December 2, 1577, he was seized on the orders of Jerónimo Tostado, the visitator of the Carmelite order, who had been appointed by the chapter of the order convened at Piacenza[122], two years earlier, in May 1575, to eliminate some apparent problems resulting from the activities of the discalced friars. He was imprisoned in a monastery at Toledo in a cell some six feet

---

120 Caraman, *Ignatius Loyola*, vii. The *Spiritual Exercises* were begun at Manresa and developed continuously thereafter during his life. They received Pope Paul III's approval in 1548. The critical edition as it appears in the MHSJ *Monumenta Ignatiana* Series 2, Madrid, 1919, is the basis of the translation by Louis J. Puhl, S.J., *The Spiritual Exercises of St Ignatius*, Chicago: Loyola University Press, 1951, used in this study (see v, n.2). The *Constitutions of the Society of Jesus* (trans. George E. Ganss, St. Louis, 1970) were finally completed by 1550. See Caraman, *Ignatius Loyola*, 167. *Discernment Log-Book, The Spiritual Diary of Ignatius of Loyola*, trans. Joseph A. Munitz, London, 1987 comprising two notebooks covering the periods 2 February to 12 March 1544 and 13 March to 27 February 1545 respectively. The full texts did not become available until 1934. The *Autobiography* was produced reluctantly at the request of his close associates. It was related to Luis Gonçalves da Câmara in three separate sessions and dictated by him to scribes. The first two in Spanish, the third in Italian. See Joseph N. Tylenda, S.J. (ed.) *A Pilgrim's Journey: The Autobiography of Ignatius of Loyola*, Wilmington, Delaware: Michael Glazier, 1985. See the introduction, ix-xiv for discussion of the circumstances of its production. There are also some seven thousand letters to persons of all degrees, see Caraman, *Ignatius Loyola*, vii. See in particular J.N. Tylenda, S.J. (ed.) *Counsels for Jesuits: Selected Letters and Instructions of Saint Ignatius of Loyola*, Chicago: Loyola University Press, 1985, Introduction ix, x.
121 Roland Barthes, *Sade, Fourier, Loyola*, trans. Richard Miller, New York: Hill and Wang, 1976, 3.
122 John of the Cross, *Selected Writings*, ed. with an Intro by Kieran Kavanaugh, O.C.D. New York, Mahwah: Paulist Press, The Classics of Western Spirituality, 1987, 17ff. (hereafter referred to as John of the Cross *S.W.* ed. Kavanaugh).

by ten, with little light, for approximately nine months. Although John was a small man in stature, four feet eleven inches, the confinement was rigorous. His imprisonment was accompanied by all the disciplinary harshness of religious orders of the time, flogging, fasting on bread and water and a harassment designed to make him renounce the Teresian way of life, the discalced reform[123].

John's imprisonment was a bi-product ultimately of the problems and misunderstandings which surrounded the implementation of the reforms of the order, conceived by St Teresa of Avila, in a climate of conflicting interpretations of jurisdiction by Philip II of Spain and the Papacy[124]. At the time he was seized, John of the Cross was acting as spiritual guide to Teresa's nuns at the Monastery of the Incarnation at Avila. He had been in the position for five years, having hitherto been encouraged by Teresa to assist in establishing the first of the reformed communities of friars in 1568 at a lonely spot in Castile called Duruelo, that is some nine years before his incarceration. It was at this time, 1568, that he changed his religious name from Juan de Santo Matia, which he had originally taken when he entered the order in 1563, to Juan de la Cruz[125].

A number of factors combined to create a situation in which he underwent a profound spiritual transformation. The circumstances of his imprisonment reacted with his aesthetic and intellectual gifts, the emerging gifts of spiritual insight and his vocation to a contemplative life (Prior to meeting with Teresa of Avila he had been considering moving to the Carthusians to pursue a more ascetic and eremitic form of contemplative life.)[126].

The deprivations of the incarceration were perhaps of pivotal importance for they plunged him into the dark night of utter destitution. It was a destitution for which the poverty and struggles of his early life had hardly prepared him, for he was deprived of the use of the physical and spiritual senses to which his being had become accustomed. He had no recourse but to live blindly in faith and hope and love, if he was not to deny his convictions. The meaning of the theological virtues seem to have been burned into his psyche during this time. The experiences he received of the unitive dimension of divine love in this dark night were like a living flame. He conceived of his experience in the biblical and bridal images of the *Song of Songs* which he knew by heart[127]. Stanzas 27 and 28 of the *Spiritual Canticle* in which the Bride speaks reflect this influence:

---

123 *Ibid.*, 19.
124 *Ibid.*, 18.
125 *Ibid.*, 14.
126 *Ibid.*, 10.
127 *Ibid.*, 213.

There he gave me his breast;
And I gave myself to him,
Keeping nothing back;
There I promised to be his bride.

Now I occupy my soul
And all my energy in his service;
I no longer tend the herd,
Nor have I any other work
Now that my every act is love[128].

He composed the first thirty-one stanzas of the *Spiritual Canticle* while he was imprisoned[129]. The remaining nine stanzas which now complete the forty stanzas of the CB redaction of the *Spiritual Canticle* in the canon of John's works, were composed after his escape from imprisonment[130].

The poetic form in which John of the Cross expressed not only the final stages of unitive love but his whole journey of spiritual development, while a reflection of the literary culture of the times, was a natural vehicle for him to express the rhythms and affective pulse of his whole spiritual experience[131]. His prose writing was incidental to the ministry he undertook after his imprisonment; the *Ascent of Mount Carmel* and the *Dark Night* were never finished. His commentaries were developed as a result of requests for explanations of his poetic work which had been composed to fulfil his own inner and overflowing need to express his thanks for the gift of divine love. In his commentary on Stanza 27 of the *Spiritual Canticle* he muses:

> What then will be the soul's experience among such sovereign graces! How she will be dissolved in love! How thankful she will be to see the breasts of God given to her with such supreme and generous love! Aware that she has been set among so many delights, she makes a complete surrender of herself and gives Him the breast of her will and love. She experiences this surrender of her soul in the way the bride did in the Canticle...[132].

---

128 *Ibid.*, 225.

129 *Ibid.*, 213. Strictly thirty stanzas were composed during his imprisonment as Stanza 11 was added later.

130 *Ibid.*, 214.

131 *Ibid.*, 32, refers to views of Federico Ruiz in the general introduction San Juan de la Cruz: *Obras Completas*, Madrid: Editorial de Espiritualidad, 1980, 14, and notes 'His works reveal a kind of sublime theological daring ... he did not think it unsuitable to turn to the use of symbols as a most effective means of explaining and communicating a *living knowledge* of the mystery of God'.

132 *Ibid. Spiritual Canticle* 27.2. See Carolyn Walker Bynum, *Jesus as Mother: Studies in the Spirituality of the High Middle Ages*, Berkeley: University of California Press, 1982, 110-169,

His teaching develops out of the commentaries in which he explains and expands the images in which his poetry is cast. The theme is divine love and the stages through which the relationship of unitive love develops. He begins chapter One of Book One of the *Dark Night* with the following explanation:

> Souls begin to enter this dark night when God, gradually drawing them out of the state of beginners (those who practise meditation on the spiritual road), begins to place them in the state of proficients (those who are already contemplatives) so that by passing through this state they might reach that of perfect, which is the divine union of the soul with God[133].

John of the Cross' treatment of the higher stages of spiritual development reveals the acute discernment with which he must have reflected upon his own dispositions as he gradually eliminated all concern with responses of his own being, both sensual and spiritual, to focus entirely on the being of the divine loved one. Thus in chapter five of Book Two of the *Dark Night* he explains:

> This dark night is an inflow of God into the soul that purges it of its habitual ignorances and imperfections ... Through this contemplation, God teaches the soul secretly and instructs it in the perfection of love without it doing anything or understanding how it happens[134] ... Yet a doubt arises! Why, if it is a divine light (for it illumines souls and purges them of their ignorances) does one call it a dark night. There are two reasons why this divine wisdom is not only night and darkness for the soul, but also affliction and torment. First, because of the height of divine wisdom, which exceeds the capacity of the soul. Second, because of the soul's baseness and impurity; and on this account the wisdom is painful, afflictive and also dark for the soul[135].

His story is about the development of a relationship in which, paradoxically, the soul is a passive partner; in which the consciousness of self is mysteriously displaced by one in which life revolves upon the divine will as the apogee of all that is bountiful and joyful. The agony associated with the displacement of self shades into a longing for the loved one to fill the void in consciousness which displacement of self creates. In turn the desperate longing of the passive nights shades into moments of betrothal and the agonies of anticipation with which that part of the relationship is characterised and in which the final traces of human weakness are eliminated. Finally the marriage takes place. The soul then enters the peace of the marriage relationship which is marred only by being confined to temporal existence and the longing for its

---

not specifically in relation to John of the Cross but to the tradition of which this passage seems a reflection.

133 *Ibid. The Dark Night* (hereafter *DN*) Bk One 1.1.
134 *Ibid.*, *DN* Bk Two 5.1.
135 John of the Cross, *S.W.* ed. Kavanaugh, *DN* Bk Two 5.2.

consummation in the glory of eternity when the divine groom is met at last face to face; a spiritual relationship is to be finally fulfilled in the resurrection of the whole human being, the body-spirit 'suppositum', in the presence of the being of the triune God. In commenting on the first verse of the *Living Flame of Love*:

> O living flame of love
> That tenderly wounds my soul
> In its deepest center! Since
> Now you are not oppressive,
> Now consummate! if it be your will:
> Tear through the veil of this sweet encounter[136]

he says,

> The soul now feels that it is all inflamed in divine union and that its palate is all bathed in glory and love, that in the most intimate part of its substance it is flooded with no less than rivers of glory, abounding in delights, and that from its bosom flow rivers of living water [Jn. 7:38] which the Son of God declared will rise up in such souls. Accordingly it seems, because the soul is so vigorously transformed in God, so sublimely possessed by them, and arrayed with such rich gifts and virtues, that it is singularly close to beatitude - so close that only a thin veil separates it ... Such is the glory this flame of love imparts that each time it absorbs and attacks, it seems that it is about to give eternal life and tear the veil of mortal life...[137].

The secret of John's story seems to lie in the depths of deprivation in which his faith in the presence of, and dependence upon, the divine love is honed and experienced not as 'gift' only but in the Holy Spirit as 'giver'. The importance of the deprivation and detachment which characterises the active and passive nights in his teaching gives it the dour and frightening character of a crucifixion. Commenting in Book One, Chapter 8:2 of the *Dark Night* he says:

> The first purgation or night is bitter and terrible to the senses. But nothing can be compared to the second, for it is horrible and frightening to the spirit[138].

Yet the deprivation which detaches the human soul from dependence on all sensible and spiritual reality is only endurable because of a concomitant growth in faith and trust which blossoms through unbearable longing for peace and fulfilment.

---

136 *Ibid.*, *The Living Flame of Love* (hereafter *LF*), 293, stanza 1.
137 *Ibid.*, *LF* stanza 1, Commentary 1.
138 *Ibid.*, *DN* Bk One 8.2.

Those seeking to follow John's teaching are left with the perplexing unknown of whether they can face the sacrifice which will be demanded of them. In *Dark Night*, Book One, Chapter 10:2 he comments:

> If there is noone to understand these persons, they either turn back and abandon the road or lose courage, or at least they hinder their own progress because of their excessive diligence in treading the path of discursive meditation[139].

It is in the progress along the unknown path which John as a spiritual director sought to assist for he recognised that informed guidance was essential and that it was his mission to provide while he could. In his lifetime he did this in a series of supervisory and teaching roles. The success of his activities as a spiritual director were to be complemented by the growth of a following which absorbed and explained his writings.

The importance of his life and work are recorded in the recognition his teaching has been accorded in the mystical theology of the Christian Church. The authenticity of the tradition is confirmed by the official recognition of John of the Cross' life and work. He was beatified in 1675. Canonised in 1726 he was ultimately declared a Doctor of the Church by Pius XI in 1926, the 'doctor spiritualis'.

It has been suggested above that the secret of his particular charisms lay in the deprivation of imprisonment in which he experienced the realisation of divine love as the fusion of giver and gift by participation in the unitive love of the Triune God, the love of the father for the son in the Holy Spirit. An alternative, if complementary, point of view is that the secret lay even deeper in his past. He was born Juan de Yepes. His father, Gonzalo de Yepes, had come from an upper-class family of silk merchants. When he insisted on marrying Juan's mother, Catalina Alvarez, a poor weaver, he sacrificed wealth and worldly status, for a relationship of love. Gonzalo died when Juan was about three. The son may have been unconscious of the love which surrounded him first in the relationship of his mother and father and subsequently after his father's death in the love of his mother. A modern view might be that the experience of Toledo may have stripped John of the Cross back to this bedrock of his formation, on which his life was founded, which itself disposed him to be capable of experiencing divine love in its fullness. It is a speculative, but perhaps plausible beginning to an explanation of the secret of the 'doctor spiritualis'.

---

139 *Ibid.*, *DN* Bk One 10.2.

7. THE CREATIVITY OF CHRISTIAN CULTURE

There is a curious sense of paradox about the experiences and lives of the mystics we have described. On the one hand the moods and aspirations of the two periods and the geographical locations, which have influenced fundamentally the histories of England and Spain, are so diverse. On the other the Christian ethos of the cultures provides the lives and experiences of the mystics with an inchoate similarity. And yet between the diversities and similarities of the two cultures, there seems to be a 'timeless creativity' which transcends the notions of diversity and similarity and which provides the cultural tradition with its dynamism. The 'creativity' is mediated by the language of 'divine love' which is the Christian mystical 'langue' and seems to have an existence independent of the 'parole' of a particular culture[140].

To introduce our problematic about how the mystics recognise the reality of the voice of divine love, we will explore in the first chapter the form in which it was mediated to them. The discussion forms a bridge between on the one hand the Prologue in which we have introduced something of the lives and experiences of the mystics and on the other their struggle to recognise in their experiences the voice of the divine spirit and understand its meaning for them.

We will divide the story of the development of the experiencing and understanding processes into two parts. Part one will deal with the mystics of the late fourteenth century and part two with those of sixteenth-century Spain. The purpose of the division is twofold. Firstly, it will be symbolic of the geographic and cultural differences which divide the two communities. Secondly, by creating a divide, as it were, between them, it will also emphasise the cross-cultural continuity of the Christian mystical traditions which, outside time and place, inform their cultures. The continuity is, however, no linear projection of similarity. The cumulative experience which develops the Christian traditions is also creative and enriching. We find that the traditions develop and respond to new historical and personal situations and reach an apogee in sixteenth-century Spain for the two aspects of divine love, 'apostolic mission' and 'contemplative union'. Our problematic is to show how these developments interrelate with the tradition of 'discernment of spirits'.

---

140 F. de Saussure, *Cours de Linguistique Générale* (1916) ed. Tullio de Mauro, Paris, 1981, Eng. trans. Wade Baskin, New York, 1959, draws the distinction between the 'deadness' of the 'parole' and the 'life' of the 'langue'. Paul Ricœur, *Interpretation Theory: Discourse and the Surplus of Meaning*, Fort Worth, Texas, 1976, quoted by Brian Stock, *Listening for the Text: On the uses of the past*, Baltimore and London: John Hopkins University Press, 1990, 101-102, notes that Saussure's emphasis upon 'langue' as the vehicle which provides meaning suggests that 'meaning' has an independent existence in which signs are irrelevant. We suggest 'cultural tradition' has a 'mediating function' which holds 'parole' and its meaning in tension.

Chapter 1

THE 'LANGUE' OF CHRISTIAN MYSTICAL EXPERIENCE

Belief in the 'reality' of different 'spiritual voices' was a common place by the fourteenth century. In England the pre-mystical consciousness of the community had been informed by the experiences of saints and cult figures. Chaucer's choice of the pilgrimage and its destination in Becket's tomb in Canterbury illustrates how eschatological notions of an encircling 'spiritual penumbra' impacted the consciousness of society. Becket's cult signifies the triumph of the 'good' over the 'evil' spirit. To awaken the 'good' spirit and the favours it might mediate may have been the object of the pilgrimage in the popular imagination but, as the Parson reminded the pilgrims, the sacrifice to be offered was 'true' contrition. The characteristics of the 'evil' spirit were portrayed in some of Chaucer's stories and, as we have seen, in morality plays and pictorial representations, as absurd but frightening; those of the 'good' spirit as sacrificial but enlivening and bountiful. Julian of Norwich's pre-mystical consciousness was probably influenced by such popular pictorial and literary images of 'good' and 'evil'.

Nevertheless, the problematic of the prospective contemplative was more profound than an awareness of the co-existence of 'good' and 'evil' spirits. The traditions of discernment of spirits and contemplation emphasised the need for divine help to revitalise the spiritual senses, the agency through which 'divine love' as 'spirit' was transmitted to the human soul to illuminate its 'raison d'être' and empower it to fulfil the demands which the spirit communicated. To 'awaken' the 'good' spirit by developing the spiritual senses, was also to 'awaken' the 'evil' spirit. Every contemplative soon became aware of the subtleties which the 'evil' spirit would deploy to exploit the emerging sensitivity for its own destructive purposes[1]. The 'evil' spirit had to be recognised and rendered impotent to infect the lives of contemplatives if the 'good' was to be enjoyed in peace. Immediate recognition of the meaning of what the spirits were saying was important so that the human intellect and will might recognise and come to desire the 'good' and reject 'evil' as a matter of habit. An explanation of the ultimate stage of the 'discernment of spirits', 'the assured under-

---

1   Cassian, for example, who we will introduce in a moment, in his *Second Conference* illustrates the point with stories of the fates of monks who had seemingly made great progress in the spiritual life and who yet failed to perceive the enmity of the evil spirit.

standing of the divine will on all occasions, in every place and in all matters'[2] of John Climacus, who we will introduce in a moment, sums up this objective; to ensure that 'divine love' and the 'divine will' may be distinguished from 'all the various forces at play in one's soul, the different kinds of love'[3] which Augustine of Hippo was to recognise.

Bernard Lonergan in his Method in Theology explains 'the divine word' as an experience of immediacy:

> Its meaning [the divine word] depends upon the human context in which it is uttered and such contexts vary from place to place and from one generation to another. But the prior word [of divine love] in its immediacy, though it differs in intensity, though it resonates differently in different temperaments and in different stages of religious development withdraws man [the human being] from the diversity of history by moving out of a world mediated by meaning and towards a world of immediacy in which image and symbol, thought and word, lose their relevance and even disappear[4].

The divine 'langue' uses human words and depends on human analogies but once discernment has reached that empathic quality of which John Climacus speaks, the world mediated by meaning (the human analogies) disappears and the mystics enter a world of 'immediacy' in which they are withdrawn from the diversity of history and the diversity of mediating analogy. This world of 'immediacy' we shall refer to as the world of the 'anagogical imagination'.

'Anagogical' is a less familiar term than 'transcendent' but, in the context of our discourse, perhaps, more useful. The etymology of the term - from the Greek 'ana', that which is above and 'agoge' that which is led - suggests the reason[5]. It is more descriptive of the operation of 'divine grace' than the term 'transcendent' which implies, perhaps, a human agency in the transcending process. 'Anagogical' feeling is more suggestive of the 'stirring' to which the mystics refer. A feature of 'anagogical stirring' is the increase in intensity as the spiritual life unfolds and which becomes so intense at the moment of participative union with the divine that the feeling represents a difference in kind rather than degree in which the world and self are 'left behind' and the mystic's soul begins to adopt a divine perspective. When mystics attempt to discuss such experiences they adopt analogies drawn from human

---

2 Climacus, *Ladder of Divine Ascent*, trans. L. Moore, London: Faber & Faber, 1939, 201 Step 26 Part 1.1.

3 Augustine, *Confessions* IV.xiv.22, quoted by Brown, *Augustine of Hippo*, London: Faber & Faber, 1967, 172.

4 Bernard Lonergan, S.J., *Method in Theology*, 112.

5 The notion of the 'anagogical' is explained by Henri de Lubac in his *Exégèse Médiévale: Les Quatre Sens de l'Ecriture*, Première Partie, Tome II. Aubier, Editions Montaigne, 1959, in a chapter entitled 'Anagogie et eschatologie', 622.

experience to describe the spiritual phenomena of the divine encounter which Rudolph Otto, in his Idea of the Holy, referred to as the experience of 'mysterium fascinans et tremendum'[6]. The mystics create the impression of difference in their descriptions of their spiritual journeys, not only linguistic but also experiential. However, they are essentially the same anagogically according to eschatological doctrine distilled from the Christian experience of the divine.

1. St John the Evangelist and St Paul

From the first it seems to have been recognised by Christians that the defining characteristic of the experience of the divinity was 'love'. However different emphases were placed upon how the 'authentic spirit' of that love was to be discerned. Neither St Paul nor St John the Evangelist among the first most articulate teachers of the meaning of Christ's life would have recognised nor acknowledged, it would seem, that the emphases in their teaching were different. Yet the circumstances of their witness seemed to emphasise what in practice were complementary tendencies.

The young St John had clearly had a special relationship with Christ as the scriptural tradition recognised. He was the one who leaned on the breast of Jesus at the Last Supper, had watched him die with the group who remained faithful at the foot of the cross and to whom Christ entrusted the care of his Mother. John, it seems, was called to an intimate personal service of Christ in his person; an archetypal 'contemplative' service[7]. The remarkable discourse which he provided in his Epistles most certainly did not neglect to emphasise Christ's teaching about love of neighbour but they went beyond all the other Evangelists and St Paul in their ecstatic emphasis that 'God is love' which emphasises the unity of the Trinity as the mystery of 'transcendent Reality'[8]. The human participation in this 'love' which he describes suggests a unitive relationship fulfils the promise that human beings may aspire to the divine likeness, and to emphasise, as Origen later perceived, Mary's 'better part' in the dichotomy between 'contemplative' and 'active' lives in the Christian biblical

---

6   Quoted by Lonergan, *Method in Theology*, 106.

7   Jn. 13.23; 19.36; 20.2; 21.7; 21.20-23, are all references to the 'disciple whom Jesus loved' and in particular 21, 20-23 to John's mission. (Jerusalem Bible). See Louis Bouyer, *A History of Christian Spirituality*, Vol. 1: *The Spirituality of the New Testament and the Fathers*. Trans. Mary R. Ryan, Burns and Oates, 1968, repr. 1982, 119:
     'St John so completely disappears [in the Johannine writings] in the very pure spiritual atmosphere he has created that the few details reported about him seem merely the projection of his Spirituality'.
     For a discussion of the problem of the Johannine writings, *ibid.*, 117-19.

8   1. Jn. 4.7-21.

Mary/Martha story. In this story Mary as the archetypal 'contemplative' participates in Christ's love with the serenity of total absorption[9].

At the same time John emphasises the dangers of self-deception and self-destruction in seeking the 'ecstatic' experience of divine love. He warns that this 'false' love is the work of the evil spirit which evidently had misled some Christians in his day; 'false' prophets he calls them who, in their extravagant and self-important enthusiasm, were deluded to suggest that their own experience provided charismatic confirmation of their relationship with the divinity and was the benchmark of divine favour and 'truth'[10].

Perhaps a similar fear led St Paul to emphasise the characteristic 'spirit' of 'Christian love' to be 'charity'; a divine gift; it is recognisable in the self-less love of Christians for their neighbours and the moral purity which should govern this neighbourly relationship[11]. His concern to ensure that the communities for whose evangelisation he was responsible did not relapse and damage the Christian reputation, perhaps, accounts for the impression that 'active' outgoing service towards neighbour rather than the 'contemplative' inward seeking of the 'giver of the gift' in prayer had primacy in Christian witness. Paul's epistles are so full of practical guides to Christian living in the world that this 'love of neighbour' perhaps seems to be a dominant theme[12].

---

9   Lk. 10.28-42. Andrew Louth, *The Origins of the Christian Mystical Tradition from Plato to Denys*, Oxford: Clarendon Press, 1985, 203/4, discusses the notion of the two lives and suggests the contrast in the Martha/Mary story was first drawn out by Origen. He also quotes Augustine from the last of his homilies on St John's Gospels, CXXIV.5 on the 'Two Lives' which draws a similar contrast between the apostles Peter and John. More recently Giles Constable, *Three Studies in Mediaeval Religious and Social Thought*, Cambridge University Press, 1995, 1-142, has discussed how the Martha/Mary story has been interpreted in history. He seems to conclude that the ambivalence with which Mary's 'better part' has been treated reflects the underlying unity of the two lives which the tradition recognises.

10   1. Jn. 4.1-6 and I. Jn. 2.18-29. The necessity of testing the spirits and how the disciples of Christ and Anti-Christ may be recognised are important themes in the first letter.

11   I. Cor. 13. See notes on love (agape) in I. Cor. 13 in the *Jerusalem Bible*, London: Darton, Longman & Todd, 1966, which also cross-references with John's first epistle.

12   Louis Bouyer, *The Spirituality of the New Testament and the Fathers*, 61:
     'In a marvellous passage of the Second Epistle to the Corinthians (which we owe to the incomparable folly of these same Corinthians) 2. Cor. 11.21-12.10 and in some other passages almost as beautiful and equally aroused by human stupidity which he seems to have suffered from as only a genius can...'.
     He goes on to suggest that the context of Paul's teaching is the instruction and admonition of the communities whom he has converted to realise what it means to be 'Christian'. Thus in discussing Pauline asceticism (86) he suggests Paul continually refers to himself as 'the slave of Christ' (Rom. 1.1; Gal. 2.10; Phil. 1.1) and invites those who wish to be his disciples to make themselves 'through charity, slaves of one another' (Gal. 5.13-15).

In neither case, St Paul nor St John, does there seem to be any intention to suggest that love of God and neighbour are not only complementary but indivisible signs of divine love working in Christian lives. Be that as it may, a variety of Christian life-styles seem to have developed which emphasise the signs of divine love which may be characterised by the concepts of agape and eros, in different combinations. Both concepts have been used with a variety of nuances in the patristic literature because they both seem to be present in the tension of a loving relationship as trust and ser-vice (agape) and longing and ecstasy (eros)[13].

2. JUDAIC AND PLATONIC INFLUENCES IN THE CHRISTIAN MYSTICAL 'LANGUE'

The characteristics of the concepts of agape and eros may also be said to reflect Judaic and Platonic emphases in the notion of Christian love[14]. The Judaic influence emerges in the many commentaries on the Song of Songs which recognise the ele-ments of fidelity and obedience to the law which are contained in the idea of 'spiri-tual marriage' as well as longing and patience which ultimately bring peace and rest in the consummation of the union. The Platonic influence is perhaps recognisable in a rigorously ascetic dialectic motivated by aesthetic peaks which finds fulfilment in 'divinisation' and which seems to bestow charismatic powers and make fruitful lives which had hitherto been dry and infertile. The ascribable Judaic and Platonic ten-dencies are perhaps already reflected in the backgrounds of Paul and John; for Paul in his pre-conversion life as a respected Pharisee and for John living in later life in Ephesus, a centre of Hellenic culture.

As Andrew Louth has pointed out in his Origins of the Christian Mystical Tradition, later Christian commentators seem to have borrowed Platonic ideology to describe and explain their own Christian mystical experiences. His work may seem to stress the influence of the Platonic tradition upon their Christian contemporaries at the expense of the Judaic. Nevertheless, the case is well made that Platonic concepts were used to rationalise and describe Christian experience. Louth identifies a Pla-tonic orientated typology among Late Antique Christian mystics concerned to ex-plain Christian notions to a post-Constantinian public. It is useful because the char-

---

13 There is an excellent discussion of this theme in Andrew Louth, *The Origins of Christian Mystical Tradition* in his final chapter, 191-204, focussed on challenging Anders Nygren, *Agape and Eros*, trans. P.S. Watson, London, 1957, and A.-J. Festugière, *L'Enfant d'Agrigente*, Paris, 1950. Other works which deal with this theme are M.C. D'Arcy, *The Mind and Heart of Love*, New York: Holt, 1947, and H.U. von Balthasar, *Herrlichkeit: Eine theologische Ästhetik* III/2, part 2, Einsiedeln, 1969.

14 Jean Guitton, *Essay on Human Love*, trans. by M. Channing-Pearce, London, 1951 (first pub-lished, Paris, Aubier, 1948, as *Essai sur l'amour humain*) 20ff. In discussing themes of exalta-tion it is suggested: 'Three great themes in history have expounded love: the Platonic theme, the theme of Solomon and the theme of Tristan. Each of these corresponds to a civilisation: the Greek, the Jewish and of the Modern World'.

THE 'LANGUE' OF CHRISTIAN MYSTICAL EXPERIENCE

acteristics seem to be identifiable in the fourteenth and sixteenth centuries as we shall see[15].

Louth identifies three strands in the later development of a Christian mystical tradition, each influenced by a distinctive Platonic school of thought, represented by the Desert Fathers, Augustine of Hippo and Dionysius the Areopagite[16]. The latter is now referred to as the Pseudo-Dionysius, an otherwise anonymous fifth-century monk. However, during the period in which we are interested, he was thought to be Dionysius the Areopagite, the disciple of St Paul. His teaching had the prestige which the connection with Paul afforded and, perhaps, gave the Platonic emphasis respectability in Christian circles. His works appeared to be authentic and have the intrinsic merit and insight to support their attribution[17].

It is perhaps convenient to begin a discussion of Louth's typology in the development of the 'mystical' tradition with the works of the Pseudo-Dionysius. He brought the use of the term 'mystical' in Christian discourse to some sort of apogee by coining the term 'mystical theology' for the final stages of spiritual development leading to a fulfilment in 'divinisation'. It was an appropriate term because it encapsulated the manner in which the Greek term mystikos, meaning simply 'hidden', had been adapted to encompass a series of meanings which reflected the 'hiddenness' of the Godhead; first of all 'hidden' in Scripture, and then in the sacraments and finally in 'participation' in its 'being' by a kind of human transfiguration in which the 'light' of the 'Godhead' shone through human flesh and lit up all around it in 'mystical' experience[18].

The modern usage of the term 'mystical theology' is similar. The Dictionary of the Christian Church describes it as 'the science of spiritual life in so far as this is dependent on the operation of Divine grace: it is commonly contrasted with 'Ascetical Theology' which treats of the spiritual life, so far as it can be pursued without supernatural assistance'[19]. In the case of the Pseudo-Dionysius 'mystical theology' does not so much 'contrast' with 'ascetical theology' as complement it as we shall see shortly. An 'ascetic' formation becomes for the mystics of Late Antiquity and

---

15 Andrew Louth, *The Origins of the Christian Mystical Tradition*, discusses in his introduction xii-xiv the development of mystical theology in the Fathers and the extent to which Platonism determines and is resisted in their thoughts. See discussion of 'love' above and the platonic notion in Jean Guitton (N.14).

16 Ibid., 161. Louth traces the Platonic influences in Pseudo-Dionysius and Augustine of Hippo in chapters vii and viii respectively. I have called the 'monastic contribution' of chapter vi 'the Desert tradition'. Louth in his Wilderness of God, London: Darton, Longman & Todd, 1991, seems to make a similar transposition.

17 Louis Bouyer, *The Spirituality of the New Testament and the Fathers*, contains a full discussion of the historical and literary problem of the Areopagite writings, 395-401.

18 Ibid., 406-412.

19 The Oxford Dictionary of the Christian Church, 952.

the fourteenth and sixteenth centuries, almost a prerequisite for spiritual fulfilment whether in the 'contemplative' or 'active' lives and an 'ascetic lifestyle' based on obedience to the divine will a necessary sign of the authentic action of divine grace in human lives[20].

3. PSEUDO-DIONYSIUS

The goal of human 'being' which Pseudo-Dionysius described as 'divinisation' was similar to that which Plato had believed might at last bring the dialectic of love to rest. Plato doubted whether the human being could ever become 'a god' for the characteristic of the God was immortality[21]. In death, perhaps, he thought Socrates might have achieved this goal. The 'divinisation' of the Pseudo-Dionysius was in some ways not dissimilar. It was, however, a rather different concept of 'immortality'; it was not existence as a 'God' but a 'participation' in the divine theophany, from an appointed place in the divine thearchy[22].

Piccarda in Dante's Paradiso explains the Dionysian concept of 'thearchy' perfectly:

It is indeed the essence of this life
That we keep ourselves within the divine will,
So that our wills may be one with his;
So that, how we are at various thresholds

---

20   Pseudo-Dionysius was well known in the Middle Ages not only for the *Mystical Theology* but also the *Celestial Hierarchy*, *Divine Names* and the *Ecclesiastical Hierarchy*. See Andrew Louth, *The Origins of the Christian Mystical Tradition*, 159-78, and R. Roques, *L'Univers Dionysien: Structure hiérarchique du monde selon le Pseudo-Denys*, Paris, 1954 and 'Denys' in *Dict. Sp.* Vol. 3, 1957, Col. 244-86 and 'Contemplation' in *Dict. Sp.* Vol. 2B, 1953, Cols 1785-87 and 1885-1911. See also Louis Bouyer, *The Spirituality of the New Testament and the Fathers*, 401.

21   See quotation from Plato's *Symposium* below and N.26 below.

22   Louis Bouyer, *The Spirituality of the New Testament and the Fathers*, 403/4. For example he suggests:
'The love of God in the universe of Platonism, of Aristotelianism and their heirs, moves the whole universe: but it is the love *with which God is loved*; *kinei hos eromenon*. For God to love anything at all would be meaningless, since there is nothing he can desire (see n.16). For 'Dionysius', on the contrary, the love that moves all beings is the love which is proper to God, to the Christian God: the agape with which he loves, pure gift, pure generosity. The eros of creatures, in this vision, is never, if it is pure, anything but a reascent of this agape towards its source'.
However as Louth, *The Origins of the Christian Mystical Tradition*, 171 points out:
'So one 'ascends' *into* the hierarchy rather than up it'.

Throughout this kingdom, pleases the whole kingdom
As it does the king who rouses us to his will[23].

Pseudo-Dionysius' concept of the hierarchical order within the 'thearchy' is

a sacred order, and knowledge and activity which is being assimilated as much as possible to likeness with God and in response to the illuminations which are given it from God, raises itself to the imitation of Him in its own measure[24].

The imitation of God leads to 'enlightenment by the unsearchable depths of wisdom'. Pseudo-Dionysius' concept of 'participative love' as 'wisdom' in the Socratic sense suggests what is to become a characteristic of the apophatic or negative way to contemplation. The following rather long passage is important as illustrative of his concept:

On no account ... is it true to say that we know God, not indeed in His nature (for that is unknowable, and is beyond any reason and understanding), but by the order of all things that He has established, and which bears certain images and likenesses of His divine paradigms, we ascend step by step, so far as we can follow the way, to the Transcendent, by negating and transcending everything and by seeking the cause of all. Therefore God is known in all, and apart from all ... and this is ... the most divine knowledge of God, that He is known through unknowing, according to the union which transcends the understanding, when the understanding withdraws from all, and abandons itself, and in them and from them is enlightened by the unsearchable depths of wisdom[25].

'Union' with the 'dazzling rays' and 'enlightenment' in this passage may be compared with Plato's ideas as expressed by Diotima to Socrates in the Symposium:

What may we suppose to be the felicity of the man who sees absolute beauty in its essence, pure and unalloyed, who, instead of a beauty tainted by human flesh and colour and a mass of perishable rubbish, is able to apprehend divine beauty where it exists apart and alone? Do you think that it will be a poor life that a man leads who has his gaze fixed in that direction, who contemplates absolute beauty with the appropriate faculty and is in constant union with it? Do you not see that in that region alone where he sees beauty with the faculty capable of seeing it,

---

23 Dante, *The Divine Comedy. Paradiso* III, 79-85, Sisson's translation, Carcanet New Press, 1980, is quoted by Louth, *The Origins of the Christian Mystical Tradition*, 171/2. I have used Dorothy Sayers' translation in the discussion of Dante in Part I below.

24 Pseudo-Dionysius, *Celestial Hierarchy* in PG III, 1f. : 164D, 165D, quoted by Louth, *Origins of the Christian Mystical Tradition*, 169/70.

25 Pseudo-Dionysius, *Divine Names* VII in PG III: 869C-872B, quoted by Louth, *Origins of the Christian Mystical Tradition*, 167/8.

will he be able to bring forth not mere reflected images of goodness but true goodness, because he will be in contact not with a reflection but with the truth? And having brought forth and nurtured true goodness he will have the privilege of being beloved of God, and becoming, if ever man can, immortal himself[26].

Both Plato and the Pseudo-Dionysius regard some transcendent metamorphosis into the divine as the human goal by which fulfilment is to be achieved. Nor does the similarity end here. The ascesis of Socrates, which although caring for other humans, denies that fulfilment can ever be achieved in an object which is changeable and will perish so that 'love' for another human being should not be an end in itself. Socrates dies for 'truth' not for 'love'. 'Love' in the sense of ecstatic delight motivates the dialectic by which 'truth' is attained[27]. For Pseudo-Dionysius, echoing St John the Evangelist, truth and love are 'one' in transcendent being. In the prayer to the 'Trinity' with which he prefaces the Mystical Theology we read:

O Trinity ... lead us to that supreme height of mystical words that transcends understanding and manifestation, there where the simple, absolute, unchangeable mysteries of theology are unveiled in the superluminous cloud of silence that initiates into hidden things, super-resplendent in the deepest depths of darkness in a manner beyond manifestation, which wholly intangible and invisible, fills to overflowing with super beautiful splendours our blinded spirits (noas)...[28] .

The Christian experience of 'love' as 'ecstatically peaceful' is explained in the langue of educated society. We do not know whether the Pseudo-Dionysius actually experienced that 'ecstatic peace' since he suggests it is mystical (hidden) and so indescribable. We only know he observed his teacher 'Hierotheos' in what the author describes as a state of ecstasy while expounding the Scriptures - 'united' with the mystery of the Word, as it were[29].

4. AUGUSTINE OF HIPPO

Pseudo-Dionysius is believed to have lived in the latter part of the fifth century in Syria, at the eastern end of the Mediterranean. Augustine, who died at the age of seventy-six in 430, lived latterly at Hippo on the northern littoral of modern day Algeria[30]. Like Pseudo-Dionysius he seems to have been deeply influenced by the

---

26 Plato, *The Symposium*, trans. Walter Hamilton, London: Penguin Books, 1951, 95.

27 See N.22 above.

28 Pseudo-Dionysius, *Mystical Theology* 1.1: P.G. III, 997A-1100A, quoted in Louis Bouyer, *The Spirituality of the New Testament and the Fathers*, 412.

29 Pseudo-Dionysius, *Divine Names* III.2 and 3 in PG III, 681D-684A, quoted by Louis Bouyer, *The Spirituality of the New Testament and the Fathers*, 411.

30 For Augustine of Hippo see Peter Brown, *Augustine of Hippo, a Biography* and Henry Chadwick, *Augustine*, Oxford: Oxford University Press, 1986. There is a considerable literature

form of Platonic thought which was dominant around the Mediterranean in his day. For Augustine the acknowledged influence was Plotinus (c. 205-70)[31], while the Pseudo-Dionysius reflected that of Proclus (411-85) to the extent he has been called the 'Christian Proclus' in his adaptation of the triadic motif of purification, illumination and union[32].

As has been pointed out by Louth, Augustine's famous account of the vision he received at Ostia which he describes in the Confessions[33], is almost identical with an account of an experience which appears in Plotinus' Enneads[34]. What the experience was really like is left to the imagination of the reader who is invited to enter into it with all the rhetorical skill which Augustine can muster. However, as he becomes more familiar with the Christian Scriptures the influence of Plotinus appears to wane.

Even in the Confessions, in which the beneficial influence of Plotinus is acknowledged, Augustine is asking himself what he really means when he says he 'loves' God. It is worthwhile quoting the passage because it seems to be so much more affirmative than Pseudo-Dionysius is prepared to be. Yet the mystery of divine love is conveyed with the same kind of ecstatic passion which Pseudo-Dionysius conveys in his prayer to the Trinity. So Augustine:

> What is it that I love when I love You? Not the beauty of any bodily thing, not the order of the seasons, not the brightness of the light that rejoices the eye, nor the sweet melodies of all songs, nor the sweet fragrance of flowers and ointments and spices; not manna or honey, not the limbs that carnal love embraces [all things which would drive the Platonic dialectic]. None of these things do I love in loving my God. Yet in a sense I do love light and melody and fragrance and food and embrace when I love my God - the light and the voice and the fragrance and the food and embrace in the Soul, when the light shines upon my Soul which

---

dealing with Pseudo-Dionysius and Augustine of Hippo. The shorter bibliographies in *The Oxford Dictionary of the Christian Church* contain information about the main primary and secondary sources and editions of their works.

31 There is an excellent account of Augustine's knowledge of Plotinus in Andrew Louth's *The Origins of the Christian Mystical Tradition*, 132-158. Augustine read Plotinus in Victorinus' translation, 132, and also Plato and Porphyry. See also Peter Brown, *Augustine of Hippo*, 122 and n.9 and 425/6, n.1; and for Porphyry 307, ns 4, 5 and 7. And Louis Bouyer, *The Spirituality of the New Testament and the Fathers*, 468-73.

32 Andrew Louth, *The Origins of the Christian Mystical Tradition*, 161, for 'Denys' as the 'Christian Proclus'. There are close verbal parallels particularly between Divine Names IV and Proclus' treatise *De Malorum Subsistentia*. Proclus' neo-platonism is discussed 162/3.

33 Augustine, *Confessions* IX and similar passages in Plotinus' *Ennead* V.1.4 and 1.2 are quoted by Louth, *The Origins of the Christian Mystical Tradition*, 138/9.

34 See Peter Brown, *Augustine of Hippo*, 129 and n.2; P. Henry, *La Vision d'Ostie*, Paris, 1938, 77, and also Louis Bouyer, *The Spirituality of the New Testament and the Fathers*, 471-473.

no place can contain, that voice sounds which no time can take from me, I breathe that fragrance which no wind scatters, I eat the food which is not lessened by eating, and I lie in the embrace which satiety never comes to sunder. This it is that I love when I love my God[35].

In this passage it is not the objects themselves that create love, it is the creator who irradiates both the mind of the observer and the signs themselves, who transfigures them with 'light'. 'Loving' remains for Augustine in this passage a kind of enlightenment which kindles warmth and peace in a tranquil satiety.

5. JOHN CASSIAN AND JOHN CLIMACUS

Cassian (c. 360-435) and Climacus (c. 570-c.649) perhaps better than any other authors in their respective periods, mediated to the mediaeval period the nature of the seminal Christian idea of 'Desert' spirituality in its ascetic manifestations. Climacus, in particular, in his Scala Paradisi conveys the experience of God as the 'quiet' of solitude and silence. Cassian suggests the experience of 'purity' in total selflessness and obedience is the prerequisite to be sought in achieving the likeness of Christ in which God may be encountered[36].

---

35 Augustine, *Confessions* X.vi, quoted by Louth, The Origins of the Christian Mystical Tradition, 141/2.
36 John Cassian's birthplace is uncertain though according to Gennadius he was a native of Scythia (writing c.480). Cassian joined a monastery at Bethlehem (c.385) but left with his companion Germanus to study monasticism in Egypt. He was an emissary of St John Chrysostom (c.347-407), patriarch of Constantinople (398) to Pope Innocent I. It is interesting to note in the light of the four ways of interpretation later advocated by Cassian that Chrysostom advocated a literal interpretation of Scripture. Cassian remained in the West after this mission and eventually founded two monasteries near Marseilles. For his works see N.37 below. The authoritative biography is that of Owen Chadwick, *John Cassian*, Cambridge, 1968, second edition. See also M. Cappuyns, O.S.B., 'Cassien' in D.H.G.E. XI, 1949, Cols 1319-48, and M. Olphe-Galliard, 'Cassien' in Dict. Sp. Vol. 2, 1953, Cols 214-276.
John Climacus, a close contemporary of Gregory the Great (540-604) studied on Mt Sinai and became an anchorite and later abbot of the monastery on Mt Sinai. His work the Scala Paradisi (see N.38 below) became influential in the West when translated from the Greek into Latin in the late mediaeval period.
Cassian adapted the practices of Egyptian monasticism for the West and influenced St Benedict and thereby the tradition of western monasticism; Climacus' work, a compendium of the early monastic authors, emphasised the Eastern tradition of 'dispassion' and the 'imitation of Christ' at a time when the ascetic foundations of contemplative prayer were perhaps losing their formative influence. A Spanish translation of one of the Latin texts of Climacus was destined to be the first book to be printed in the New World (Mexico, 1532). See Guerric Couilleau, 'Jean Climaque' in Dict. Sp. Vol. 8, 1974, Cols 369-89. Also Kallistos-Ware's introduction to the Scala Paradisi in the Classics of Western Spirituality series, trans. C. Luibheid and N. Russell, London: SPCK, 1982, and M. Heppel's introduction to the translation of *The Ladder of Divine Ascent* by Archimandrite Lazarus Moore, London: Faber & Faber, 1959.

Cassian does not write from the standpoint of his own first-hand experience but from that of his meetings with a range of desert fathers in which he was accompanied by Germanus. Thus Cassian in the Institutes and Conferences writes as an observer of a practice which he wishes the monks of his foundations in Gaul near Marseilles to adopt[37]. Climacus in turn is apparently responding to a request by a brother abbot to share the spiritual wisdom for which he is renowned, with others who are attempting to acquire it[38].

In both cases the emphasis is placed on 'morality' as 'obedience' and conducting oneself with a Christ-like humility which it has been suggested owes something to a tradition of scriptural exegesis practised by Origen and the Alexandrines[39]. They both temper the Judaic tradition of witness, that is the obedience to the Law as the sign of right conduct, with the Christian notions of humility and trust in the mercy of God. This is not to suggest that Augustine or the Pseudo-Dionysius are unconcerned with witness and conduct as the signs of the presence of true, divinely inspired, wisdom. Cassian and Climacus however are particularly concerned with the practical problematic of achieving it rather than penetrating to the essence of wisdom. Divine wisdom they suggest to the mediaeval monastic tradition is to be recognised in the monk in the expression of a Christ-like humility both physical and intellectual,

---

37 Cassiani *Opera Omnia*, ed. A. Gazet, Douai, 1616. Reprinted J.P. Migne, P.L. XLIX-L. The *Conferences (Collationes)* and *Institutes (De Institutis Coenobiorum)* in Crit. Ed. M. Petschenig in *CSEL* xiii, 1886 and xvii, 1888 respectively. Fr. trans. of the former by E. Pechery, O.S.B. and J.C. Guy, S.J., the latter in *Sources Chrétiennes*, Paris, xlii, liv, lxiv, 1955-9 for *Conferences* and clx, 1965, for *Institutes*. See also J.C. Guy's *Jean Cassien. Vie et doctrine spirituelle*, Paris, 1961.

38 There is no critical edition of the *Scala Paradisi* of Climacus and there is a diverse manuscript history (The translation I have used is taken from the editio princeps first published in Paris in 1633, ed. Matthew Rader and later reprinted in Migne, P.G. Lxxxviii, cols 569-1209). Much of the ground covered is similar to a 5th-Century ascetical compilation known as *the Book of Holy Men*, a collection of sayings (*Apothegmata*) attributed to the Desert Fathers (see Heppel's introduction N.36 above, 10 n.2). They are displayed as thirty steps in an ascent to God corresponding to the thirty years of Christ's life before his Baptism. The relative importance attached to each subject follows closely the *Book of Holy Men*. For example, Book X of the *Book of Holy Men* and Step 26 of the *Ladder* dealing with discernment are closely related. The dedication suggests it was compiled at the request of John, Abbot of Raithu on the Sinai peninsula, who sought to utilise Climacus' experience for the benefit of his own monks (see J. Gribomont, 'La Scala Paradisi, Jean de Raitou et Ange Clereno' in *Studia Monastica* ii, 1960, 345-58). It has been suggested that some of the ideas in the *Scala Paradisi* have points in common with the Jungian system of analytical psychology. Heppel *op.cit.* 16, n.3, refers to M.O. Sumner in the Guild Lecture No.83 of the Guild of Pastoral Psychology, Jan. 1953.

39 Louth, *The Origins of the Christian Mystical Tradition*, 54, suggests Origen's real concern was the interpretation of Scripture, 'the heart of his life's work' despite his contribution to the tradition of intellectual mysticism developed by Evagrius and passed on to the Eastern Church, 74.

which is trust in and dependence on God. This trust and dependence they regard as
the essence of faith and of Christian love[40].

6. REFLECTION : A GRAMMAR OF LOVE

The authentic 'langue' of mystical experience then is 'divine love'. It is 'anagogical'
in character because it depends upon the divine gift and its recognition. Participation
in the 'gift' draws the participant into 'union' with the divine 'giver', into a time-
lessness which 'withdraws' the participant from history, into the world of immediacy of 'divine love', of the anagogical imagination.

We have referred to some of the expressions of this imagination, in the apostolic age
in St John the Evangelist and in St Paul, and in the post-Constantinian age, in
Pseudo-Dionysius, Augustine of Hippo, Cassian and Climacus. Their voices, as they
mediate the 'immediacy' of their experiences of divine love, depend on human
analogies which they are conscious are inadequate to express the 'feeling' of the
'mysterium fascinans et tremendum'.

Yet the words of these mystics have been recognised as classical expressions of the
'mystery'. Their works are 'classics' in the sense that David Tracy uses the term in
his *The Analogical Imagination*[41]. They are expressions of a universally recognised
'reality', the power of which impregnates, as we shall see, the pre-mystical consciousness of contemplatives in the centuries ahead.

The common feature of these diverse expressions of the 'reality' of 'divine love' is
the emphasis placed upon the revitalisation of the spiritual senses to complement the

---

40 See Louis Bouyer, *The Spirituality of the New Testament and the Fathers*, 426, suggests of
    Climacus that, 'he means to lead the monk from the novitiate to perfection, which for him, is
    the same thing as perfect charity ... The theme of the imitation of Christ is set up as the princi-
    ple of everything else'.
    And similarly he quotes (503) Cassian in the first Conference vii: 'Purity of heart is ... the
    unique end of our actions and desires ... [in order] to keep our heart invulnerable to all the
    wicked passions and to mount, as by so many degrees, even to the perfection of charity'.
    'Perfection of Charity' is the end he says to which the apostle Paul refers when he said 'if I do
    not have charity this [all other good works and ascetic practices] will prove useless to me'.
41 David Tracy, *The Analogical Imagination*. New York: Crossroad, 1991. See in particular chap.
    5, 193-229. See also 149, n.96 where Tracy refers to Paul Ricœur's notion of 'imagination' as
    developed in his lectures (believed to be unpublished) on the positions of Aristotle, Spinoza,
    Ryle and Sartre on imagination as (1) 'a rule-governed form of invention (alternatively a norm-
    governed productivity)' and (2) 'the power of giving form to human experience'. The latter,
    Tracy suggests, enables Ricœur to retrieve 'mimesis' as a 'creative redescription' and to de-
    velop the notion of fiction as a redescription of reality challenging everyday descriptions. I am
    using 'imagination' in a similar sense.

physical. The revitalisation is the work of the 'grace' of the Holy Spirit as it makes itself felt in consciousness.

The common problematic recognised by the apostles and experienced by the mystics is to recognise 'divine grace' and exclude from consciousness the many other forms of 'spirit' which the revitalisation of the spiritual senses awakens. The discipline of a tradition of 'discernment of spirits', 'to test the spirits', is the instrument that evolved for this purpose. That tradition, as it were, becomes a 'grammar' of love, the evolution of which we may recognise in the classical mystical expressions of late fourteenth-century England and sixteenth-century Spain as we shall see[42].

---

42 I use 'grammar' in the same sense as John Coulson in his *Religion and Imagination*, Oxford, 1981, 87, n.3 as 'underlying form and structure, which we discover as we learn and use a language'.

PART I

FROM VIRGIL TO DANTE AND CHAUCER

Allegories of the Mystical Poetic

INTRODUCTION

Dante Alighieri has described in *Vita Nuova* how a chance meeting at a May Day party in Florence, when he was nine years old, opened up for him a new aesthetic and spiritual dimension of consciousness[1]. He fell in love with Beatrice, the young daughter of the Florentine, Folco Portinari, at whose house the party was held. The experience of love with its power to change the way Dante regarded the world and those about him henceforward became a dominant inspiration in his life. Beatrice became for him a 'God-bearing image': Beatrice's role in the *Divine Comedy* points to what this means[2].

In the story, Virgil, the 'poet of the gate', has been Dante's guide through Hell and Purgatory. Virgil's role as guide, perhaps, personified for Dante the apogee of what might be achieved by natural wisdom unaided by supernatural illumination[3]. When Beatrice approaches them like a divine illumination, in the final stage of the journey to the threshold of Paradise Virgil disappears. As for Dante, so for us, as we shall explain.

In contrast to Dante's Beatrice, the 'God-bearing image of love', Chaucer's Criseyde is a tragic figure symbolising the destructive power of human love. When

---

1   Dante Alighieri, Vita Nuova, trans. with intro by Mark Musa, Oxford: Oxford University Press, 1992, II, 4. Dante describes Beatrice and the effect she had on him rather than the location and occasion of the meeting which scholars have subsequently reconstructed.

2   D.L. Sayers' Introduction to her translation of Dante's Divine Comedy, London: Penguin Books, reprinted 1955; 1 Hell, 28 (hereafter: The Divine Comedy/1. Hell/2. Purgatory/3. Paradise); also 26 n.1 quotes Vita Nuova, 'Ecce Deus fortior me, qui veniens dominabitur mihi'. See also Charles Williams, The Figure of Beatrice, London: Faber, 1943; P.H. Wicksteed, From Vita Nuova to Paradiso, London: Longmans, 1922 and Dorothy Sayers, Introductory Papers on Dante, London: Methuen, 1954 and her Further Papers on Dante, London: Methuen, 1957. In this context see Étienne Gilson, Dante the Philosopher, trans. David Moore, London: Sheed and Ward, 1948, 294. He sounds a caution about associating the figure of Beatrice with any particular abstractions, such as 'Christ' or 'Contemplation' or 'the Church'. Mark Musa in the introduction to Vita Nuova (see N.1 above) suggests, xix, 'Again and again Beatrice is presented as a reflection of Christ'. The distinction is drawn between a 'reflection' and an 'abstract symbol'.

3   Divine Comedy, 1 Hell, 67.

Troilus and Criseyde was read to the English Court in 1387 it is said that Queen Anne imposed on Chaucer a penance for having dared to suggest that a woman could be false in love. The penance was to write *The Legend of Good Women*. It is a charming anecdote which perhaps well illustrates the dramatic impact of Chaucer's work. He was well aware of the contrast between the ideal which Beatrice symbolised in the *Amour Courtois* tradition of a supernatural love, which is eternally faithful, and a natural human love. In the mouth of Pandarus he places the truism for his day:

> Was nevere man nor womman yet begate
> That was unapt to suffren loves hete
> Celestial, or elles love of kynde[4].

The point is well made for in Chaucer's day the normal alternative to matrimony was a monastery or convent.

Troilus and Criseyde is a poetical study in a classical setting, in which Christian ethics in sex did not apply, of natural human love, fully romantic, fully sexual. It is an apposite setting in another sense. In the Middle Ages the Troy story was part of the national myth. It was derived from Geoffrey of Monmouth (d. 1154) who declared on what he believed to be good authority that England, originally called Albion, was inhabited by giants. It was invaded by Felix Brutus, a Trojan Prince, and great-grandson to Aeneas (Virgil's hero) in the year 1116 BC. Brutus landed at Totnes, defeated the giants and renamed the country after himself. In Chaucer's day this was so flourishing a tradition that there was a movement during his lifetime to rename London, 'Troynovant', New Troy. All that concerned Troy was therefore of great patriotic as well as poetic interest[5].

However this may be, in the dramatic last moments of the story of Troilus and Criseyde, in the Palinode, this human love is suddenly placed in the context of a higher love, the love of God. Virgil's poetic inspiration is not rejected but his 'eschatology' is. We follow Troilus after his 'tragedye' is over, out of this world as he looks down with new awareness and prays. This is a different reaction from that which Virgil gives the departing soul of Turnus as he slips vengefully to the shades in the closing moments of *The Aeneid*.

---

4   Nevill Coghill's Introduction to his trans. of Geoffrey Chaucer's Troilus and Criseyde, London: Penguin Books, 1971, xx, quoted from F.N. Robinson's edition of Troilus and Criseyde Bk. 1, 977-9.

5   Ibid., xvi. Geoffrey of Monmouth's famous Historia Britonum was probably completed in 1139 but the surviving text seems to have been from 1147. Geoffrey acquired a reputation which no historical criticism could diminish.

An Allegory of 'Love' in the 'Amour Courtois' Tradition of Spirituality

Christ, standing on the book of scriptures, crushes evil spirits while he rewards the hero. In the foreground, the theological virtues of 'faith', 'hope' and 'love', depicted as beautiful maidens, protect the members of the pilgrim Church from their own 'animality', depicted as 'Hell' in the form of a whale. Painted by El Greco before his arrival in Spain, and while under the influence of the Venetian school.

El Greco, Coronation of a Saint or King (Modena Polyptych), before 1570.

Troilus' prayer concludes with some words borrowed from Dante:

> Thou Oone, and Two, and Thre, eterne on lyve,
> That regnest ay in Thre, and Two and Oon,
> Uncircumscript, and al maist circumscrive,
> Us from visible and invisible foon
> Defende: and to thy mercy everichon,
> So make us, Jesus, for thi mercy digne,
> For love of mayde and moder thyn benigne[6].

Chaucer in a dramatic volte-face does not judge the human love story. The feelings of despair alternating with bliss are all part of the experience of human love, its beauty, its sorrows and perhaps impermanence. If human beings are to escape its impermanence he seems to say, it is necessary to recognise a higher love of which human love is a shadow; that is 'eterne on lyve', which will 'falsen no wight'. El Greco's representation in Figure 2 perhaps symbolises this ideal in the '*Amour Courtois*' tradition.

There is perhaps no better introduction to the fourteenth century English mystics as they explore the recognition of this 'eterne on lyve' and attempt to unravel the substance from the shadow on the high road to mystical knowledge of 'loves hete Celestial'. Julian of Norwich's *Showynges* perhaps approaches Chaucer's *Troilus and Criseyde* as a dramatic presentation of the experience of 'loves hete Celestial'. The counterpoint she unfolds between experience and doctrine is a perfect case study in dramatic form of the practice of 'discernment of spirits'.

---

6   N. Coghill, op.cit., xxv/vi, quoted without identification of source. Note 10, 309 points out that the first three lines of the final stanza are directly translated from The Divine Comedy, 3. Paradise, XIV, 28-30.

Chapter 2

JULIAN OF NORWICH

1. '[THE LORD] REVEALED IT BECAUSE HE WANTS TO HAVE IT BETTER KNOWN'

We have already introduced Julian's *Showings* in the Prologue[1]. They represent the core of experience, the drama, around which 'doctrine' as the symbol of authority weaves its counterpoint confirming here and challenging there her recollections of the visions and locutions and authenticating her story of divine love as she experienced it.

We might begin by considering her doctrine because it is the conformity of her teaching with the traditional teaching of the Church by which her audience would first judge the authentic flavour of the drama she presents:

> For truly I saw and understood in our Lord's meaning that he revealed it because he wants to have it better known than it is[2].

Her experience of the showings and her reflections upon them provide a very personal flavour to the meaning of the faith as practised in her day. Her story is a cogent example of personal experience mediated by the Christian culture of the day which the tradition of discernment of spirits validates and absorbs into itself.

As we have seen she was apprehensive from the first that her *Showings* would be ridiculed as the product either of the hallucinatory effects of fever or as misplaced enthusiasm. She was certainly right to be apprehensive. On the one hand, there was apparently a genuine fear among those contemporaries, who regarded contemplation and mystical experience as the high point of Christian development, that the whole tradition of contemplative prayer would be discredited by enthusiasts who regarded extraordinary experiences as a sign of God's favour and their absence as disfavour[3].

---

1   The conventions to be used in this chapter for Julian to identify sources are the same as used in the Prologue. See Prologue, N.29.
2   *Showings, trans. L.T.* ch.86, 342 and Crit.Ed. *L.T.*, 732,7-9.
3   See Prologue, N.38 above.

On the other, there were many 'actives', as the *Cloud* author infers[4], bishops among them, who were thoroughly sceptical of the legitimacy of contemplative tradition which was not strictly circumscribed by enclosure or a religious rule. For example, Julian's bishop in the diocese of Norwich was responsible for her enclosure. He was Henry Despenser (Bishop 1370 to 1406), a soldier-bishop 'in the crusading tradition', who organised and commanded a military expedition against the French in the Low Countries, albeit disastrously unsuccessful[5]. As he showed subsequently in his vengeful treatment of the dissidents after the collapse of the Peasants Revolt in which the Archbishop of Canterbury had been murdered, he had little inclination to be forgiving and regarded the Church, it seems, as the protector of the established social and political order[6]. To such a man ideas which might lead to religious enthusiasm and disrupt the even tenor of church life might seem dangerous and unnecessary. The dissemination and eventual condemnation of Lollard opinions in the latter part of the fourteenth century would have given such views a degree of legitimacy![7].

We can therefore understand how Julian would be motivated to test the orthodoxy of her account of her experiences and their meaning. Her standard was principally conformity to Church doctrine and practice as she understood them to be. Her texts in this regard may be treated from two points of view. On the one hand, there is the teaching, the mediated message and its conformity with doctrine; on the other, there is the process of reflection and meditation with its 'infused' insights by which she established the meaning of her experiences, the mediating process, and its confor-

---

4   *CL* H.27.5-6. See Prologue, N.63, for abbreviations and conventions used relating to the *Cloud* Author.

5   Peter Heath, *Church and Realm 1272-1461; Conflict and collaboration in an age of crises*, London: Fontana Press, 1988, 111 and 195-7. For Despenser's ultimate impeachment (1383) see M. Aston, 'The Impeachment of Bishop Despenser' in *BIHR*, xxxviii, 1965, 127-48. See also B. McNab, 'Obligations of the Church in English Society: Military Arrays of the Clergy 1369-1418' in *Order and Innovation in the Middle Ages: Essays in Honour of Joseph R. Strayer*, ed. W.C. Jordan, B. McNab and T.F. Ruiz, New Jersey, 1976, 293-314.

6   For Peasants Revolt of 1381 Heath, *Church and Realm*, 192-5 and A.J. Prescott, *Judicial Records of the Rising of 1381*, London University Ph.D. thesis, 1984. Also C. Oman, *The Great Revolt of 1381*, 2nd Ed. Oxford, 1969; R.B. Dobson, ed. *The Peasants Revolt of 1381*, London: Macmillan, 1970; 2nd Ed., 1983; R.H. Hilton and T.H. Ashton, eds, *The English Rising of 1381*, Cambridge, 1984. McFarlane, *John Wycliffe and the Beginnings of English Non-conformity*, 187, singles out Despenser, 'the loud-mouthed and bloodthirsty', as the only bishop who 'showed delight' in the sport of persecuting Lollards, though his actions were less ruthless than his reported speech. For Archbishop Sudbury (1375-81) see Heath, *Church and Realm*, 193-4 and W.L. Warren, 'A Reappraisal of Simon Sudbury' in *JEH*, x, 1959, 139-52.

7   Wycliffe's writings were condemned in 1382 at the Blackfriars Council. See H. Workman, *John Wyclif*, Oxford, 1926, Vol. 2, appendix T, 416ff. and McFarlane, *John Wycliffe and the Beginnings of English Non-conformity*, chaps 4 and 5, 89-159. See also chap. 6 which deals with Oldcastle's rising in 1414, 160-185. See also A. Hudson, 'Lollardy: the English Heresy' in *SCH*, xviii, 1982, 261-83, and M. Aston, 'Lollardy and Sedition' in *Past and Present* xvii, 1960, 1-44.

mity to established 'contemplative' practice. The processes of authentication and understanding were reciprocal. It is not possible to distinguish separately the evidence which she adduced to satisfy herself about authenticity and that she was not deceiving herself, from that which related to their meaning. In practice her understanding of the meaning reinforced her conviction that she was having and subsequently that she had had, a most powerful experience of divine self-revelation.

2.'LOUE WAS HIS MENYNG': THE MESSAGE MEDIATED

'Loue': 'Þi thurst of god'[8].

The understanding of Julian's spiritual vision hinges on her treatment of 'love'. As we have seen she begins the final paragraph of the Long Text with the words:

Thus was I lernyd, þat loue is oure lordes menyng[9].

The concept of 'loue' encapsulated the product of an extended learning process.

And fro the tyme þat it was shewde, I desyerde oftyn tymes to wytt in what was oure lords menyng. And xv yere after and mor, I was answeryd in gostly vnderstondyng, seyeng thus: What, woldest thou wytt thy lordes menyng in this thyng? Wytt it wele, loue was his menyng. Who shewyth it the? Loue...[10].

The 'infusion' of 'gostly vnderstondyng' to integrate the 'acquired' knowledge of the Pauline and Johannine traditions with her own experience in the *Showings* suggests the insight which enables her to appropriate and assimilate both in such a way that 'loue' becomes the pivot of her spiritual understanding and vision of life's purpose.

The discernment of love and 'what-is-not-love' becomes the mediating process, the dialectic which grounds her idea of how the individual responds in the existential situation to the knowledge given by the insight of what love is and means:

---

8   *Showings*. Crit.Ed. *L.T.*, 678.5.
9   *Ibid.*, 733.20. Oliver Davies, 'Transformational Process in the work of Julian of Norwich and Mechthild of Magdeburg' in *M.M.T. of Eng.*, 1992, 39-52, suggests "love is his meaning' seems less a resolution of this paradox [a God who is with us but transcends understanding] than its whole hearted embrace'. This perhaps emphasises that the processes of authentication and understanding were reciprocal as suggested above.
10 *Ibid.*, 732.13-17.

Alle this lesson of loue schewyth ... þat alle that is contraryous to this is nott of hym but it is of enmyte ... know it by þe swete gracious lyght of hys kynde loue[11].

The notion of 'lyght' is explained in the transposition of the term 'loue' into 'charite':

Thys lyght is charite[12].

The transposition serves to integrate the Pauline concept of charity with the Johannine teaching that God is love. She seems to imply that there is an element of fruition in the concept of 'charite' for 'at þe ende alle shalle be charite'[13]; that it relates to an object rather than an 'affectio':

I had iij manner of vnderstondynges in this lyght of (c)ha(r)ite. The furst is charite vnmade, the seconnde is charyte made, the thyrde is charyte gevyn. Charyte vnmade is god, charyte made is oure soule in god, charyte gevyn is vertu, and þat is a gracious gyfte of wurkyng, in whych we loue god for hym selfe, and oure selfe in god, and alle þat god lovyth for god[14].

The objects are God, as Trinity, the soul of the human being, and virtue as behaviour. 'Loue' is a relationship which bonds or brings the three aspects of 'charyte' together. The use of 'lyght' to represent the relationship reflects the conscious realisation of it through the affections which it stirs and awakens in subliminal being.

The ultimate explanation of this subliminal relationship is in the mystery of creation:

In oure makyng we had begynnyng, but the loue wher in he made vs was in hym fro with out begynnyng[15].

In the order of 'loue' the human being moves from the infinite to the finite and back again. The problem of what is made of this life and this love is shrouded in eschatological mystery. Julian recognises that knowledge of divine providence beyond this point is dependent on revelation in the order of faith and she counsels respect for God's 'prevytes'[16]. It is good manners to avoid prying into the matters which God does not wish to have known. Sufficient to recognise that as was conveyed to her:

---

11 *Ibid.*, 719.23-26.
12 *Ibid.*, 726.1.
13 *Ibid.*, 727.3.
14 *Ibid.*, 727.10-15.
15 *Ibid.*, 734.24.
16 *Ibid.*, 430,1-7:

'I kepe the full sykerly'[17].

The idea of creation as an act of love and the sense of security which flows from this knowledge is confirmed by the symbolism of the hazelnut in the first revelation. It is such a small and insignificant thing but it owes its continued life to the power which brought it into being; a power which is now recognised as love[18]. Yet, the soul of the human being is actually made in the image of God: 'charyte made is oure soule in God'. It participates in the divine 'charite'; that is it takes the form of God as revealed in the second person of the Trinity and is kept in being by the divine creative power. The creation is not just a single act without further consequence.

The metaphor of motherhood, 'thys feyer louely worde: Moder'[19], so prominent in Julian's exposition of her experience of Christ the 'very mother of lyfe and of alle'[20], is the one that is most apposite to convey in human terms the creative process and the relationship which flows from it. It symbolises in practical terms an ideal of participative being, nurture and care, and a special relationship which exists between mother and child throughout life. It also conveys the idea of the desire for ultimate success in the creative venture, for the child to reach maturity and fulfilment, and ultimate reunion in the eschatological order.

The ideal also includes the concept of mercy to which special attention must be paid in a moment. The ground of mercy is love, its working is 'kepyng in loue'[21];

for vs behovyth nedys to dye in as moch as we fayle syghte and felyng of God that is oure lyfe[22].

While motherhood symbolises affectively the creative relationship which Julian wishes to convey, there does not seem to be an intention to idealise motherhood for

---

'Oure lord shewyd two maner of prevytes. One ... hyd in to the tyme that he wylle clerly shew them to vs. That other ... hym selfe shewyd openly in thys reuelation ... þat we wytt that it is hys wylle we knowe them'.

See Ritamary Bradley, 'Christ the Teacher in Julian's *Showings*: the Biblical and Patristic Traditions' in *M.M.T. in Eng.*, Exeter, 1982.

17 *Ibid.*, 719.20 and 609.72 'I kepe the fulle suerly'.

18 The first revelation is in two parts; corporeal and spiritual. The corporeal was of blood trickling down Christ's face from where the crown of thorns was thrust down on his head. The spiritual was the hazelnut image as a symbol of his familiar love. *Showings*, trans. *S.T.* chaps 3 and 4 respectively; see Kenneth Leech, 'Hazelnut Theology: Its Potential and Perils' in *Julian Reconsidered*, Fairacres, Oxford: S.L.G. Press, 1988. Associated with the spiritual part was a spiritual vision of our Lady. In the Long Text (chap. 4) she associates the corporeal vision of Christ with the Trinity.

19 *Showings*, Crit. Ed. *L.T.*, 578.45.

20 *Ibid.*, 598.47.

21 *Ibid.*, 501.14.

22 *Ibid.*, 502.21-22.

its own sake. There is a perfect example of the ideal qualities of motherhood in the Lady Mary, the mother of Christ, to whose qualities her attention is drawn in the *Showings*

> I vnderstode thre maner of beholdynges of motherhed in god. The furst is grounde of oure kynde makyng, the seconde is takyng of oure of kynde and ther begynnth moderhed of grace, the thurde is moderhed in werkyng. And therin is a forth sp(r)edyng by the same grace of lengt and brede, of hygh and of depnesse without ende: and all is one loue[23].

Sr. Benedicta Ward has suggested that Julian may well have been a mother who had lost a child in the plague epidemic of 1369[24]. This suggestion is based not only on the particular sensitivity which Julian displays in her treatment of motherhood - a sensitivity which suggests, for Ward, 'experience' - but on the vision she describes in the fifteenth showing. The image is of a foul and decaying corpse from which a little child emerges and 'glydyd vppe in to hevyn'[25]. It is possible that the vision is directed to an experience of Julian and intended to bring to mind both the sense of helplessness at the loss of a child in such circumstances and also the supreme value placed upon the child by its parents and the distress associated with such apparently wanton destruction of an innocent by disease. However, the vision might equally well exemplify a general experience of death with the purity of the child and the affective resonances associated with it symbolising purity and innocence and the eschatological end of the body/soul resurrection. The second alternative would seem more likely, particularly in view of the emphasis placed by Julian on the generality rather than the particularity[26] of the meaning of the visions and the emphasis placed

---

23 *Ibid.*, 593.43-48. There are a number of works dealing with the 'gender', 'motherhood' and 'compassion' aspects of Julian's texts. Margaret Ann Palliser O.P., *Christ, Our Mother of Mercy. Divine Mercy and Compassion in the Theology of the Shewings of Julian of Norwich*, Berlin and New York: Walter de Gruyter, 1992, is perhaps the most comprehensive and contains a very full bibliography. See also Brant Pelphrey's works *Christ our Mother. Julian of Norwich*, London: Darton, Longman and Todd, 1989 and his *Love Was His Meaning: The Theology and Mysticism of Julian of Norwich*, Salzburg: Institut für Anglistik und Amerikanistik, Universität Salzburg, 1982; Robert Llewelyn, ed. *Julian: Woman of our Day*, London: Darton, Longman and Todd, 1986 and his *With Pity Not With Blame*, 1983, by the same publisher.

24 Sr Benedicta S.L.G. 'Julian the Solitary' in *Julian Reconsidered*. Convent of the Incarnation, Fairacres, Oxford: SLG Press, 1988, 17-29. She bases her suggestion on three considerations: external evidence; absence of evidence; and internal evidence of the *Short Text* itself. As Andrew Louth suggests in his chapter on 'Mediaeval Anchorism and Julian of Norwich' in *The Wilderness of God*, 65, n.7, Sr Benedicta's argument remains speculative and simply demonstrates how speculative our knowledge of Julian's historical circumstances are. For the Plague see A.H. Thompson, 'The Pestilences of the Fourteenth Century in the Diocese of York' in the *Archeological Journal* lxxi, 1914, 97-154.

25 *Showings*, Crit.Ed. *L.T.* 623.35.

26 *Ibid.*, 646.64.

by Christ, as recorded in the Gospels, on the need for the human soul to become childlike in its trust, a point which Julian emphasises in her reflections[27].

The quality of the Lady Mary on which Julian places primary emphasis is symbolised by the location in which the vision and locutions are set at the foot of the cross. It is compassion. Julian's idea of the greatest pain is to 'se the louer to suffer'[28]. Through Mary's motherhood compassion is also a quality attributed to the creator, as the divine Mother, and Christ, as Mother of the new restored Adam[29]. The passion of Christ becomes the supreme act of compassion; mercy as the quality expressing the divine love is fulfilled for Julian in the compassion of Christ. In the visions he told her 'yf I myght suffer more, I wolde suffer more'[30]. The act of voluntary self-sacrifice is an act which symbolises both the sorrow and joy of love. The wounds which the Passion evokes of contrition, compassion and longing to take upon oneself the afflictions of the loved one resonate 'in charite gevyn' the virtues of faith, hope and love[31].

---

27 *Ibid.*, 607.55-57, is illustrative of Julian's treatment of these themes. The Gospel references I have in mind are Mt. 19.14; Mk. 10.14; Lk. 18.16. See also Colledge and Walsh in the Introduction to their translation of the *Showings*, 87, where a comparison is made of Anselm's and Augustine of Hippo's treatment of the 'Christ as Mother' theme. Paul Molinari in his *Julian of Norwich: The Teaching of a 14th Century English Mystic*, London: Longman's, Green & Co., 1958, 171, quotes A. Cabassut, 'Une dévotion médiévale peu connue' in *RAM*, 25, 1949, 239: 'The *Oratio 65* [of St Anselm (1022-1109)] was certainly a source of inspiration ... The theme of the motherhood of Christ owes much to him either directly or indirectly ... [that is] the fundamental idea that Christ has given birth to us by dying on the cross, and that the pains of his passion have been the sufferings of our spiritual forthbringing'.

The mother and child imagery is also found in the *Ancrene Riwle* (written for anchoresses), trans. M.B. Salu, Orchard Books, 1955, chap. 61, suggesting this analogy was already well established in England as an appropriate way to convey to women the idea of spiritual rebirth. The child is the image of innocence and faith of the soul. Molinari, 193, n.3, refers to M. Viller and P. Pourrat, 'Abandon' in *Dict. Sp.* I, 1940, cols 1-49, who point out that St Francis de Sales conceived abandonment more or less as the spirit of the child and St Teresa of the Infant Jesus recommends 'the way of spiritual childhood' as the way of perfection. See Mgr Laveille, *Sainte Thérèse de l'Enfant Jésus*, Lisieux, 1926, chap. 14, 377. It would seem therefore that no particularly personal significance need be attached to Julian's usage of the imagery either of motherhood or the child. For a full discussion of the historical development of the 'Jesus as Mother' theme, see Carolyn Walker Bynum's *Jesus as Mother: Studies in the Spirituality of the High Middle Ages*, *op.cit.* See Prologue N.132 above, at 111, n.3 she cites other recent works dealing with the same theme. See also Valerie Lagorio, 'Variations on the Theme of God's Motherhood in Mediaeval English Mystical and Devotional Writings' in *Studia Mystica* 8 (Summer 1985), 15-37.

28 *Showings*, Crit.Ed. *L.T.* 365.59.

29 See N.27 above.

30 *Showings*, Crit.Ed. *L.T.* 382.6. Trans. *L.T.* chap. 22, 216 and *S.T.* chap. 12, 144.

31 *Ibid.*, 332.72. 'The sekyng with feyth, hope and charitie plesyth our lord'.

They seem to suggest for her three ways of contemplating the Passion

> The furst is the harde payne that he sufferyd with a contriccion and compassion[32].

The lessons which Julian learns and conveys to her readers in her reflections is that love is as much a matter of pain or sorrow as it is of joy, and regardless of your sin, she is told, one way or another you will suffer, 'for loue and drede are bredryn'[33]. The Passion represents the withdrawal of the object of love if only for a short time. It is the temporary nature of this loss which Julian emphasises. By the juxtaposition in the *Showings* of the event of the Passion with the infinity of the order of creation she symbolises both the short run and long run implications of her understanding of the meaning of the Passion in the finite human order. In the long run the human being experiences death and hopefully resurrection with Christ; in the short run an alternation of consolation and desolation. Without pain we cannot recognise joy as an absolute good.

> A properte of blessyd loue that we shalle know in god, whych we myght nevyr have knowen withoute wo goyng before[34].

> Here saw I a grett onyng betwene Crist and vs, to my vnderstandyng; for when he was in payne we were in payne, and alle creatures that myght suffer payne sufferyd with hym[35].

The notion of the sacred heart seen through the wound in Christ's side further symbolises the concept of self-sacrificing love[36]. It links the event of wounding and the flow of water and blood from his side with the purifying effect of the sacrifice, its salvific value; the suffering of pain is a purifying process. The wounds of contrition, compassion and longing for which Julian had asked in childhood are linked in this image of a pierced and riven heart not only with Mary's supreme suffering as mother[37] as she watches a loved one suffer and die, but also with the healing properties of the wounds[38].

The ideas of salvation, redemption and fulfilment in everlasting life beyond death are linked with the idea of joy in the spontaneous mirth with which she greets the vision of Christ's death as overthrowing the devil, the evil in the world, which the

---

32 *Ibid.*, 378.34-35. Trans. *L.T.* chap. 20, 234.
33 *Ibid.*, 673.20.
34 *Ibid.*, 503.46-47. Trans. *L.T.* chap. 48, 263.
35 *Ibid.*, 367.14.
36 *Ibid.*, 394ff. Trans. *L.T.* chap. 24, 220-21; *S.T.* chap. 13, 146.
37 *Ibid.*, chap. 18, 366ff. and chap. 25, 398ff.
38 *Ibid.*, 377.31; 'whych paynes shal be turned in to everlastyng joy by the vertu of Cristes passion'.

visions bring to the forefront of her attention[39]. Laughter destroys pain, literally in the context of the sickness with which her revelations were associated; on the point of death herself, she is restored to life[40], an experience, the symbolic significance of which did not escape her; from life to death in the finite order to life in the order of infinity. The vision of the glorified Christ which she receives symbolises the fulfilment which Christ's death has mediated and which make the wounds of life bearable[41].

The symbolism of the visions distils for her the manner of creative love. There are three ways of 'longyng in God'[42]; ways in which God's love is expressed; 'to lerne vs to know hym and to loue hym evyrmore'; 'to have vs vppe in to blysse'; and 'to fulfylle vs of blysse'[43]. The important point is that God loves us first and it is he who teaches us to know him and then to love him forever. He wants us to experience the joy of his presence and the healing which that joy will accomplish: 'God is our very peas'[44]. For Julian the process is God initiated; he teaches, we learn.

However the reason for our 'traveyle' is 'vnknowyng of loue'[45]. We recognise God's power and wisdom but not his love:

... but for felyng of loue in oure party, therefore is alle our traveyle[46].

God's love, she believes, never fails; the failure is ours and this leads to her treatment of sin as the absence of love[47]. The positive and negative elements in the dialectic become love and its absence. The paradox is posed of a loving self-sacrificing God and an untrusting, suspicious creature, failing to recognise all the evidences of divine love because it fails to understand what love truly means.

---

39 *Ibid.*, *L.T.* chap. 13, 348.25-350.49.
40 *Showings*, Trans. *L.T.* chap. 13, 202. *S.T.* chap. 8, 138. Julian notes that when she laughed, those around her bedside laughed too, which pleased her. She wishes all her fellow Christians would laugh too. Those at her bedside perhaps recognised in her laughter, the first signs of her recovery.
41 In the *Showings* Trans. *L.T.* in the following chap. 14 (6th Revelation), 203 and *S.T.* chap. 9, 139 and also *L.T.* chap. 26 (12th Revelation), 223. The *S.T.* reference chap. 13, 147, adds that those who look and seek will see Mary and pass on to God through contemplation.
42 *Showings*, Crit.Ed. *L.T.* 679.9.
43 *Ibid.*, 679.11-12, 680.13, 680.14-15.
44 *Ibid.*, 508.40.
45 *Ibid.*, 667.25.
46 *Ibid.*, 444.24-25.
47 *Ibid.*, 406.26-28 'But I saw nott synne ... no maner of substannce, ne no part of beyng, ne it might not be knowen but by the payne that is caused therof' and 431.23-26 'for in the thyrde shewyng, whan I saw that god doyth all that is done, I saw not synn, and than saw I that alle is welle. But whan god shewyde me for synne, than sayde he: Alle schalle be wele'; see also 337.8 'nothyn is done' by 'happe ne by aventure but alle by the for[eseing] wysdom of god'.

3. 'IT WAS NO RAVYNG': THE MEDIATING PROCESS

Authenticity and Understanding. 'Answeryd in my reson'[48].

The purpose of this section is to explore Julian's approach to the process of discernment; how she framed the problematic and how she addressed it. It takes as its premise an acceptance that the *Showings* were genuine or rather that there is no reason on balance to suppose they were not. It is concerned only with Julian's own ways of satisfying herself not only that the *Showings* were authentic but also that the rational process by which she established what they meant was objective and verifiable by external criteria; that is, how they fitted into the framework of faith she had acquired in her Christian formation and how they extended and deepened it.

The fact that she was powerfully aware of the problem of authenticity is clearly established. As we saw in the Prologue she knew that she would have difficulty in persuading other people that the experiences were genuine. Her first reaction when faced with a visitor, of religious persuasion, whether priest or religious is not clear, was to disown the experiences. They had resulted from the fever; she 'ravyd' she tells him[49]. However, she was immediately distressed by her denial, 'ashamyd and astonyd for my rechelenesse'[50]; the more so since her visitor took seriously the account of her vision of the bleeding Christ on the cross at the foot of her bed. She was distressed by her lack of trust because she was convinced at the time of the *Showings* that they were of divine origin:

> Nott with standing I beleft hym truly for the tyme þat I saw hym; and so was than my wylle and my menyng ever for to do without end. But as a fole I lett it passe oute of my mynde[51].

There is no archness in Julian's account. On the one hand she was aware of her conviction that the *Showings* were genuine; on the other that people would be inclined to disbelieve her; that in fact the fever had caused her to hallucinate in an imaginative way. The dilemma for her was to reconstruct in her imagination the series of experiences and the process by which her conviction had been formed that they were of divine origin; not only of divine origin but also to expose those which were of diabolic origin.

---

48 *Ibid.*, 365.57-58. See also 364.51-52 'fylle me with mynde' and 639.1 'opynnyd my gostely eye'.

49 *Ibid.*, 633.17. See D. Rogers, 'Psychotechnological Approaches to the teaching of the Cloud-Author and to the *Showings* of Julian of Norwich' in *M.M.T. in Eng.*, 1982, particularly in relation to our references to Paul Molinari's *Julian of Norwich; the teaching of a fourteenth century English mystic*, NN.69 and 81 below.

50 *Ibid.*, 633.20.

51 *Ibid.*, 634.26-29.

She recounts two types of experiences in the *Showings* which she judged to be of diabolic origin. The first was in the form of a temptation; to look away from the cross which had been the focus of her attention in the *Showings*[52]. The alternative she was presented with was not in itself evil; to look up to the Father in heaven. Later she interpreted the temptation as an attempt to get her to abandon the sight of the suffering Jesus; to seek disengaged tranquillity as opposed to God revealed in Christ. She tells us that she was glad she chose the suffering Jesus and resisted the impulse to take, what she interpreted as, an easier path. It was through his Passion and death that Jesus overcame the devil. The experience confirmed her understanding of the close association between love and suffering[53]. No human suffering, however unjust it may seem, can match the injustice in which the creator is the victim of the creature. The willing self-sacrifice of Christ offering himself as the sacrificial victim of such 'inhuman' justice restores the relationship of love between creator and creature because Christ as true man and true God represents the bridge over which the creature must travel to rejoin the creator.

And the cause why that he sufferyth is for he wylle of hys goodnes make vs the lyers with hym in hys blysse[54].

It also teaches her to recognise that love means self-sacrifice and whatever suffering may attend it;

therfor we be indysees and traveyle with hym as our kynd askyth[55].

It highlights for her too the dilemma of the Church's teaching about the fate of the damned, those who are judged to have dissociated themselves from the merits of Christ's sacrifice, and the fear and anxiety which the doctrine of damnation instils. Julian is particularly concerned to promote, what she regards as one of the lessons of her experiences, a right attitude to fear and anxiety.

In some ways the second type of diabolic intervention which she experienced reinforces her conviction that the evil effects of suffering and fear are overcome by an appreciation of the nature of divine love[56]. The personification of evil in the form of the fiend is particularly vivid in the mediaeval imagination; however the modern imagination is no stranger to the fear and anxiety which are part of the finite effects of the destructive forces which seem to pervade the human psyche. During the sixteenth *Showing*, Julian describes an almost continuous physical attack by the fiend[57].

---

52 *Ibid.*, chap. 19 and *S.T.*, chaps 10 and 11.
53 *Ibid.*, *L.T.* chap. 20.
54 *Ibid.*, 381.23.
55 *Ibid.*, 381.22.
56 *Ibid.*, chap. 67.
57 *Ibid.*, chap. 69.

It is recalled in specific physical detail; not only the physical assaults but also the accompanying effects of foul stench and smoke. Bystanders did not sense any of these effects. They seem to have been interior experiences similar to those experienced in nightmares:

> Me thought that besynes myght nott be lykened to no bodely lykenesse[58].

The important point for Julian seems to have been the way she combatted the fear which the assault created rather than the assault itself. Throughout she says she kept her eyes fixed on the cross:

> Mi bodely eye I sett in the same crosse there I had seen in comforte afore þat tyme[59].

For her the experiential certainty that fixing attention on Christ and his Passion can overcome the ill-effects of demonic intervention was the most profound lesson to be appreciated. The deliberate choice of the cross suggested to her that this was no ordinary dream; there was a consciousness of an association between the preceding *Showings* and the experience of demonic activity in the dream.

> [I]t was gruzyng and dawnger of the flesch without assent of the soule ... two contrarytes whych I felt both at that tyme; and tho be two partes, that oon outward, that other inward. The outwarde party is our dedely flessch ... the inward party ... is more pryvely felte; and this party ... I chose Jhesu to my hevyn[60].

It further reinforced her conviction in the reflection upon the meaning of the Passion and its fundamental message of love. For her the Passion became the bridge which provided the transition from darkness to light; in the same way that trust and hope provide the nexus which link love and the effects of its absence in her vision of the spiritual life.

> [I sett] my tong with speþch of Cristes passion and rehersyng the feyth of holy church and my harte to fasten on god with alle the truste and þe myghte[61].

The Passion is an indissoluble bridge for her to which the creature always has access through faith.

These two particular descriptions of demonic activity which Julian provides in the *Showings* depict a reality with which she had no difficulty in associating. Whereas

---

58 *Ibid.*, 649.13-14.
59 *Ibid.*, 650.1.
60 *Ibid.*, 372.23-32.
61 *Ibid.*, chap. 70, 650.2.

for the modern mind they might seem to represent an extravagant and over-credulous flight of imagination, for Julian the affective contrast which the experiences provided with her reactions to the Passion, assisted her in re-affirming the authenticity of the overall experience of the divinity in the *Showings*:

> For if oure feyth had nott enmyte, it shulde deserue no mede, as by the vnder-standyng that I haue in oure lordes meynyng[62].

The feelings of compassion and contrition, the alternating experiences of consolation and desolation, which the showings of Christ's sufferings evoked, were in direct contrast to the fear which the diabolic intrusions produced. However, for Julian the touchstone of affectivity was insufficient to rule out the possibility of self-deception. The main touchstone of authenticity was whether or not the teachings of the visions and locutions conformed with those of 'Holy Church';

> I beleue þat he is oure sauyoure that sh(e)wed it, and that it is in þe feyth that he shewde, and therfore I loue it evyr joyens. And therto I am bounde by alle hys owne menyng, with the nexte wordes þat folowen: kepe thee there in, and con-forte thee ther with and truste therto[63].

Julian takes it for granted that there is no ambiguity in the teaching of 'Holy Church'; she speaks of 'the ordynannce of holy chyrch'[64]. She does not indicate that she has any doubt that the authentic voice of the Church can be heard; that there may be differences of opinion among theologians or different liturgical and canonical interpretations of teaching. She is conscious of the fallibility of individuals within the Church but that the teaching might be perverted does not seem to be a serious possibility. When she compares her understanding of what the *Showings* mean with the Church's teaching, she is aware of paradox, but never is she in any real doubt that apparent differences are reconcilable. She is inclined to doubt her own understanding rather than the teaching on which her own religious formation was based. Her concept of Church is mystical. The Church is guided by the Holy Spirit; it is the mystical body of Christ[65].

Nevertheless, there is no conflict in her mind between the organs of the institutional Church and the concept of the mystical body. The institutional Church exercises authority in the finite dimension; the mystical body is its substance in the infinite

---

62 *Ibid.*, 656.16. See Jean Leclercq, *The Love of Learning and the Desire for God. A Study of Monastic Culture*. Trans. C. Misrahi, New York: Fordham University Press, 1961, 93 on the power of the imagination of mediaeval people compared with people today; cited by Colledge and Walsh in the Introduction to the *Showings*, Crit.Ed., Vol. 1, 131.

63 *Ibid.*, 652.23-27.

64 *Ibid.*, 668.33.

65 *Ibid.*, 414.5-7, and also 607.55-64 and 612.23-613.30.

dimension. There is almost a distinction similar to that in human being; substance and sensuality. There is no difficulty in extending to the Church the two aspects of Christ; on the one hand he is man; on the other he is god. Both aspects are the reality of his existence. To say there is no difficulty is perhaps a misnomer. It was not until she had solved the riddle of the Lord and Servant example that she felt she understood the concept of the two orders of being operating on the same plane rather than as two separate layers of existence[66]. But it is true she never doubted that there was a reasonable explanation. The full explanation was simply a 'prevyte' of God until such time as he was prepared to enlighten her understanding.

It is difficult to accept that both before and after her enclosure, Julian did not engage in spiritual discourse in addition to her prayer-life, *lectio divina*, and spiritual reading. From the evidence of Margery Kempe, it is known that she was a spiritual director of considerable reputation[67]. On the other hand, particularly in the early days following, for example, the showings and the writing of the short text, it is difficult to believe she did not receive direction herself or did not seek it. The events leading to her enclosure, must have brought to the attention of the ecclesiastical authorities the substance of the *Showings*. Indeed there may well have been some attempt made to down-play their importance and to test their authenticity, against the longer-run behaviour of Julian. After all a key test of exposure to divine touchings was the quality of life which they induced. Was Julian's attitude and life consistent with the holiness which such experiences would be expected to engender? Moreover, Julian was well aware of the prejudice with which 'visions' received by women were regarded by the ecclesiastical authorities, especially in the late fourteenth century. She knew she would be expected to deport herself with humility and submissiveness[68].

---

66 *Ibid.*, chap. 51. See D.N. Baker, *Julian of Norwich's 'Showings': From Vision to Book*, Princeton, New Jersey: Princeton University Press, 1994. See also Henri de Lubac, *A Brief Catechesis on Nature and Grace*, 35, n.46, quotes Karl Rahner, *Mission et Grâce, op.cit.*, Vol. 1, 65-67: 'Grace is essentially a determination, an elevation and divinisation of nature ... Let us not therefore imagine it as though it were a higher storey that the heavenly architect in his wisdom would have added to the bottom one (nature) in such a way that the lower floor, keeping intact the structure which belongs to it as such, would merely be a support to this upper one'.

67 See Prologue, N.28.

68 See for example Prologue, N.57 for John Gerson's attitude. See also the excellent introduction to *The Chastising of God's Children and the Treatise of Perfection of the Sons of God*, ed. J. Bazire and E. Colledge, Oxford: Blackwell, 1957. *Chastising* is a late 14th century Middle English work whose author remains anonymous. Although concerned with the profit to the human soul of spiritual and physical afflictions (41), the author of *Chastising* identifies himself with the attitude that much of the spiritual malaise evident in his day had its roots in 'contemplatives gone wrong' (47) and while drawing in part on Alphonse of Pecha's *Epistola Solitari*, an apologia for *St Bridget of Sweden's visitations and revelations*, uses the ideas in quite the opposite manner to Alphonse, to warn the unwary of how easily they may be deceived by the devil (48). Margery Kempe's *Book* also provides a record of how suspiciously women's 'enthusiasms' were regarded in their day.

Perhaps it was this consciousness of the need to establish credibility and authenticity that made Julian so careful to be accurate and precise in her descriptions of the nature of divine communication. Fr. Molinari in his *Julian of Norwich, the Teaching of a 14th Century English Mystic*, has made a careful comparison of the terminology used by Julian to describe her experiences with that used in the contemplative tradition[69]. His analysis relates both to the visions and locutions themselves and also to the process of verification. The particular feature of Julian's descriptions on which he believes she places primary emphasis is the infused understanding which is unaccompanied by either vision or locution; it is a process of enlightenment in which the understanding is brought about not so much by reasoning and logical process but by direct insight, the intuitive grasp of a truth.

> Alle this blessyd techyng of oure lorde god was shewde by thre partys, that is to sey by bodely syght, and by worde formyd in myne vnderstondyng, and by gostely syghte ... for gostely syghte, I haue seyde some dele, but I may nevyr fulle telle it[70].

It can subsequently be verified by rational process but the insight itself is inspired. The inspiration may have resulted from subliminal activity, below consciousness, but is attributed to the Holy Spirit working from the depth of the soul. Julian is aware that self-deception is possible in such insight and is therefore rigorous in applying objective criteria; reason, the Church's teaching and the experience of the contemplative tradition.

There is a certain tension in her emphasis upon trust and the need for rigorous verification of the source of her insights. Trust, of course, is not an absolute; there are degrees of trust. Trust grows with knowledge and the experience of love. At any one time trust may be deficient even in the experienced contemplative. It is the dialectic between verification and experience which builds the quality of discernment. Ultimately paradox must be understandable and resolvable or the significance of the experience must be doubted. Whatever raises doubts and is in conflict with trust, is likely to have its source in the 'enmyte' of human being. Ultimately trust is rational because the individual understands that reason has limits and experience is verifiable. Trust of this kind is based upon verifiable experiences supported by rational ordering within a philosophical/theological horizon[71].

---

69   Fr. Paul Molinari, S.J. *Julian of Norwich*, 140-45 and the Appendix 60-70.
70   *Showings*, Crit.Ed. *L.T.*, chap. 73, 666.2-4 ... 6-7.
71   *Ibid.*, 323.22-28 'the feyth of holy chyrch which I had before hand vnderstondyng, and as I hope by the grace of god wylle fully kepe it in vse and in custome, stode contynually in my syghte, wyllyng and meanyng never to receyve ony thyng that myght be contrary ther to. And with this intent and with this meanyng I beheld the shewyng with all my dylygence, for in all thys blessed shewyng I behelde it as in gods menyng'.

Another source of tension in Julian's account of her experiences is the question why
she should be chosen to receive this revelation. Her initial explanation is that the
vision is associated with her own imminent death. Her recovery from the sickness
leaves the question unresolved. In the meantime the conviction of the authenticity of
the *Showings* has been formed and she becomes aware that she has been the channel
of a divine revelation. It has become her responsibility to disseminate the message[72].
By the same token she denies that this duty or the *Showings* themselves result from
any merit of her own[73]. It is perhaps easier for an objective observer to recognise the
qualities of contrition and compassion and indeed intelligence, that might have made
Julian the ideal choice for such a role. Her own genuine humility would naturally
cause her to deny the qualities. In the matter of love the human being will always be
imperfect and unworthy. However, she had displayed the attributes which the tradition has associated with outpourings of divine love because those attributes are the
necessary pre-conditions for the divine love to be recognised and returned. For
Julian her own role remained a mystery. The very unobtrusiveness of her subsequent
life suggests a quality of humility and 'dyscrycion' which acknowledges a total
dependence on divine direction. If it is the divine will that his message be understood and disseminated, then he would provide the means and the direction. Her
own task is to pray for understanding and guidance. The time lapse between her
experiences of the *Showings* and her final understanding of the meaning of the Lord
and Servant example, which illuminated the meaning of not only the parable but also
the *Showings* themselves, provided the occasion for the testing of her faith and perseverance, qualities which would ensure the divine message would be powerfully
represented[74].

The explanation that is given by Julian for the suppression of the Lord and Servant
parable in the short text is that at the time she did not understand it. It is possible,
though purely speculative and unverifiable, that Julian may have initially considered
that an account without theological explanation, might have evoked political conno-
tations. The Christian *Weltanschauung* so dominated mediaeval thought, Marsilius
of Padua's *Defensor Pacis* notwithstanding[75], that the relationship of Lord and Servant was the archetypal social compact. It was not regarded as political or social or
economic in the orientation of mediaeval thought; society was regarded as holistic;
social gradings were in natural order of things and accepted. However, in the late

---

72 *Ibid.*, chap. 8, 320.34-40 'And therefore I pray yow alle for gods sake, and counceyle yow for
    yowre awne pro(f)yght, þat ye leve the beholdyng of a wench that it was schewde to ... for it is
    goddes wylle that ye take it with a grete ioy and lykyng as Jhesu hath shewde it to yow'.

73 *Ibid.*, chap. 9.

74 *Ibid.*, chap. 51, 519.74-85 and 520.86-88.

75 Marsilius of Padua (c. 1275-1342). Crit.Ed. of *Defensor Pacis* by C.W. Previté-Orton, Cam-
    bridge, 1928. See the note in *The Oxford Dictionary of the Christian Church*, 878. The work is
    one of the most challenging of the Middle Ages. According to Marsilius the church must be
    completely subordinate to the state. See also W. Ullmann, *A History of Political Thought: The
    Middle Ages*, 204ff.: 'The People as Sovereign Legislator'.

fourteenth century, the feudal relationship was coming under strain both at the social and economic level and also at the political level. The tensions were inchoate but as the Peasants' Revolt[76] was to show and the difficulties arising from the lack of strength in the monarchy to emphasise, they were persistent. The descending theory of authority, which Dante espoused[77], was still in the ascendancy but it was coming under pressure both in the ecclesiastical and secular spheres. It seems unlikely that Julian would have suppressed the allegory without a powerful reason. It was pivotal to the expansion of the short text into the longer version and to her conception of the nature of sin and to her understanding of the Passion and mercy of God.

The reflections on the Lord and Servant allegory provide the most substantial part of the differences between the two versions of the *Showings*[78]. The realisation that the Lord and Servant symbolised the duality of being; the co-existence of a natural and 'supernatural' for want of a better term, dimension of being in humanity.

> whych syght was shewed double in þe lorde, and the syght was shewed double in the servannt. That one perty was shewed gostly in bodely lycenesse. The other perty was shewed more gostly withoute bodely lycenes[79].

Both the old and the new Adam are represented in the servant. The lord represents both the temporal reflection of the triune God in his church and the internal spiritual reflection in the relationship of the Trinity to the son. The sacramental relationship is the nexus which binds the two aspects of being in their human and spiritual realities. The theological significance of Julian's reflections on the allegory is not so important for the present purpose, as its symbolic significance for Julian herself as illuminating the whole of her experience. Suddenly everything falls into place. She appropriates the *Showings* in a new way; they are no longer the means for the strengthening of faith but they now reveal the wonder of God's love and of his providence. The allegory provides the medium for an infused insight into the divine operation and into the Trinity itself; it is not a full understanding, but it is an understanding of a different kind than she had previously achieved. It is a difference of kind rather than degree[80].

---

76 See N.6 above.

77 See W. Ullmann, *A History of Political Thought: The Middle Ages*, 189-195. Also A.P. d'Entrèves, *Dante as a Political Thinker*.

78 See Introduction by Edmund Colledge and James Walsh to their translation of the *Showings*, 23.

79 *Showings*, Crit.Ed. *L.T.*, 514.4-7.

80 *Ibid.*, chaps 52, 53, 53, 55 in which she recognises the soul as a created Trinity like the uncreated blessed Trinity and 58 in which she explains her understanding of the properties of the Trinity as 'fatherhood', 'motherhood' and 'lordship' in which the human being has 'being', 'increasing' and 'fulfillment' or 'nature', 'mercy' and 'grace' and these become 'might', 'wisdom' and 'love'. See Vincent Gillespie and Maggie Ross, 'The Apophatic Image: The Poetics of Effacement in Julian of Norwich' in *M.M.T. in Eng.*, 1992, 53-78, esp. 53. I find it difficult taking Julian's experience as a whole to agree that it is appropriate to apply to her, as

The experience of her struggle to understand the allegory, teaches her the difference between the exercise of reason and the infusion of understanding which the gift of the Holy Spirit provides[81]. It is a gift which follows faith and perseverance; not so much as a reward for their pursuit as a necessary preparation for the receipt of the gift. The gift will never be lacking but the necessary conditions for its appropriation take time to emerge; some of the reasons why this is so are known - doubtful dread, sloth, impatience - the imperfections of spirit which disable it and lead to spiritual blindness; others are locked amongst the 'prevytes' of God which, she understands, it is not necessary for the creature to penetrate but 'it longyth to the to take hede to alle þe propertes and þe condescions, that were shewed in þe example though þe thyngke that it be mysty and indefferent to thy syght'[82]. In other words, 'be attentive'[83].

4. DISCERNMENT: 'DYSCRECION'

A key in understanding the role of discernment in Julian's treatment of spiritual development is the text.

---

the authors seem to, the notion of Rowan Williams' 'any speech about God is a speech about absence'. They quote Jacques Derrida, 'Structure, Sign and Play in the Discourse of the Human Sciences' in *Writing and Difference*, trans. A. Bass, London, 1978, 278-93, esp. 279 and 292 on 'absence'. 'It extends the domain and play of signification infinitely' and 54 they quote Samuel Terrien, *The Elusive Presence*, New York, 1978, 476, 'Presence dilutes itself into its own illusion whenever it is confused with spatial or temporal location'. Both quotations are admirable comments on the apophatic experience but would seem more appropriate to the *Cloud* Author or John of the Cross than to Julian.

81 Molinari, *Julian of Norwich*, 137-39 notes that:
'Julian is very much at home with the anagogical sense of Scripture, which for so many of the Fathers expresses the whole of the Christian mystery, and, as such, absorbs the allegorical and tropological senses, and [quoting H. de Lubac, *Exégèse Médiévale: Les Quatres Sens de l'Ecriture*, 2.631-633] makes the synthesis of the 'sensus spiritualis seu plenior''.
So much of Julian's contemplation is anagogical; 'it could with justice be described as the meeting place of her developing understanding of Scripture and of the infused contemplative graces bestowed on her'. Her struggle to understand the 'Lord and Servant' parable is a case study in the development of the anagogical imagination. See also Jean Leclercq's 'Preface' to the Colledge and Walsh translation of the *Showings*, 8-11, where he makes the connection between Julian's theology of the Trinity and the symbolism of the Motherhood of God as an original contribution in which 'the harmony between theology and poetry' is exemplified (9), and B. Lorenzo, 'The Mystical Experience of Julian of Norwich with reference to the Epistle to the Hebrews, ch. ix: Semiotic and Psychoanalytic Analysis', trans. Yvette le Guillou, in *M.M.T. in Eng.*, Exeter, 1982, 161-181.
82 *Showings*, Crit.Ed. *L.T.*, 520.87-521.89.
83 *Ibid.*, 439.46 'Intende to me'.

Sekyng is comyn and that ech soule may haue with his grace and owyth to haue dyscrecion and techyng of holy church[84].

Seeking is a part of 'being' itself; manifested in the attempt to understand the desire for knowledge which humans observe to be a part of their make-up. The pursuit of this understanding leads to God when guided by the revelation which is the basis of the Church's teaching. However, an essential ingredient in the search, if it is to be successful, is the exercise of 'dyscrecion' which is itself a grace.

The role of 'discrecion' is further developed in her treatment of prayer in Chapter 41:

... it plesyth hym that we werke in prayer and in good lyvyng by his helpe and his grace, resonable with discrecion kepyng oure myghtys to hym tyll whan we haue hym that we seke in fulhede of joy that is Jhesu[85].

Both prayer and the way of life are to be pursued using reason and the special judgement which is derived from grace, until God reveals himself. 'Discrecion' is the essential adjunct, quality of judgement, to the exercise of the powers of reason, which will lead to the desired end:

Thou shalt haue me to thy mede[86].

The fullest explanation of what she means by 'discrecion' is offered immediately prior to the exposition of Lord and Servant parable at the close of Chapter 50. Julian is plucking up the courage to ask God to clarify the difficulty she has in reconciling what she has seen in the *Showings* with the teaching of the Church and she says three considerations prompt her boldness. The third of these

... is that it nedyth me to wytt, as me thyngkyth, if I shall lyve here, for knowyng of good and evyll, wher by I may by reson and by grace the more deperte them a sonder, and loue goodnesse and hate evyll as holy chyrch techyth[87].

She realises that in the practical situations which have to be faced in life it is not always so easy to apply the Church's teaching and distinguish good from evil. This requires the exercise of reason enlightened by grace. It especially requires love of goodness which is itself a grace so that good is chosen and evil rejected. There are two aspects to the practical business of good living; to love goodness, that is ultimately to wish to do God's will, and to know what it is in any particular situation. Both require help from God but the exercise of reason is also necessary; it is a com-

---

84   *Ibid.*, 334.84-86.
85   *Ibid.*, 465.51-466.54 'dyscrecion' above becomes 'discrecion'.
86   *Ibid.*, 466.55.
87   *Ibid.*, 512.32-35.

bination of reflection and prayer which provides the quality of judgement which she denotes by the word 'discrecion'. It is an 'infused' gift:

> and this is his owne werkyng in vs, and of his goodnesse openyth the ey of oure vnderstanding, by whych we haue syght, somtyme more and somtyme lesse, after þat god gevyth abylte to take...[88].

In this context she is particularly referring to the desire to do God's will. It is not always felt to the same degree, despite a basic disposition to do 'good':

> And now we be reysyde in to that one, and now we are sufferyd to fall in to that other[89].

The 'medle' is so 'mervelous' that one scarcely knows where one stands. It is an alternation between 'feeling' God and 'blyndnesse'. The basic disposition to do 'good' is faith; to trust, in this context of alternating light and blindness that light will return, which:

> may now be seen and feelt in mesure by the gracious presence of oure lord whan it is[90]

but

> oure feyth is contraryed in dyuerse maner by oure owne blyndnesse and oure gostely enemys within and withoute[91].

We are helped 'with goostely lyghte and tru techyng on dyuerse manner within and withoute, where by þat we may know hym'[92].

Faith grows with the exercise of 'discrecion' and the experience this provides of God's goodness and love. The individual grows in this dialectic process of love and its absence:

> Perfore it is goddes wille and oure spede that we knawe thamm thus ysundure[93].

---

88 *Ibid.*, 547.17-548.20.

89 *Ibid.*, 548.20-21.

90 *Ibid.*, 628.12-13.

91 *Ibid.*, 654.6-7.

92 *Ibid.*, 654.8-655.10.

93 *Ibid.*, *S.T.*, 278.33-34. This follows a description of the disturbing kinds of fear which she suggests should be rejected as one would an evil spirit, whose attributes she thus describes. Reverent fear develops from the peace and rest which is the characteristic of God's love and which the Christian fears to lose.

That is good and evil. By learning (meke knowyng) and with 'contrycion and grace'[94], the individual will be transformed in the ability to judge 'alle thyng þat is not oure lorde'[95] and then the ultimate purpose is achieved. God will 'cure vs and oone vs to hym'[96].

The characteristics of an action which conforms to God's will are the opposite to those, by which evil is recognised. All that opposes the 'homely' nature of his love, 'it is of the enmy and nott of god'[97].

> And be the grett desyer that I saw in oure blessyd lorde that we sulle lyue in this manner, that is to sey in longyng and enjoyeng, as alle this lesson of loue schewyth, ther by I vnderstonde þat alle that is contraryous to this is nott of hym, but it is of enmyte. And he wille þat we know it by þe swete gracious lyght of hys kynde loue[98].

5. JULIAN'S POSITION WITHIN THE TRADITION OF 'DISCERNMENT OF SPIRITS'

'For he it is holy Chyrch'.

For Julian 'holy Chyrch' means more than the institutional church. It signifies the mystical relationship which exists between Christ, the founder of the institution and those who are incorporated within it by baptism. It is Christ who inspires the institution and guarantees its teaching as a true reflection of his spirit[99]. The foundation of Julian's discernment, the criterion of 'truth', is the conformity of her *Showings* with the teaching of the Church. 'Holy Chyrch' is the mind of Christ. Whatever is in conflict with the teaching of the Church is likely to be inspired by the evil spirit. She places her trust first in the Church and only secondly in her interpretation of the *Showings*. In her concern to be obedient to the Church's doctrine, she points in the direction of Ignatius of Loyola and his 'rules for discerning with the Church' which provide an unequivocal endorsement of Julian's implied view that the spirit of discernment is first given to the Church and through the Church to individuals. So there can be no conflict[100].

On the other hand, her long struggle to reconcile the visions she received of Christ's love and mercy, which was central to the *Showings*, with the Church's teaching on

---

94 *Ibid., L.T.,* 698.33.
95 *Ibid.,* 678.24.
96 *Ibid.,* 699.25.
97 *Ibid.,* 705.26.
98 *Ibid.,* 719.22-26.
99 *Ibid.,* chap. 26.
100 *Ibid.,* 607.55-608.64 ... 612.23-613.30.

sin and damnation, lead her towards an Augustinian interpretation of the mystical relationship between the temporal Church and the *Civitas Dei*. Whether or not she was aware of Augustine's *De Civitate Dei*, we do not know. Nor do we know the source of the spiritual direction it is probable she received. However, through her meditations on the 'Lord and Servant' parable she came to understand the distinction between a descendent Christ and a transcendent Trinitarian God as two planes of existence, as it were, for the Church, the temporal and the spiritual. So she can say, 'for he it is, holy Chyrch', that is 'he' both Christ and Trinitarian God[101]. The latter we can only know through faith in the temporal institution of the Church[102]. Her notion of Church, whose teaching is the basis of meditation, reflects the tradition of self-understanding which the mediaeval Church had gradually developed as the institutional Church pondered the insights of Augustine and the other Fathers.

By the same token, she seems to react against a false Augustinianism, perhaps prevalent in the aftermath of the plague which failed to understand that Augustine's consciousness of the sinful nature of man was but a reflection of his awareness of the absolute love and mercy of God. Sin for Augustine was a very deep mystery because he could never reconcile the human tendency to sinfulness with the knowledge of the depth of divine love. For Augustine sin was something deeply rooted in human nature by the original disobedience of Adam which distorted even the human capacity to reason. The crippling effect of sin might only be overcome by recognising the merits of Christ's sacrifice[103]. The major lesson which Julian understood from the *Showings* was just this point. Only by keeping her vision fixed on the Crucifix at the foot of her bed was she able to overcome the activity of the devil, seeking to distract and destroy her. She understood that absolute trust in the merits of Christ's sacrifice and by extension his whole life and teaching was the fundamental basis of discernment. This seems to encapsulate the ancient tradition of meditative prayer on Scripture as the basis of the ascesis which leads, with God's grace, to the kind of discernment which Cassian and Climacus had in mind; to acquiring the capacity to see, as it were, through God's eyes. The concomitant notion implicit in Julian's teaching on discernment is that the human will is guided by the analogical imagination which deals with human images but to understand the divine will, it is necessary to develop an anagogical imagination which is fed by divine spiritual 'images'.

This is perhaps what Julian means when she says: 'Seeking is comyn and that ech soule may haue with his grace and owyth to haue dyscrecion and techyng of holy

---

101 *Ibid.*, 431.17.
102 *Ibid.*, 431.12-14.
103 Julian's preoccupation with reconciling 'synne' and God's 'loue' is perhaps a reflection of a prevailing preoccupation with 'synne' in the Church of the day, reflected also in Walter Hilton and the *Cloud* Author.

Chyrch'[104]. This statement seems to capture, for her generation, the spirit of the contemplative tradition of faith seeking understanding through personal humility and meditation. She seems unconscious of the crisis of confidence in the teaching of the temporal Church which will soon begin to engulf it. The scenario with which Ignatius of Loyola and John of the Cross will be faced in the sixteenth century in attempting to discern divine 'truth', is the battleground, to restore the confidence 'of' and 'in' 'holy Chyrch', which seems to have dissipated in the intervening decades of the fifteenth century.

---

104 *Showings*, Crit.Ed. *L.T.*, 334.84-86. - The number of times we come back to this theme suggests it might be a leitmotiv.

Chapter 3

THE *CLOUD* AUTHOR

1. 'ÞE SOUEREINNEST POINTE OF CONTEMPLATIFE LEUING'

The unknown author of the *Cloud* canon[1] is no less cautious than Julian about the possible reception of his message. He wishes to confine it to an audience which will

---

[1]   N.63 of the Prologue describes the Cloud-canon and the sources used. In addition to the passages in Hodgson's introduction referred to there, see James Hogg, 'The Latin Cloud', in *M.M.T. in Eng.*, 1984 and A. Minnis, 'The Sources of the Cloud of Unknowing: A Reconsideration' in *M.M.T. in Eng.*, 1982. The modern titles and abbreviations used in this chapter are the same as those in the Prologue, but I have used Middle English titles on their first appearance and abbreviated forms thereafter. The conventions used are as follows:

Modern English Title	Middle English Title	Abbreviated Title	Footnote Reference
The Cloud of Unknowing	Þe Clowde of vnknowyng	the Cloud	CL
The Book of Privy Counselling	Þe Book of Priue Counseling	Priue Counseling	PC
An Epistle of Prayer	A Pistle of Preier	Preier	P
An Epistle of Discretion of Stirrings	A Pistle of Discrecion of Stirings	Stiring	ST
Denis Hid Divinity	Deonise Hid Diuinite	Hid Diuinite	HD
The Study of Wisdom	A tretyse of þe Stodye of Wysdome þat men Clepen Beniamyn	Benjamin	B.M.W.
The Treatise of Discerning of Spirits	A Tretis of Discresyon of Spirites	Spirites	S

Richard of St Victor's work is referred to as *Benjamin Minor*; Pseudo-Dionysius work is referred to as *The Mystical Theology*. I have quoted from Abbot Justin McCann's modernised version of *The Cloud of Unknowing and Other Treatises* (*The Cloud, Priue Counselling* and *Hid Diuinite*) and as indicated for the other treatises. The translations have been checked against Phyllis Hodgson's Critical Edition, *The Cloud of Unknowing and related treatises*, Analecta Cartusiana Salzburg, Austria: Institut für Anglistik und Americanistik, 1982.
In the footnotes references have been indicated by both the source of the translation and the critical edition thus:

not be misled by misinterpretation. The message itself is not elitist; on the contrary, it is concerned with a state of maturity to which all beings, he believes, are ultimately destined. However he wishes to address only those who are already conscious of this destiny and have progressed some way along the path to its realisation. So he begins the *Þe clowde of vnknowyng* with a cautionary prologue, for it is a dramatic theatrical performance through which his audience learns by the experience of participation:

> I charge thee and I beseech thee, with as much power and virtue as the bond of charity is sufficient to suffer, whatsoever thou be that this book shalt have in possession, whether by property, or by keeping, or by hearing as a messenger, or else by borrowing, that inasmuch as in thee is by will and advisement, thou neither read it, write it, nor speak it, nor yet suffer it to be read, written or spoken, by any other or to any other, unless it be by such a one or to such a one as hath (in thy supposing) in a true will and by a whole intent *purposed him to be a perfect follower of Christ*. And that not only in active living, but also in the *sovereignest point of contemplative living*[2].

He is enjoining his audience to participate in good faith by being party to an agreement, a covenant, expressed almost in 'legal' terminology, not to let his text fall into the wrong hands.

He wishes to address only those who 'in thy supposing' - an important qualification - are committed to trying to be 'perfect' followers of Christ. They are not however beginners. They have already demonstrated their good intentions in 'active Christian living' but have come to realise there is a further step along the path to perfection. Furthermore, they wish to proceed to this 'sovereignest point' of becoming a contemplative. To guide his audience to this furthest point along the path is the *Cloud* author's objective. Later on in the *Cloud* narrative he explains the reason for his caution:

> Beware of error here, I pray thee; for ever the nearer men touch the truth, the more wary must men be of error[3].

Work (e.g. CL),   M. chapter (chap.) page (p.);   H. page (p.) Line (L)
          M ≡ McCann   H ≡ Hodgson

I decided to use modernised quotations in this chapter since in the previous chapter on Julian the variant spellings of the same word in Middle English were a distraction and the origins of the variations were not usually relevant to my discourse. Moreover, Justin McCann's translations which I have used where available follow the Middle English text closely.

2   *CL*: M. Pro., p. 8; H. 1, 8ff. See also *CL*: chap. 74; H. 72, 25-73, 17 [my italics].

3   *CL*: M. chap. 21, p. 37; H. 30, 24. The *Cloud* Author's caution contrasts with the use made of his texts today as a basis for prayerful reflection. See for example, A. Cooper, *The Cloud. Reflection on Selected Texts*, Homebush, N.S.W.: St Paul Publications, 1989.

Our author must have been conscious that in the Church of his day there was considerable misunderstanding of what 'contemplatives' were trying to achieve and, may be even scepticism about whether contemplation was indeed the 'sovereignest point' of Christian perfection. The scepticism may reflect more widespread realisation in that time that 'the devil also had his contemplatives'[4], those who have fallen into error, the possibility of which our author refers to. Nevertheless he urges:

> Actives, actives! Make you as busy as ye can ... And meddle you not with contemplatives. Ye know not what aileth them. Let them sit in their nest and in *their play* with ... the best part of Mary[5].

We must return to the Martha-Mary story, to which 'the best part of Mary'[6] refers, later. Suffice it to say that he identifies, as many mediaeval authors did, the Mary of the Martha/Mary gospel story with Mary Magdalene the reformed sinner.

He may perhaps use Mary Magdalene's experience as symbolic of the Christian's progress from sinner to contemplative in *Þe Book of Priue Counseling*:

> all the men of this life may be divided in three: in sinners, in actives, and in contemplatives[7].

The gradations reflect various degrees of divine involvement but

> Himself [our Lord] saying 'without me you can do nothing'[8]

and our author goes on to offer an explanation for the ascending scale in his typology,

> Without me - either only suffering and not consenting as in sinners; or else both suffering and consenting, as in actives; or (that more than all this is) principally stirring and working, as in contemplatives - 'ye may do nothing'[9].

---

4   *CL*: M. chap. 45, p. 63; H. 48, 2-3. From the context, see H. 47, 43, this may be a reference to the Lollards.

5   *CL*: M. chap. 21, p. 37; H. 30, 24-29. See Hodgson's Commentary at page 164, 30/28, for significance of 'play' (pley) particularly the use in Ancrene Wisse (Ancrene Riwle). The idea of 'play' seems to have been taken up by Marion Glasscoe in the subtitle 'Games of Faith' of her book on *English Mediaeval Mystics: Games of Faith*, London and New York: Longman, 1993. [my italics]

6   See Hodgson's Commentary, 161, 17/9-21 and 17/22-23 and Chap. 1. N.9 above for Giles Constable's discourse on the subject.

7   *PC*: M. chap. 10, p. 128; H. 93, 39-40.

8   *PC*: M. chap. 10, p. 126; H. 92, 39. Jn. 15, 5.

9   *PC*: M. chap. 10, p. 128; H. 93, 42-94, 3.

The contemplative, in other words, is being led by God to his 'sovereignest point', this 'best part', - for which Mary is the archetype - where Christian perfection is to be found. Those who rest in the 'active' Christian life may be completely unaware of the powerful stirrings which 'aileth' contemplatives. Our author's 'play' is about how God's lead may be recognised and followed through the metamorphosis which transforms the 'active' into the 'contemplative'.

The achievement of Christian perfection is in our author's view a literal metamorphosis, in which the Christian sheds his skin of sensuality, like a suit of clothes, to be clothed by God in a new skin and emerge a transformed being by the experience of 'oneing' in which the metamorphosis takes place[10].

The author's story is about this intensely painful process of metamorphosis which he tells in vivid physical and psychological metaphors. He tells the story from the beginning of the Christian pilgrimage because, although he is primarily concerned with the final most painful stages of metamorphosis, he nevertheless suggests that the stages of sinful and active life are not so much to be forgotten as seen in a different light by those who achieve their goal of 'oneing' or 'union' with the divinity.

So his 'play' unfolds in a number of scenes. The first may be called 'steryng of loue'[11]. It is the metaphor of the 'blind stirring of love'. In it 'being' is stirred to emerge from the darkness of the mire in which it has been sunk, in response to some 'blind' unrecognised goad. It emerges from the mire in the second scene which may be called the 'stynche' of 'synne'[12] in which it recognises its foulness in contrast to some primeval memory of the smell of pure air. It is then led to strip off the foul accretions of mire which had stained its clothing. This scene may be called 'the nakedness'[13]. In it the powerful and painful process of forgetting and shedding the mire and the stench of sin takes place. As this process of forgetfulness of the past develops the pure, clear light of the future shines through and is blinding in its intensity. In the fourth scene, therefore, the being suffers 'the blindness' of 'unknowing'. The being 'feels' and gropes the way forward guided by the warmth from the source of light. In the final scene it experiences 'the oneing'[14] in which the metamorphosis is completed. Sight returns and with it the view of all things is transformed.

For this author his audience is elitist or exclusive only in the sense that he wishes it to be confined to people who have experienced this 'stirring' so powerfully that they are moved by it. They do not possess any particular personal merits or intelligence.

---

10 *PC*: M. chap. 6, p. 118; H. 86, 26-27.
11 *CL*: H. 9, 12 and 15, 1.
12 *PC*: H. 77, 15 and 72, 12.
13 *PC*: H. 86, 24 cf. 'nakid blynde felyng'.
14 *CL*: H. 67, 10 e.g. 'onyd to God'. See Robert K. Forman, 'Mystical Experience in the Cloud-Literature' in *M.M.T. in Eng.*, 1987.

On the contrary, it is the divine 'stirrer' who initiates everything. The simplest person can participate. The only requirement they must possess is to have been goaded by the 'stirring' to 'be' Christians, and to have faithfully followed the teaching of the Church. The contemplative life is an aspect of church life; the 'sovereignest' aspect albeit. Our author conceives of the contemplative living a life within the Christian community; not outside it or apart from it. The contemplative is an integral part of the community in this life. So our author's epilogue is about 'Holi Chirche'[15], not only as a temporal community, but also as a mystical community combining a natural and a supernatural existence as the body of which Christ is the head.

The texts in which our author's 'play' are to be found expound a unified conceptualisation of the contemplative life and of the process of contemplation but they deal with them with different emphases. Our reconstruction follows the process through which discernment of spirits develops from recognition to faith and love by successive stages in a total metamorphosis. Paradoxically it is not so much a process of ascent to enlightenment but a progressive denuding from within as the contemplatives descend down into the depths of the human psyche in nakedness and blindness. The dramatic denouement, which is the reward of faith and perseverance, is restoration of sight, totally transformed. The author seems to believe it is a 'full' enlightenment, which is possible only when the roots of sin are destroyed and which cannot be achieved in any other way. The restoration of sight in the return to health and wholeness is totally gratuitous but never withheld from those who trust completely in the divine mercy. This, our author believes, is the way of the cross. The 'resurrection' process through which the contemplative passes in the 'oneing', is an experience of such sublimity that our author will not defile it by attempting to describe it with his 'blabryng fleschely'[16] tongue.

2. 'STERYNG OF LOUE'

The *Cloud* author's 'stirring' which ultimately guides contemplatives to seek their vocation in 'contemplation' is the same impulse, perhaps, that led Chaucer's pilgrims to undertake their pilgrimage. It is felt with varying intensities, but, in our author's experience, 'blindly'. The great seventeenth-century English contemplative, Augustine Baker, to whose initiative, as we have seen, has been attributed the preservation of Julian of Norwich's long text[17], interpreted our author's 'stirring' in the following way:

---

15 *CL*: H. 35, 13. A variant is 'Holy Chirche', 33, 34.

16 *CL*: M. chap. 36, p. 43; H. 34, 37. See also 'boystouse beestly tonge' at *PC*: M. chap. 7, p. 117; H. 87, 17.

17 See Prologue N.31 above and Hodgson's Introduction to the Critical Edition, xvii-xix, for Augustine Baker's involvement with the Cloud texts.

For what is stirring but motion? And he calleth it a 'blind stirring' because it is without use of the understanding, the which is termed the eye of the soul. And he calleth such exercise a 'stirring of love' because the soul thereby heaveth herself up towards God, out of the interior affection she hath towards him, choosing him and seeking after him for his sake[18].

The use of the metaphor of 'heaving', which implies great exertion, suggests a 'grabbing hold', the role of those who heave themselves up as they are pulled out of the mire by the unrecognised source of the stirring. Someone or something is needed to overcome the inertia. That someone or something is 'love' which is both rescuer and the motivating power which supplies the energy to begin the heave.

The *Cloud* author refers to the 'blind stirring' variously as this 'secret little love', 'the naked intent of the will', 'the blind outstretching', 'the meek stirring of love', 'this working' and sometimes simply as 'it'[19]. Augustine Baker's interpretation seems to gather up all these various usages. It is a 'secret' 'meek', 'little' love; not a boisterous physical thing which stirs from without, but something gentle which stirs from 'within'. It is perhaps this very gentleness that makes it the object of 'choice'; something to be sought with the 'naked intent of the will'. Such a thought suggests that it is the agent for transforming the will. 'Naked' in such a context implies 'singleminded', without any other intent; to be sought after for its own sake in a 'blind outstretching' which becomes a 'working' when it is harnessed to power and is called 'a heave'. This 'blind love' starts as 'little' but becomes in the 'working' a mighty 'heave'. It is something which wants to be harnessed but the object to which the harness is attached is 'felt' but remains 'unknown' and the harnessed being 'blind'.

The *Cloud* author uncovers the object and source of this 'love'

> that devout stirring of love ... is wrought in his will not by himself but by the hand of Almighty God[20].

And

> Almighty God with his grace must always be the chief stirrer and worker, either with means or without, and thou [in this case the person to whom *Priue Counseling* is addressed], or any other like unto thee, but the consenter and the sufferer[21].

---

18 Justin McCann's modernised version, *The Cloud of Unknowing and Other Treatises*, also contains Baker's Commentary on the *Cloud*.

19 See William Johnston's, *The Mysticism of the Cloud of Unknowing*, Wheathampstead, Herts: Anthony Clarke, repr. 1980, 98. I am greatly indebted to this work and where I have referred to it hereafter I have used the abbreviation 'J'.

20 *CL*: M. chap. 26, p. 42; H. 14, 9-11.

The passivity of the contemplative is apparently always the starting point. He speaks with scorn of those who think they can appropriate the divine love by their own initiative;

> in confusion of their erring presumption, that in the curiosity of their learning or their natural wit will always be principal workers themselves, God but suffering or only consenting; when verily the contrary is truth in things contemplative[22].

And this of course is the reason why actives sometimes misunderstand the contemplative vocation:

> So that, in things active, man's learning and his natural knowledge shall principally abound as in working - God graciously consenting ... But in things contemplative, the highest wisdom that may be in man, as man, is far put under, so that God be the principal in working and man but only consenter and sufferer[23].

And the 'contemplative' finds it difficult to persuade the 'active' of his *bona fides* unless the 'actives' have experienced the stirring for themselves in the way in which the 'contemplatives' have.

> And if thou ask me by what means thou shalt come to this work, I beseech Almighty god of his great grace and his great courtesy to teach thee himself. For truly I do well to let thee know that I cannot tell thee. And that is no wonder. Because it is the work of *only God*, specially wrought in whatever soul he liketh, without any merit of the same soul. For without it no saint nor angel can think to desire it[24].

The essential difference, perhaps, which our author is trying to draw between the 'stirring' of the 'contemplative' and that of the 'active', is the context. The 'active' is drawn to good works and teaching by perceiving a need outside himself and the action of God is to endorse the work with, perhaps, a sense of peace or the success of the work itself. In the case of the 'contemplative', however, the stirring originates from within, without apparent external cause. He advises the person wondering whether to undertake the life of the 'contemplative' to seek advice, 'counsel' or 'spiritual direction', to be obedient to the Church and faithful to Scripture. He insists the would-be 'contemplative'

---

21   *PC*: M. chap. 7, p. 121; H. 88, 21-23.
22   *PC*: M. chap. 10, p. 127; H. 92, 42-93, 3.
23   *PC*: M. chap. 10, p. 127; H. 93, 17-23.
24   *CL*: M. chap. 34, p. 48; H. 38, 6-12 [my italics].

should be such a one as doth all that in him is, and ... hath done long time before, for to able him to contemplative living, by the virtuous means of active living. For else it accordeth nothing to him[25].

Contemplation, then, is the object of the Christian's pilgrimage. It is the summit. The progress through the life of 'sinner' and 'active' to 'contemplative' is a natural progression; a development and an extension of each moment of life in which all three phases are present in some degree, to a more specialised series of moments where each successive phase becomes dominant. So the 'contemplative' should aim, in our author's view, to seek a life at the summit.

And how is this to be achieved? By cultivating this 'little love', this stirring, so that it becomes the dominant guide in the 'contemplative's' life:

All thy life now must always stand in desire, if thou shalt advance in degree of perfection. This desire must always be wrought in thy will, by the hand of Almighty God and thy consent[26].

The consent takes the form of 'passivity' of a kind, a 'stand in desire' to advance in perfection; it is passive in the sense that it seems to be an orientation towards perfection which is characterised by sensitivity towards and maintaining a constant look-out for the 'stirring' of this 'little love'.

However, there is a difference between 'stirrings'; they may be of two kinds[27]. The one signifies 'ordinary' grace, the natural delight which arises from reflections and evidences of God in one's daily routines; the other is a 'special' grace which urges the recipients on to the life of perfection and encourages them as in 'pleye' between, for example, father and son, to more perfect performance[28]. In the *Priue Counseling*, in particular, our author describes how a prospective 'contemplative' may become aware of the 'special' grace[29].

He draws a distinction between a 'stirring' which arises from within and one from without. Neither is indubitable evidence of this 'special' grace on its own but when they are experienced together, it is very probable that the 'stirring' is evidence of a special calling. He goes on to explain what he means by this distinction.

---

25 *CL*: M. Prol. p. 3; H. 1, 19-21.

26 *CL*: M. chap. 2, p. 7; H. 8, 36-9, 3.

27 *PC*: H. 94, 20.

28 *PC*: H. 95, 33f. See also M. P. 130, n.1 and Hodgson's Commentary 181.95/33 (for variant spelling of 'pley' see H. Glossary, 218/9) and *CL*: M. chap. 66, p. 64; H. 48, 35-37. See also Hodgson's Commentary 170, 48/35, 36; 'he shuld fele [God] gamesumli pley wiþ hym, as fadir doþ wiþ þe childe'.

29 *PC*: M. chap. 11, pp. 128-30; H. 94, 11-95, 36.

The interior mode of 'stirring' is like a blind desire which nourishes and feeds daily devotions. It seems to be a feeling that grows and which seems to bring with it the joy of spiritual insight. If it is connected with spiritual exercises, such as an aware-ness of personal wretchedness or the passion of Christ, exercises which are basic to the prayer-life of a Christian, then it is probable the stirrings are part of the 'ordi-nary' graces which strengthen and encourage Christians in their daily living. In our author's view these kinds of stirrings are not in themselves indicative of a special call to the contemplative life.

The other kind of stirring he identifies results from an external source. He explains that they are pleasurable feelings which arise when a person reads about contempla-tion for example. They come through the windows of the senses. If this pleasure is short-lived it is probably evidence of an ordinary grace. On the other hand, if it per-sists and squeezes between the person and his prayer, if it is so overpowering that it is present at bedtime and on awakening, and continues through all daily activities intruding into prayer and making a deep impression on the whole outlook, so that the stirring from without becomes indistinguishable from the effects of a stirring from within, then probably it is sure evidence of a special calling[30].

He describes the effects on the individual who experiences this kind of stirring in the following way:

> Thou lovest to be alone and sit by thyself: men would hinder thee, thou thinkest, unless they wrought with thee; thou wouldst not read books nor hear books but only of it[31].

So persons in this position only want to be with 'contemplatives' and talk about the experience of this stirring. They would run a thousand miles to talk about it with someone who was known to have really experienced it[32]. In its intensity the stirring seems to dominate the personality.

Yet the stirring and the elevated feelings which have accompanied it may suddenly cease[33]. The person is left longing for it to return and famished by its absence. Our author's explanation for this apparent loss of grace is twofold. First of all, he sug-gests, it is to teach the would-be 'contemplative' the difference between grace which is spiritual and the feelings which signify its presence which are physical. The ab-sence of feeling and stirring does not mean that grace is absent. Grace is God him-self who cannot be comprehended in his essence or nature. The contemplative has to learn to recognise on the one hand, as it were, a silent spiritual presence and on the

---

30 *PC*: H. 95, 22-25.
31 *PC*: M. chap. 11, p. 130; H. 95, 33-35.
32 *PC*: M. chap. 11, p. 130; H. 95, 26-28.
33 See *PC*: M. chap. 12; H. 95, 37-98, 7 for what follows.

other the accustomed feelings which accompany the presence. The second point about the apparent loss of grace is that the would-be 'contemplative' has to learn to live in faith and hope without the physical benefits and comfort of elevated feelings. God dispenses grace according to his pleasure as if in 'pleye' perhaps. It is not something that the 'contemplative' can command by the exercise of the will. The will must be trained, he explains, to be docile and thus sensitive to the insights which flow from stirring from within. Such insights, he believes, have to be tested against the canons of reason, Scripture, counsel and 'conceyence'[34].

However, our author is equally certain that for those who are called to the contemplative vocation the stirrings will not be absent for long and will return with ever increasing intensity. This is the little lesson of 'love'[35]:

all that is spoken of it is not it, but of it[36].

In the *A Pistle of Preier* which is in fact a lesson of love he refers to the perfection of love being recognised when

affection is stirred unto God *without mean*, that is without messenger of any thought in special causing that stirring[37].

It is a blind and naked outreaching of affection welling up from the unplumbed depths of the psyche spontaneously which suffuses the whole person:

This is the work of love that none may know but he that feeleth it. This is the lesson of our Lord when he saith, 'Whoso will love me, let him forsake himself'[38].

The particular form of ascesis, which our author so graphically expounds, by which the stirring may be cultivated and by which the 'contemplative' may learn to 'forsake himself', is itself dependent on learning to recognise 'the stirring'. The 'work', the series of operations, by which the growth in intensity of the stirring may be encouraged is inter-active. It involves both recognising the source and directing the whole of one's being towards it by the occlusion of other sources of 'stirring'.

In the *A Pistle of Discrecioun of Stirings*, our author deals, in his usual forthright style, with teaching how the recognition of the 'blind stirring' may be developed as the criterion for the direction of life. Our author is addressing a person who has sought his advice about how 'contemplatives' may make ordinary decisions about

---

34 *PC*: M. chap. 12, p. 133; H. 97, 40-98, 1.
35 *PC*: H. 87, 43-44 in which he directs attention to 'lityl pistle of preier'.
36 *PC*: M. chap. 7, p. 19; H. 87, 20-21.
37 *P*: H. 105, 30-32; J pp. 107-8.
38 *PC*: M. chap. 8, p. 122; H. 89, 18-20.

regulating their activities of silence and of speaking, of common dieting and of singular fasting, and of 'dwelling in companye & of only - wonyng by þiself'[39]. In the highly regulated life of the monastery or the hermitage, such decisions become matters of conscience. Our author directs his enquirer to consider the source of stirring which underlies the decision: 'if grace only be the cause ... [or] ... if it be otherwise then there is but peril on all sides'[40]. To judge reasonably the motions of grace in the soul one must have much experience. The experience he refers to is 'the clear and true knowing of himself and all his inward dispositions'[41] which initially comes from seeking counsel about what is experienced. Yet he insists that true discernment in spiritual matters comes from within the heart not from outside:

> And touching these stirrings, of the which thou askest my opinion and my counsel: I say to thee that I conceive of them suspiciously; that is that they should be conceived on ape manner. Men say commonly that the ape doth as other seeth. Forgive me if I err in my suspicion, I pray thee[42].

In other words, is the doubt about what to do genuine or is it a motion prompted by discussion or the observation of other people's experience? The source of the motion is all important:

> And therefore beware and *prove* well thy stirrings and whence they come. For howso thou are stirred, whether from within by grace or from without on ape manner, God wot and I not[43].

Only the person experiencing the stirring can really recognise its source.

> Look that thy stirrings to silence or to speaking to fasting or to eating, to onliness or to company, whether they come from within *of abundance of love and devotion in spirit* and not from without by windows of thy bodily wits, thy ears and thine eyes[44].

He then presents the crux of the matter when choosing, for example, between silence and speaking: 'Choose thee a thing the which is hid betwixt them'[45]. For he goes on:

> It is God for whom thou shouldst be still, if thou shouldst be still; and for whom thou shouldst speak if thou shouldst speak; and for whom thou shouldst fast; and

---

39 *ST*: H. 109, 1-4.
40 *ST*: H. 109, 13-16; J. p. 120.
41 *ST*: H. 110, 18-19; J. p. 120.
42 *ST*: H. 113, 1-4; J. p. 120.
43 *ST*: H. 113, 18-20; J. p. 121 [my italics].
44 *ST*: H. 113, 23-26; J. p. 121 [my italics].
45 *ST*: H. 114, 34-35; J. p. 121.

for whom thou shouldst be alone, if thou shouldst be alone; and for whom thou shouldst be in company; and so for all the remnant, whatso they be[46].

The criterion of choice is always 'God' and recognising that God is not an activity but a desire, 'the true lovely will of thine heart'.

For silence is not God, nor speaking is not God ... nor yet any of all the other such two contraries. He is hid betwixt them, and may not be found by any work of thy soul but only by love of thine heart. He may not be known by reason. He may not be thought, gotten nor traced by understanding. But he may be loved and chosen with the true lovely will of thine heart. Choose thou him; and thou art silently speaking and speakingly silent, ... and so forth of all the remnant[47].

As this 'lovely' stirring grows stronger it intrudes upon every action. It orders the 'contemplatives' to choose God, and if they do not follow the command it wounds them and gives them no peace until they do its bidding,

Then that same that thou feelest shall well know *how to tell thee* when thou shalt speak and when thou shalt be still. And it shall govern thee discretely in all thy living without any error, and teach thee *mystically* how thou shalt begin and cease in all such doings of nature with *a great and sovereign discretion*. For if thou mayest by grace keep it in custom and in continual working, then if it be needful to thee for to speak, for to eat in the common way, or for to bide in company, or for to do any such other thing that belongeth to the common true custom of Christian men and of nature, it shall first stir thee softly to speak or to do that other common thing of nature, whatso it be; and then, if thou do it not, it shall smite as sore as a prick on thine heart and pain thee full sore, and let thee have no peace but if thou do it. And in the same manner, if thou be speaking or in any such other work that is common to the course of nature, if it be needful and speedful to thee to be still and to set thee to the contrary, as is fasting to eating, being alone to company and all such other, the which works of singular holiness, it will stir thee to them[48].

Providing therefore that the contemplative 'stands in desire'[49] for God, the stirring, the motions of the heart, will guide the will to choose how to act in accordance with God's will. The stirring becomes a 'bright flame' in the very depth of the soul where no evil spirit can penetrate. He makes the point in the *Cloud*.

---

46   *ST*: H. 114, 39-115, 4; J. p. 121.
47   *ST*: H. 115, 4-13; J. p. 122.
48   *ST*: H. 117, 23-39; J. pp. 122-23 [my italics].
49   *CL*: H. 9, 1; 'stonde in desire'.

Trust then steadfastly that it is only God that stirreth thy will and thy desire, plainly by himself, without means either on his part or on thine. And be not afraid of the devil, for he may not come so near. He may never come to stir a man's will, except occasionally and by means from afar, be he never so subtle a devil. For sufficiently and without means may no good angel stir thy will; nor, shortly to say, anything but only God[50]

and he reiterates it in the *Stiring*. This guidance of God Himself is true discernment and true wisdom. It is the gift for which one must strive:

with all the love of thine heart, utterly voiding from thy ghostly beholding all manner of sight of anything beneath him[51].

The *Cloud* author, for all the vigour and novelty of his presentation, is not putting forward new ideas. He is interpreting what seems to be a very vivid personal experience of established contemplative practice. The marrying of a thoroughly grounded practice with the personal experience of following it is forcefully expressed in the *Cloud*:

But since all reasonable creatures, angel and man, have in them, *each one by himself*, one principal working power, the which is called a knowing power, and another principal working power, the which is called a loving power. Of the which two powers, to the first, the which is a knowing power, God who is the maker of them is evermore incomprehensible; but to the second, the which is the loving power, he is *in every man diversely*, all comprehensible to the full. Insomuch, that one loving soul alone in itself, by virtue of love, may comprehend in itself him who is sufficient to the full - and much more without comparison - to fill all the souls and angels that ever may be[52].

All human beings have a knowing power, 'each one by himself', to a degree he seems to say which varies among them. However, regardless of how well endowed they may be with this particular power, God remains incomprehensible to them. On the other hand, although the loving power is also present 'in every man diversely', yet in whatever degree it is possessed, God is comprehensible to it. The nature of the love is such moreover that each soul can comprehend God 'who is sufficient to the full', 'without comparison' to fill it (the capacity of the soul) to the brim. The reasoning power, it might be concluded, is the servant of its twin the loving power, which can subsist on its own, if needs be.

---

50 *CL*: M. chap. 34, p. 50; H. 39, 11-17.
51 *ST*: H. 117, 13-14; J. p. 124.
52 *CL*: M. chap. 4, pp. 9-10; H. 10, 31-40 [my italics].

Notwithstanding the very clear position he takes about the primacy of the loving over the reasoning power in the works he is addressing to prospective 'contemplatives', the emphasis is different in *A tretyse of þe Stodye of Wysdome þat new clepen Beniamyn*. As we have noticed this latter work is a free translation of the twelfth-century allegory of Richard of St Victor[53]. These different emphases simply reinforce the warnings he gives in the Prologue to the *Cloud* about his purpose. The particular point which concerns us here and which is made in *Benjamin* is that 'discretion', represented by Joseph, in the allegory, is the first born son of Rachel who represents 'reason'. 'Contemplation', represented by Benjamin, is the second born son of Rachel who dies after giving birth to him. 'Discretion' then precedes 'contemplation', and both are the progeny of 'Reason', but once discretion is in place and contemplation is born, reason disappears[54]. In *Benjamin* the importance of discernment is heavily underlined:

> Thus it seemeth that the virtue of discretion needeth to be had, with the which all others may be governed. For without it, all virtues be turned to vices. This is he, that Joseph, that is the late-born child. But yet the father [Jacob ≡ God][55] loveth him more than them all, for why truly without discretion may never goodness be gotten nor kept. And therefore no wonder if that virtue be singularly loved without which no virtue be had nor governed[56].

However discernment is a gift, a grace, which seems only to be obtained after a great deal of experience, of many falls, failings and mistakes:

> a man learneth by the proof that there is nothing better than to be ruled after counsel, the which is the readiest getting of discretion[57].

This notion seems to echo the teaching of the Desert Fathers as recorded by both Cassian and Climacus.

The *Cloud* Author goes on to make the point that love alone cannot give this virtue but only reason.

> And here is the open reason that neither Lya [affection], nor Zelfa [sensuality], nor Bala [imagination] [all women who bore children by Jacob] can bear such a child, but only Rachel [reason]. For, as it is said before, out of reason springeth

---

53 See Prologue N.63 above. See also *B.M.W.*: H. 129, 1 and Hodgson's Commentary, 195. I am assuming in the discussion which follows that the *Cloud* Author is the translator of this work, which remains an open question. See N.66 below.
54 *B.M.W.*: H. 130, 22ff. for diagrammatic representation of relationships.
55 *B.M.W.*: H. 129, 9-10 and 141, 28.
56 *B.M.W.*: H. 141, 32-38; J. p. 128.
57 *B.M.W.*: H. 142, 16-18; J. p. 128.

right counsels, the which is very discretion understood by Joseph the first son of Rachel[58].

The emphasis on securing 'right counsel' once again echoes the teaching of the Desert Fathers who also believed that it was primarily the linking of meditative prayer and the counsel of a spiritual director which formed the virtue of discretion. This teaching moreover does not conflict with the position the *Cloud* Author takes in *Priue Counseling*:

> And I would think that it were impossible to man's understanding - although God may do what he will - that a sinner should come to be restful in the ghostly feeling of himself and of God, unless he first saw and felt by imagination and meditation the bodily doings of himself and of God, and thereto sorrowed for that that were to sorrow, and made joy for that that were to joy[59].

A great deal of 'work' must be done and experience gained before the graces of contemplation are likely to be received. However, the *Cloud* Author is careful to suggest that the advice is based on common experience and that this in no way restricts God's freedom of action to dispense grace in whatever manner he pleases. He illustrates what is meant in *Benjamin* in his depiction of Rachel. The union of Jacob and Rachel represents in the allegory the union of reason with God which brings forth first 'discretion' and then 'contemplation'. Rachel as 'reason' is portrayed as a woman of flesh and blood, no cold abstraction - we are reminded of Dante's portrayal of Beatrice in the *Divine Comedy*[60]. Rachel is an expectant mother longing for the birth of her child:

> And therefore she multiplied her study, and whetted her desires, each desire on desire, so that at last, in great abundance of burning desires and sorrow of the delaying of her desires, Benjamin is born, and his mother Rachel dieth[61].

Meditation and the reasoning processes which accompanied it 'whetted' her desire and then the desires intensified to an almost intolerable degree. It is like the stirring perhaps of Benjamin in the womb and the labour of giving birth. Reason has no part to play in these final stages of labour in which 'contemplation' is born. It is the desire to give birth that takes over. And so the *Cloud* Author says,

---

58 *B.M.W.*: H. 142, 22-25; J. p. 128.
59 *PC*: M. chap. 9, p. 114; H. 90, 29-34.
60 When Dante is reunited with Beatrice in the *Divine Comedy*. 2. *Purgatory* she is revealed as a real woman of flesh and blood, no icon of the *amour courtois* tradition.
61 *B.M.W.*: H. 144, 15-18; J. pp. 129-30.

For why in what time that a soul is ravished above himself by abundance of desires and a great multitude of love, so that it is inflamed with the light of the
Godhead, surely then dieth all man's reason[62].

'Man's reason' dies to be replaced by 'high ghostly wisdom'[63]. 'Reason' is transformed into 'wisdom' in the final metamorphosis. In *Priue Counseling*, commenting
on the text 'Beatus homo qui invenit sapientiam', he says,

He is a blissful man that may find this *oneing wisdom* and that may abound in
this ghostly working ... in offering up of his own blind feeling of his own being,
all curious knowledge of learning and of nature far put back[64].

The 'oneing wisdom' takes over; it is 'the high wisdom of the Godhead graciously
descending into a man's soul'[65].

There is undoubtedly a different emphasis between the *Benjamin* and the author's
'counselling works'[66]. It has led to the suggestion that this translation might not be
the author's work. It is, of course, a free interpretation of Richard of St Victor's text.
But like his other translations, of Pseudo-Dionysius' *Deonise Hid Diuinite* and of
two of Bernard of Clairvaux's sermons in his *A Tretis of Discresyon of Spirites*, it
seems he wished to make available in the vernacular the primary sources of his own
understanding and teaching. He seems to recognise that the transcendent wisdom of
which the *Benjamin* speaks, is the fruit, the ripe fruit, of contemplation[67]; it is not the
result, usually, of a miraculous conversion such as that of St Paul. It is rather the
fruit of much work not only of the reason applied in meditating sacred authors, but
also the work involves a recognition and nourishing of this 'blind stirring', which
starts as 'meek' but grows in intensity until Benjamin is born. In his counselling
works he does not discount the power and use of reason, he simply emphasises that
the 'blind stirring' of love is a better guide to attainment of the 'oneing wisdom'
than reason can be. Rachel, as reason, cannot satisfy her own desires but she can
recognise them as beyond her own power to satisfy.

---

62 *B.M.W.*: H. 144, 18-21; J. p. 130.
63 *PC*: H. 82, 12; J. pp. 135-6.
64 *PC*: M. chap. 5, p. 12; H. 81, 40-82, 4.
65 *PC*: M. chap. 5, p. 112; H. 81, 30-31.
66 Yet see *PC*: H. 85, 11-29, where he refers to Richard of St Victor's allegory. For Richard of St
    Victor see Hodgson's Commentary, 195. See also Prologue N.63 above and N.53 in this chap-
    ter.
67 *PC*: H. 87, 43-44 and *P*: H. 106, 1-3.

3. THE SPIRITUAL MARRIAGE: '*ONEHEAD OF LOUE*'

The 'oneing' is analogous to marriage:

> And in this onehead is the marriage made betwixt God and the soul, the which
> shall never be broken, though all the heat and fervour of this work cease for a
> time, but by deadly sin. In the ghostly feeling of this onehead may a loving soul
> both say and sing, if it will, this holy word that is written in the Book of Songs in
> the Bible: 'Dilectus meus mihi et ego illi'. That is 'my loved unto me and I to
> him' understood 'shall be knitted with the ghostly glue of grace on his part and
> the lovely consent in gladness of spirit on thy part'[68].

And speaking of the love which is consummated in the peak experience of contemplation:

> And in this time is thy love chaste and perfect. In this time it is that thou *seest*
> thy God and *thy love* and nakedly *feelest* him also by ghostly oneing to *his love*
> in the sovereign point of the spirit, as he is in himself, but blindly as it may be
> here, utterly spoiled of thyself and nakedly clothed in himself, as he is, unclothed
> and not lapped in any of these sensible feelings - be they never so sweet nor so
> holy - that may fall in this life. But in purity of spirit properly and perfectly he is
> perceived and felt in himself as he is, far removed from any fantasy or false
> opinion that may fall in this life[69].

In this 'oneing' the two loves, that of the contemplative and that of God, are united
at that 'soueryn poynte of Þi spirit'. There is feeling but it is 'naked', 'spoiled' and
'unclothed' of self; clothed only in God. There is seeing but it is 'blind', enclosed as
it were deep within the being itself at the 'soueryn poynte'.

The *Cloud* author is at pains to dissociate this experience of God from any 'sensible
feelings', yet he is perceived and felt in himself as he is. The perception and feeling
cannot however be associated with any image or product of a disturbed imagination
taken from this life. He goes on to emphasise

> This sight and this feeling of God (thus in himself as he is) may no more be sepa-
> rated from God in himself (to thine understanding that thus feelest or thus seest)
> than may be separated God himself from his own being, the which be but one
> both in substance and also in nature. So that as God may not be from his being,
> for onehead in nature, so may not that soul (that thus seeth and feeleth) be from
> that thing that he thus seeth and feeleth, for onehead in grace[70].

---

68 *P*: H. 126, 14; J. p. 247.
69 *PC*: M. chap. 12, pp. 132-33; H. 97, 14-22 [my italics].
70 *PC*: M. chap. 12, p. 133; H. 97, 23-29.

It seems that the *Cloud* author is taking very great care with his explanation to avoid suggesting that he can describe what he sees and feels. He is suggesting, perhaps, that the mystery is somewhat akin to the mystery of the Trinitarian nature of the Godhead. There is both oneness and distinction. The experience is real; the spiritual senses register it as 'seeing' and 'feeling' but what is seen and felt cannot be separated from within the experience itself. One perhaps experiences the wholeness, the unity of being as God experiences the created universe.

The mirror motif perhaps explains what the *Cloud* author means by the experience of the wholeness of created being. In *Priue Counseling* he says, 'Let that meek darkness be thy mirror and thy mind wholly'[71]. The darkness may be that blindness at the sovereign point of the spirit. The mirror does not operate effectively if the darkness is not perfect. Thus in the *Benjamin* he adds:

> his soul, the which is as a mirror *in the which all thing is clearly seen* when it is clean. And when the mirror is foul then mayest thou see nothing clearly therein[72].

However the last word about this experience may be the comment in the *Cloud* in which our author suggests the supreme union is one of consummate love in response to vision. The union seems to be an engagement of the individual being with the 'whole' being of creation which transforms its outlook. One of the difficulties in describing the union may be that it is a different experience for different individuals according to their particularity. He says

> but to ... the loving power, he is, in every man diversely, all comprehensible to the full[73].

The experience seems to be an intuitive reflection in the loving power of the fullness of divine love which encompasses not only individuals in their singularity but the whole of creation in which individuals recognise they are loved with the same perfect fullness as the whole of creation.

4. 'TREWE EXPERIENCE': A REFLECTION ON THE 'DISCERNMENT OF SPIRITS'

The *Cloud* Author and Julian, it seems, approach the tradition of 'discernment of spirits' from different standpoints in experience. Unlike Julian, the *Cloud* Author is not concerned with authenticating his own mystical experience, of which he is deliberately reticent, before describing its meaning. His works do not have the character of a case study in the discernment of spirits. Julian's starting point is a vivid and,

---

71 *PC*. H. 75, 29.
72 *B.M.W.*: H. 143, 18-20 [my italics].
73 *CL*: M. chap. 4, p. 10; H. 10, 36-37.

for her, an astonishing and unexpected experience. The *Cloud* Author by contrast is attempting to guide a person, real or symbolic, along a well-trodden path already illuminated by a tradition which incorporates the experience and discernment of others and confirmed by his own experience. In doing so he is using his own experience discreetly, as a reference point, but without seeking to create expectations which may inhibit the recognition of the individuality of contemplative experience. 'Trewe experience'[74] is not necessarily uniform, he seems to say. This is perhaps why he is so positively reticent. Julian refers to the teaching of the Church to mediate the authenticity and meaning of her experience of the divine love and mercy; the *Cloud* Author uses his knowledge of the contemplative tradition and reflection on its meaning to mediate his experience and teaching for those seeking a contemplative vocation. The *Cloud* Author speaks, it seems, from the standpoint of an established 'contemplative' for the prospective 'contemplative'; Julian speaks from the standpoint of a person initially unaccustomed to contemplative experience but led to explore its nature and meaning through meditation on Scripture and the contemplative tradition, and for the benefit of all her fellow Christians rather than a particular group.

We have seen how the *Cloud* Author attempts to ensure that his teaching in the *Cloud* is restricted to those who have demonstrated by their 'active' living that they have the necessary 'graces' to proceed to contemplation. The 'advanced actives' seem to be his target audience. Just as the Pseudo-Dionysius described in the *Mystical Theology* the final stages of the ascent to the summit of contemplation through the clouds after a long and arduous climb which he had described in his other works, so the *Cloud* Author pre-supposes that the prospective 'contemplative' he is addressing is equipped with the training necessary to undertake the final assault on the summit, which he is about to describe.

He adopts the apophatic approach as he understands it in his translation of the Pseudo-Dionysius' *Mystical Theology*. However, he places it in a wider context of subsequent mystical experience. The twelfth-century mystics, St Bernard of Clairvaux, William of St Thierry and the Victorines had made outstanding contributions to the contemplative tradition in their accounts of the experience of divine 'love' which seems to have impressed Dante as reflected in the *Divine Comedy*[75]. The *Cloud* Author seems to be aware of their work. He is believed to have been as we have seen the author of a Middle English translation of Richard of St Victor's, *Benjamin Minor* and makes use of Richard's allegory in his own work. Moreover, he bases his work *Spirites* on two of Bernard's sermons and interpolates references to divine love into his translation of the *Mystical Theology* which were not in his Latin

---

74 *PC*: H. 97, 39.
75 See *Divine Comedy*. 3. *Paradise*, Canto x for Richard of St Victor, Canto xii for Hugh of St Victor, and Canto xxxi for St Bernard. William of St Thierry is not mentioned specifically but his 'Golden Epistle' was attributed to Bernard in Dante's time.

source, and which may reflect the influence of Bernard or William of St Thierry. His apophatic approach to contemplation reflects the fundamental influence of the Pseudo-Dionysius, therefore, but incorporates within it other recognisable influences which seem to make him cautious of creating expectations about what the 'ultimate' experience will be.

The *Cloud* Author's approach to contemplation might be regarded as eclectic if it were not so particularly concerned with reconciling Scripture and tradition, with the unity between Christian revelation and the diversity of Christian experience, with a God who cannot be known in 'trewe' essence but is recognisable in human experience. This is the crux of his teaching. He cannot say what the 'trewe' experience will be like but he can recognise its signs and moreover he can suggest how prospective 'contemplatives' may come to recognise for themselves 'trewe' from false experience of the divinity. The essence of the apophatic ascetic is to eliminate the possibility of falsehood, by purifying the consciousness. Yet 'purifying' consciousness for the *Cloud* Author means abandoning consciousness of self and the world and placing absolute trust in divine love and its fulfilment in a transforming union. He regards it as a frightening test of faith in divine love, similar to that which Christ undertook in his Passion. The human being cannot undertake it without divine help mediated in part by the teaching of Scripture, human counsel and conscience[76].

The transformation which takes place in the 'oneing' process is not, as it were, the result of acquiring some ultimate insight by rational process. He recognises with Richard of St Victor that the rational process must beget 'discernment', the recognition of the limitations of 'knowledge' before contemplation can be born. Discernment matures into wisdom, as reason dies when contemplation is born. 'Wisdom' is being assimilated into the divine, seeing through Christ's eyes, as it were[77]. Just as Julian understands that Christ views the sinning human being with mercy and compassion, so the *Cloud* Author understands that the inherent tendency to disregard God, to sin, which has weakened the power of the soul, is finally rooted out, burnt out, in the flame of participation in the divine union. Then the 'contemplative' begins to see creation through the eyes of the Creator. After the implied spiritual marriage is consummated and contemplation born, discernment may become 'creative' rather than cautionary. The *Cloud* Author cannot explain the transformation; 'spiritual marriage' is perhaps a too corporeal image for him. Prospective 'contemplatives' have to experience this for themselves.

Nevertheless, in the tradition of the Desert Fathers, although the mature power to discern as 'wisdom' is not achieved until the discursive reason is abandoned, there is a preparatory learning process in which discursive reason plays a prominent part. 'Sinners' and 'actives' learn that 'discernment', the ability to recognise good and

---

76   *PC*: M. chap. 12, p. 133; H. 97, 39-98, 1.
77   See N.65 above.

evil, is necessary in order to make progress in the spiritual life. Discernment and contemplation are the offspring of God and Reason in the allegory. However, since the reasoning faculty has been impaired by the inherited taint of disobedience, it must be complemented with guidance from a Spiritual Director, obedience to a religious rule or the Church. Without the acquisition of a capacity to discern, to become acquainted with the commandments and counsels of the Church and their application, and the caution it engenders about the pitfalls of spiritual development, the attempt to embark on a contemplative vocation is likely to end in disaster.

The *Cloud* Author's consciousness of the consequences of sin does not mean in his view that 'contemplatives' should be so preoccupied with sin that they forget they have been ransomed. Human beings are unresolved 'lumps of sin' but that does not mean they should forget that they have been saved. They must present themselves 'as they are' to God 'as he is', naked and blind.

They are 'nothing' compared with God, but they may become 'as Gods' by participating in the divine love and sharing his life and love. They may not know what such an experience is like and they should not be anxious to know. Their task is to fan the stirrings of divine love into a flame. He points forward to John of the Cross who finds a language to evoke the wonder of the experience of divine love in his poetry and prose, not so much as personal experience but as a divine experience.

But there is perhaps more to the difference between the *Cloud* Author and John than language. It also is more profound than the fear of over-familiarity. John of the Cross evokes the wonder of a divine experience because he believes the consciousness of individuality and its personal appropriation will be expropriated by God. The *Cloud* Author is conscious that individuals respond in different ways to the divine experience and the infinity of the divine cannot be communicated except as personal experience, which introduces limitations and finiteness. In this regard he also points forward to Ignatius of Loyola who recognises that Christ, as it were, calls the individual by name. The individuality of the individual is not eliminated or expropriated by answering the personal call, it is perfected. The *Cloud* Author was perhaps conscious of the experience of Mary Magdalene in recognising Christ's call in the garden. She recognised him as the Christ of her experience rather than the triune God. The nature of her experience perhaps was of 'love' unbounded; it may be expressed as God wishes it to be expressed as the presence of his being at once paradoxically veiled and illuminated by a human form.

Chapter 4

WALTER HILTON

1. AN 'ANAGOGIC' COMMUNION

The third of the middle English mystics was introduced in the Prologue not in his own right so much but as the foil who illuminates the unique approach to contemplation of the *Cloud* Author. Walter Hilton's work, however, is more than a foil which enables us to understand more clearly the approach of others to the role of discernment in the contemplative tradition. His work is a mediating bridge between the contrasting polarities which the works of Julian and the *Cloud* Author exhibit. It is also a bridge between late mediaeval experiences of contemplation and those which constitute the tradition which guided them. The first book of his major work, the *Scale of Perfection*, is a finely balanced synopsis of the received tradition of contemplative experience. The second book seems to recount his own insights drawn from the experience of his attempts to follow the traditional practice[1].

---

1   The canon of Hilton's works is listed in the Bibliography. His major work now generally referred to as *The Scale of Perfection* (*Scale*) is in two books. They were written in Middle English but a Latin translation had been made within a few years of Hilton's death. The title of these books is however editorial. In one manuscript they are entitled *De Vita Contemplativa* (British Library Add, MS 11748) and *The Reformyng of Mannys Soule* in another (British Library, MS Harley 2397); in others they are untitled. It is generally accepted that some time elapsed between the writing of the two books. The first is addressed to an anchoress and was probably written in the late 1380's. The second purports to take up several questions raised by the first but Hilton seems to have in mind a wider audience (see appendix below). The two books of *The Scale of Perfection* summarise his teaching for which his other works provide a counterpoint. The *Scale* seems to incorporate (especially *Scale 2*) his own spiritual experiences and insights which, like Julian's, are weighed against the accepted teaching of the Church on spiritual development as reflected in the writings of other masters of the spiritual life. His sources have been carefully researched by J.P.H. Clark and are discussed in the Introduction to the edition of *The Scale of Perfection*, to which I have principally referred (Clark, J.P.H. and Dorward, R. eds, *The Scale of Perfection*. New York: Paulist Press, 1991, in the Classics of Western Spirituality series, 21-27). The sources appear to have been well 'chewed'. Clark's introduction to the *Scale* also discusses the other works in his canon (13-21). This edition of the *Scale* seems to me the most authoritative available at the time of writing and my references are taken from it quoting *Scale 1* or *Scale 2*, chapter and page number. I refer also to 'Clark's Introduction' from this publication. A critical edition of the work is being prepared for press by Dr M.G. Sargent. The editors have based their text on the manuscripts which have been se-

The second book of the *Scale* is thought to have been written towards the end of his life[2]. When one comes to reflect upon it after reflecting upon Julian's *Showings* and the *Cloud* Author's works, there is a curious sense of *déjà vu*. On the one hand, the style and context of the work is completely different. Yet, on the other, the impression lingers that this second book of the *Scale* is the outcome of an intense dialogue between Hilton, on the one hand, and the *Cloud* Author and Julian on the other. The impression does not derive only from some similarities, perhaps derived from Scripture, in the images used by the authors, though these are striking. Some of the characteristic images used by Julian of a 'courteous' Lord and the 'homeliness' of Christ, the mutterings of the devil, to say nothing of her Christological emphases, jump from Hilton's pages. Similarly, the images of 'passivity', such as nakedness and blindness, nothingness and darkness, and even clothes changing, which are so characteristic of the *Cloud* Author, are interwoven into Hilton's text. The impression of unity is principally derived however from the way in which the contrasting approaches to the imagery of Christ which is reinforced in Julian's work and relegated in the *Cloud* Author's, are reconciled in Hilton's. Hilton's distinction between a reformation in faith and a reformation in both faith and feeling seems to unify what appear to be the contrasting insights of Julian and the *Cloud* Author, without in any way detracting from the power of their particular insights. This is not to say however that there is any conclusive historical evidence to suggest that Hilton knew of either author or their work, though there is a possibility that the *Cloud* Author and Hilton knew each other[3].

The works of Julian and the *Cloud* Author are classics in their own right both in style and insight. Hilton's *Scale of Perfection* is also a classical spiritual text which in the succeeding century appears to have had an even greater circulation than the

---

lected as the best texts. This, in the case of Book 1, was CUL 6686 and for Book 2, Harley 6579. The editors have checked the texts against the Latin translation of the Carmelite, Thomas Fishlake (York Minster Chapter Library MS XVI K5 made about 1400). This latter manuscript provides a valuable reference because of the diversity of the manuscript tradition in Middle English. There are some forty-five extant manuscripts for *Scale 1* and twenty-five for *Scale 2*. The number and distribution of the preserved manuscripts suggest they were highly valued works, reflecting a well accepted tradition of spiritual teaching, which would have justified and been consistent with the patronage of Thomas Arundel (see appendix below).

2   See the Appendix at the end of this chapter for a discussion of what is known of Hilton's life in the context of the *Scale of Perfection*.

3   It has been suggested (Clark, Introduction, 25) that the *Cloud* Author may have been acquainted with Hilton's work since he refers to 'another man's work' on three occasions in the *Cloud* (chaps 35, 48, 68); the first, on reading, meditation and prayer as a means to contemplation; the second, on the discernment of good and evil in regard to sensory religious experience; the third to argue against possible misunderstanding of the language of recollection and introversion. The references are considered suggestive because, other than Hilton's Latin letter, *Epistola de Lectione* there is no other work that deals with all three points.

work of the *Cloud* Author[4]. The manuscript tradition has been so complex that only now is a critical edition of the *Scale of Perfection* in the process of publication[5]. More is known of Hilton's life than of the other two authors' lives. Yet there are many gaps in our knowledge despite the achievements of the scholarly work which has been devoted to illuminating Hilton's background.

We wish to concentrate principally on the two books of the *Scale of Perfection* in our attempt to understand how Hilton perceived the role of discernment of spirits in the practice of contemplation. In these two books he seems to identify two complementary functions of the imagination, the analogical and the anagogical. He sees them as different modes of imaginative operation and the process of spiritual development as the full realisation of each mode. However the immediacy of the anagogical function seems to supersede the mediatory analogical in contemplation; and in the aftermath of continuous experiences of contemplation seems to take precedence over the analogical in the way experience is understood[6].

The mystics, as we have seen in the cases of Julian and the *Cloud* Author, are extremely sensitive to the anagogical functioning of the imagination. They are aware of its supreme value as the medium for divine communication and they are equally aware of the possibility that the devil or a disordered unconscious may use this same medium of communication. They approach its manifestations with great caution and take very considerable precautions to distinguish a divine from some other manifestation. Julian was concerned with establishing that the manifestations of spirit she received in the *Showings* were divine as well as understanding their meaning. The *Cloud* Author was principally concerned with preparing the way for a divine communication by purifying the consciousness by eliminating as far as possible all

---

4   T.W. Coleman, *English Mystics of the Fourteenth Century*, London: Epsworth Press, 1938, 106: '... it is true to say no other mystical work in our tongue has had a deeper or more abiding influence than this'. The evidence relates to the number of extant manuscripts, some of which are authorial, and the range of dialects of the copyists. See A.I. Doyle, 'A Survey of the Origins and Circulation of Theological Writings in English in the 14th, 15th and early 16th centuries with special consideration of the part of the clergy therein', Diss. 2301-2, Cambridge University, 1953.

5   See Clark's discussion of textual problems in his Introduction to the Classics of Western Spirituality edition, 53-56.

6   The distinction between the analogical and anagogical imaginations is exemplified in the concluding paragraph of *Scale 2* chap. 44, 298: 'But you say, 'What are these spiritual things?'. For I often speak of spiritual things. To this I say in reply that all the truth of holy Scripture may be called a spiritual thing, and therefore a soul that can see the truth of it by the light of grace *sees spiritual things...*'. The 'immediacy' of the anagogical function is suggested in *Scale 2* chap. 46, 301, e.g. 'And you must know that a pure soul can see by the same light of grace the self-same truth of the blessed Trinity that these holy teachers, inspired through grace, write in their books for the strengthening of our faith'. The 'immediacy' seems to be brought about by the operation of grace. For a discussion of the notion of 'anagogic' see Henri de Lubac, *Exégèse Médiéval. Les Quatre Sens de l'Écriture*, see Chap. 1, N.5.

sources of stimuli which were recognisable, so that in contemplation the human being might be free to participate in the divine and achieve spiritual fulfilment.

Julian's teaching about the anagogical imagination seems to be based on the specific experiences of the *Showings*[7]. The *Cloud* Author's teaching seems to be no less experientially based than Julian's. However, while in the experiencing, his insights may have come suddenly and spontaneously, they seem to arise from expectations formed in a specific tradition of spirituality. The 'oneing' was sought in his case whereas in Julian's it was unsought except to the extent that she linked her *Showings* to the three childhood wishes. However those wishes themselves seem to tap a powerful source of spiritual tradition which we have suggested may have been imaginatively stimulated by impressions created from viewing the mediaeval play cycles[8].

Julian's spirituality might be characterised as 'redemptive'. While it is focussed on the crucifixion and the sorrow and suffering with which she identifies, its power is the 'love' theme. Christ's great suffering, she understands, is in proportion to his great love, which would have been greater still if it could have been. The meaning she extracts from the *Showings*, is not, as we might expect, about the magnitude of the sin which brought about the suffering but rather about the great trust which so much suffering should stimulate in the redemptive power of Christ's love.

The *Cloud* Author's emphasis is different. We might characterise his spirituality as 'incarnational'. His 'nothingness' precedes the creative act which brought humanity into being. His 'darkness' is the darkness of the womb before the spirit enlightened it. His 'purity' is that of the Lady Mary's sinlessness and virginity. His spirituality is focussed upon recreating the circumstances of the incarnational process by which the human being may be recreated in the divine metamorphosis which occurs in the cloud of unknowing. This is a love differently imagined from Julian's. It has no recognisable human analogy and even the humanity of Christ is deliberately put to one side.

These are the two poles of spirituality which Walter Hilton seems to unite from the understanding of his own spiritual experience and the Augustinian tradition which he adopted as an Augustinian canon in the last years of his life. His spirituality might be characterised as 'resurrectional'. It is influenced profoundly by the Augustinian teaching about the existential power of grace and of the spirit as a Trinitarian manifestation of unity. Julian, in describing the first of her *Showings*, suggested that

---

7   The recognition of the meaning of the allegory or parable of the 'Lord and Servant' for Julian was distinct from the 'showing' itself. She believed she received an infused 'anagogic' insight before she could appropriate its full significance.

8   The connection between Julian's childhood wishes and their recall at the time of the 'Showings' is perhaps illustrative of her appropriation of the 'Showings' as 'real'. There is, as it were, an 'anagogic' insight which influenced her attitude to all the 'Showings'.

by the manifestation of Christ she understood 'the Trinity'[9]. She seemed to wish to convey her conviction that the showing of Christ she received was both divine and human. Hilton, while fastening on to the cleansing power of the *Cloud* Author's 'incarnational darkness' seems to be unwilling, as we shall see, to dismiss Christ from the imagination in the darkness which he believes must precede the 'reformation in feeling' and which he says must take place before 'contemplation' of the Godhead may be experienced[10].

It is possible that the *Cloud* Author, when describing Mary Magdalene's contemplation of Christ in the context of the Martha/Mary biblical story, may also have had in mind Mary's meeting with the risen Christ following her discovery that the tomb in which Christ had been placed was empty. His emphasis in the exegesis of the Martha/Mary story was placed upon the way Mary had been able to forget her previous sins in her total concentration on the divinity of Christ which is the ultimate reality[11]. Hilton, however, refers explicitly to the incident in which Mary meets and fails initially to recognise the risen Christ. She only does so when Christ calls her by name[12]. He uses the incident to illustrate his notion of a reformation in feeling. It is not the sight of Christ which Mary recognises. It is his voice, and his aura, as she attempts to embrace him. His exegesis is a powerful illustration of the experience of the special grace of a contemplation which is essentially a 'feeling' of Christ. In the encounter with Mary following his 'resurrection' but before his 'ascension', Christ grants her, as he does the other Apostles, the special privilege of a vision of the divine being in a form recognisably human but without the finiteness of its human bodily nature. The power which in the Augustinian exegesis complements the Trinity is not revealed until Pentecost when the spirit carries the power and manifests it to the assembled apostles[13].

Hilton's 'darkness' also differs from the 'darkness of unknowing' of the *Cloud* Author. Rather than a darkness of 'unknowing' in the sense of being unable to remember and recognise, Hilton's darkness has two characteristics. The first is a lack of understanding rather than a lack of recognition[14]. The second is a darkness of the

---

9   See for example *Showings*, Crit.Ed. *L.T.* chap. 4. The reference to the Trinity in the *Long Text* is not included in the *Short Text*. See also Nicholas Watson, 'The Trinitarian Hermeneutic in Julian of Norwich's Revelation of Love' in *M.M.T. in Eng.* 1992, 79-100.
10 *Scale 2* chap. 24, 234-38 and *Scale 2* chap. 25, 238, 239. See Tarjei Park, 'Reflecting Christ: The Role of the Flesh in Walter Hilton and Julian of Norwich' in *M.M.T. in Eng.*, 1992, 17-38. She notes, 37, 'where in Hilton the signs of 'sizt' and 'Jhesu' are emptied of physicality, Julian's expand in celebration of the Incarnation and Passion, of birth in death, of our organic humanness in Christ'. Hilton's 'emptying' however, only occurs in the stage of reformation in faith and feeling.
11 *CL*: chap. 16 through chap. 22.
12 *Scale 2* chap. 30, 255.
13 *Scale 2* chap. 30, 256.
14 *Scale 1* chap. 52, 123, 124.

'image of sin' which like the *Cloud* Author he refers to as a covering, a clothing[15]. The 'image of sin' is a recognition of the human being's total inability to avoid and to subsequently recover from sin, without the assistance of the divine goodness. This recognition of the gulf separating the creature from the creator is what he means by 'reformation in faith'. It is a rational process which ultimately suggests that reason has finite bounds and that the human being must in the last resort rely on the experience of 'grace' as 'feeling' in order to escape the darkness of the 'image of sin' and put on 'Christ', as it were, as a suit of clothes[16]. Nevertheless, 'reformation in faith' which leads into his 'darkness' must precede 'the reformation in feeling' and lead to an existential experience of 'reformation in faith and feeling' as a new existence.

Hilton's exegesis of the spiritual pilgrimage, which in the second book of the *Scale* he refers to as the parable of the pilgrimage to Jerusalem[17], is very much about discerning the Holy Spirit as 'grace' and recognising the counterfeit spirits which 'ape' it, to use the *Cloud* Author's term. It is unfolded as a learning process and, paradoxically, bearing in mind the disputation between Cassian and Augustine on the subject of the human contribution to reformation of the human being[18], uses the same imagery as Cassian used to explain the difference between the various ways in which 'Jerusalem' might be interpreted. Hilton's description of the pilgrimage to Jerusalem in fact combines Cassian's ways of interpreting the meaning of 'Jerusalem', as we shall see, as historical, tropological, allegorical and anagogic[19]. The 'reformation in feeling' illustrates the anagogic mode of interpretation which displaces the other analogical modes with a special infusion of grace in which the 'giver' and his 'gift' are fused in the soul of the contemplative while the sojourn in Jerusalem lasts[20].

According to Hilton the visit to Jerusalem in this life is of variable length and frequency[21]. That is as it would be for a pilgrimage. He foreshadows a final resting place in the spiritual Jerusalem in the life of the resurrection. Just as in this life the consciousness of special grace is unlikely to be other than of varying length and frequency, so in the life of eternal union with God the enlightenment and joy will be

---

15 *Scale 1* chap. 53, 124, 125.

16 *Scale 1* chap. 51, 123 and *Scale 2* chap. 5, 199, 200.

17 *Scale 2* chap. 21, 226ff. and n.102, 309. It is suggested that the specific source may be St Bernard's *Sermo in Quadrigesima 6*. 'There was a man wanting to go to Jerusalem' suggested the parable of the Good Samaritan. Augustine in *Quaestiones Evangeliorum* 2.39, PL 35.1340, suggests the Good Samaritan is Christ himself.

18 Owen Chadwick, *John Cassian*, 120-35 and Phillip Rousseau, *Ascetics, Authority and the Church*, 231-34.

19 *Scale 2* chap. 43, 294 and n.369, 326. Cassian, *Conferences* 14.8 on the senses of 'Jerusalem'.

20 *Scale 2* chap. 25, 238, 239; *Scale 2* chap. 26, 242; *Scale 2* chap. 19, 223 and n.89, 308; *Scale 2* chap. 21, 227 and n.105, 310, for Jerusalem as 'sight of peace' which 'stands for contemplation in perfect love of God, for contemplation is nothing other than a sight of Jesus, who is true peace'.

21 For example see *Scale 2* chap. 25, 238, 239.

perpetual. However, even in this life once the wonder of the eternal city has been experienced and the reformation, which its 'feeling' brings with it, is accomplished, it will remain an absorbing memory to be repeated as often as may be. Just as the meeting with Christ for Julian and the fusion with the unimaginable Godhead in the soul for the *Cloud* Author, so the Trinitarian experience of Christ enthroned in glory in Jerusalem for Hilton is an experience of contemplative enlightenment and joy[22]. But whereas however for Hilton the experience also represents the fusion of faith and feeling in an enlightened wisdom, for the *Cloud* Author it remains a dark wisdom while life lasts. For the *Cloud* Author it is the wisdom of blind faith just as for Julian the experience is of a peace in contentment and trust which surpasses all understanding[23].

Jerusalem with all its biblical and Christological associations is for Hilton a unifying symbol for his discourse, just as the tomb of Becket at Canterbury is for Chaucer in the *Canterbury Tales*. The Parson's tale, delivered in the form of a prose homily rather than, as in most of Chaucer's other tales, in poetic narrative, emphasises by contrast the symbolic significance which the object of pilgrimage has for Chaucer[24]. Becket's death seems to have symbolised in the imagination of the English the victory of the Church in the struggle for independence from the secular authority. Henry II's public penance symbolised the recognition of victory[25]. So the Parson's homily emphasises the need for contrition before Chaucer's pilgrims present themselves at the tomb and seek Becket's intercession. In similar fashion the reformation which must precede the contemplative's entry into Jerusalem in Hilton's teaching, reflects the oblation and forgiveness which Christ's final entry into Jerusalem presaged in the Christian imagination[26]. The symbols of Jerusalem and Canterbury are rich in analogical associations but in both works, the *Scale of Perfection* and the *Canterbury Tales*, their meaning, like life itself in fourteenth-century England, is anagogic and designed to stimulate the anagogic imagination to seek the mystery of

---

22 *Scale 2* chap. 32 and *Scale 2* chap. 33, 259-63. See in particular the references to the Trinity in *Scale 2* chap. 46, 301 and n.404, 328.

23 See for example *CL* H. 68.7-21 and commentary 68/7-8 and *Showings*, Crit.Ed. *L.T.* chap. 68 and sixteenth revelation.

24 Chaucer, *Canterbury Tales*, ed. Cawley, Introduction xiii and Parson's Prologue, 531 L.L.49-51:
'To shewe yow the wey, in this viage,
Of thilke parfit glorious pilgrymage
That highte Jerusalem celestial'.

25 Becket was murdered at Christmas 1170. It is generally accepted that Becket as a symbol was more important in death than in life. His 'victory' was symbolic as a clerical rallying point though it is said Alexander III sent more papal missives to England after his death than to the rest of Europe put together, see G.O. Sayles, *The Mediaeval Foundations of England*, London: Methuen, 1948, 350, for a discussion of the immediate impact of Becket's death.

26 All the gospels refer to Christ's entry into Jerusalem but John 12:14-16, points up the prophetic significance of the occasion.

life's meaning in a commitment of feeling: prophetic in Hilton's case, and perhaps poetic in Chaucer's.

Chaucer's poetic intent may have been to stimulate a new consciousness of the world and its curiosity in his readers. Hilton's might seem to be to create a new consciousness of the extraordinary promises of Christ in his readership. In neither case is the direction of development in consciousness left to chance. Chaucer, in his tales, covers the whole span of life and people in contemporary England. Each tale and each individual has a place in his tableau. Even the Pardoner has some redeeming or redeemable features which make the tale both moral and memorable in its imagery, like a morality play[27]. Hilton likewise is thorough in the manner in which he unfolds his discourse to develop a discerning consciousness of the anagogic meaning of the Christian revelation. It is no accident that nearly every chapter of the work turns out to be an exegesis of a scriptural passage. Every step the pilgrim is to take has a scriptural signpost to direct attention to the original supernatural authority for that particular direction[28]. Hilton links the notion of the Church as a living spiritual communion to interpretation of Scripture[29].

The soul, he says in chapter 43 of *Scale II*, is stirred to see Jesus in Holy Scripture. He is hidden there. Truth and humility, the characteristics of Christ, are like faithful

---

27 Stephen Knight, 'Chaucer's Religious Canterbury Tales' in *Mediaeval English Religious Literature*, 156-66. He suggests, however, the Pardoner's Tale is 'deeply revolutionary', 162.

28 This is not surprising in view of Hilton's attitude to the interpretation of Scripture; e.g. in *Scale 2* chap. 43, 293-298. However, M.G. Sargent in his 'The Organisation of the Scale of Perfection' in *M.M.T. in Eng.*, 1982, 232, argues that Hilton 'seems to have derived his organisational methods from those of scholastic exposition' rather than the forms of monastic devotional literature in which 'rumination' on Scripture was central. The scriptural citations and allusions in the *Scale* are still in my view a feature of the texts and also the textual 'organisation' and 'exposition' as a whole. Biblical texts are frequently quoted in Latin and translated and interpreted for the benefit of the 'unlettered' to illustrate and support his theme as the basis for its authority. The life and example of Christ as a text seems to be the organisational theme as Sargent points out in the transformation of the 'image' in the human being to the 'likeness' of Christ, 'to see Jesus in holy scripture', as Hilton says in *Scale 2* chap. 43, 293. As Sargent points out S.S. Hussey in his article 'Walter Hilton: Traditionalist' in *M.M.T. in Eng.*, 1980, 7, suggests that Hilton seems in *Scale 2* 'largely to discard categories in favour of analogies'. In my view his intention might have been to elucidate the anagogical reality hidden in the analogies, particularly 'Jerusalem' as the location of Temple, whose stones 'speak' and enlighten the 'image'.

29 Hilton refers to the Church as 'spiritual mother', *Scale 2* chap. 10, 207, and as 'laboring in this life', *Scale 2* chap. 45, 299. There is a considerable literature on the situation in the English Church which provides some perspective on a far from 'uniform' institution. - See for example: Eamon Duffy, *The Stripping of the Altars, Traditional Religion in England c.1400-c.1580*, New Haven and London: Yale University Press, 1992, which is primarily concerned with the 15th and 16th centuries but also provides an insight into the vibrant church life of the 14th century.

sisters[30]. He may even have Martha and Mary in mind when he uses this metaphor to suggest the active and contemplative aspects of the Church united in faith in the interpretation of Scripture. He uses the Emmaus example to illustrate the need for faith in interpreting Scripture. He refers to a grace-given disposition to understand what is written. Of the disciples on the road to Emmaus, he says, *apperuit illis ut intelligerent scripturas*. The purpose of Christ's appearance was to reveal to them how the events which they had just witnessed in Jerusalem fulfilled what had been foretold and recorded in Scripture. In a similar way Hilton suggests the lover of Jesus receives the insights of Holy Scripture from him as they apply to the conditions of the day. The sense of Scripture may be expounded literally, morally, mystically and heavenly if the matter allows it[31]. By the letter, or literal interpretation, the body may find comfort; by a moral interpretation vices and virtues may be recognised; by a mystical interpretation, and this is particularly interesting, Scripture is illuminated to see the works of God in 'Holy Church' and apply the words of Christ, 'our head', to his Church the mystical body. The heavenly interpretation concerns the working of love, when all truth in Scripture is applied to God's love. In Scripture God shows his mysteries as to a true friend, not serving him in fear like a slave. The Scriptures must be 'chewed' by the grace of spiritual understanding because in them is the hidden life of the Spirit. This life is not revealed to heretics and lovers of the flesh and so they are not able to get the inner flavour of it. The mystery of Holy Scripture is sealed by Jesus under a key which is the Holy Spirit.

Hilton's views on the interpretation of Scripture might suggest that any Christian under the guidance of the Holy Spirit might be able to extract the true flavour. Indeed this is what the Lollards were suggesting though they favoured a literal interpretation and the importance they attached to the availability of the Scriptures in the vernacular was to enable all Christians to read and interpret them literally at first hand[32]. Clearly Hilton's intentions were quite different. He regarded the interpretation of Scripture as a professional task requiring spiritual awareness, learning and knowledge of the Church's tradition of exegesis. His use of Scripture in the texts of both parts of the *Scale of Perfection* underlines his view of its importance to confirm and support his teaching. Discernment in this context is a matter for professionals but professionals who have 'chewed' the Scriptures thoroughly to extract the spiri-

---

30 He refers to 'truth' and 'humility' as 'faithful' sisters joined together in 'love' and 'charity', like 'Father' and 'Son', perhaps, joined by the Holy Spirit in love, and he goes on 'for this reason there is no break in counsel between those two'. They rely on each other just as the 'active' and 'contemplative' lives perhaps rely on each other too.

31 *Scale 2* chap. 43, 294, see n.369, 326.

32 See for example K.B. McFarlane, *John Wycliffe and the Beginnings of English Non-Conformity*, 13. See also reference to Wycliffe's *On the Truth of Holy Scripture*, defending the literal interpretation of the Bible, 90, 91, and references to others including Marsilio of Padua who had urged the literal interpretation. See also 118 and 119 on the deficiencies of the first translation of the Bible; the second free vernacular translation was completed in 1396, the year of Hilton's death, 149.

tual flavour[33]. The 'chewing' or meditation is a necessary preliminary to the diges-
tion. It is an operation similar to that advocated by Cassian and indeed Hilton seems
to be in a tradition of exegesis which goes back at least to the Desert Fathers and
probably owes much to Origen and Clement of Alexandria and their predecessors.

The dilemma which faced Hilton in attempting to provide lay people and unlettered
religious with the means to develop their spirituality is illustrated by the hermeneutical problem. This is not to suggest that Hilton was conscious of the dilemma. But on
the one hand 'reformation in faith' is in part dependent on the Church's teaching and
the traditional exegesis of Scripture which provides knowledge of the faith. While
on the other the 'reformation in feeling' leads to the acquisition of spiritual understanding which would enable the person who is 'reformed in faith and feeling' to
interpret Scripture for themselves in the context of their own existential lives. In the
first book of the *Scale*, he does not face the problem directly because he suggests
that very few, if any, unlettered or lay persons will be able to so divorce themselves
from the world and the dependence on the analogical imagination to reach the level
of spiritual understanding characterised by the third degree of contemplation[34]. In
the Second book, however, he is by no means so elitist. Those who receive the special graces and cooperate with them may reach this third degree of contemplation
which he characterises as 'reformation in faith and feeling'. They thus may acquire
the spiritual understanding to interpret Scripture in the context of their own lives.
Julian of Norwich may perhaps be one such person, though without more definitive
knowledge of her background we cannot be sure whether she was lay or religious,
and when she tells us she was unlettered we need hardly take her modest disclaimer
at face value[35].

2. REFORMATION IN FAITH AND FEELING

Faith and Feeling

The 'feeling' which is such an important concept in Hilton's discourse is neither
divorced nor dissociated from discursive reasoning. In some devout folk, he suggests, there does not appear to be any conscious separation of feeling and faith. In a
similar way with such people faith and reasoning are almost simultaneous processes;
it seems 'right' to trust what one has been taught. The authority of the teacher is not

---

33 *Scale 2* chap. 43, 294 and n.375, 326. See also Beryl Smalley, *The Study of the Bible in the
    Middle Ages*, Oxford, 1964 and her 'Ecclesiastical attitudes to Novelty, c.1000-c.1250' in
    Church, Society and Politics, ed. Derek Baker, Studies in Church History 12, Oxford, 1975.
34 *Scale 1* chap. 9, 83.
35 See Prologue 2, 16, N.56 above. In chap. 51 of Julian's *Long Text* it has been estimated there
    are at least 30 allusions to the Pauline letters in the Vulgate. See Introduction to the critical edi-
    tion, 139. St Paul is considered to be the father of exegesis based on the four senses of the text.

questioned and there is no desire to disobey what faith enjoins. Feeling, faith and reason are in harmony. Moreover, their feeling is more often than not, more than simply the wish to obey what is accepted, it is an enthusiastic espousal of the teaching and a love of what is done. He attributes this harmony to the operation of 'grace' which is unconsciously accepted. However, with the literate people Hilton is primarily addressing in his *Scale*, there is a much greater degree of intellectual self-consciousness which recognises a distinction between faith and reason on the one hand and faith and love on the other. Faith may be proved and tested by reason, he suggests, but while the satisfaction of reason may be a prerequisite for faith in such people it does not necessarily produce the feeling which grows from desire or enthusiasm into love. Hilton maintains it is necessary to acquire this 'feeling' before the journey to Jerusalem can be completed[36].

He further observes that the newly converted frequently exhibit more spiritual feeling and fervour than those who are 'perfect'[37]. They are in a condition of partially reformed feeling in the sense that they are experiencing grace for the first time in a new way. This he suggests is God's way of purifying them. He uses the analogy of new wine in old casks. Souls experiencing the feeling of grace are weakened by habitual love of the world. They are unable to contain the new wine without signs of great stress as the new wine continues to ferment. Not until the fermentation is complete will they be still. He also uses the analogy of the pilgrim again. Having suffered the discomforts of the journey pilgrims reach an inn at night and obtain refreshment. The refreshment does not last[38]. Only when the pilgrim reaches Jerusalem and is made 'perfect' will there be lasting refreshment in that they no longer need fresh infusions of grace. They are habitually in love with Jesus and in this state the former worldly loves no longer trouble them. Their souls 'magnified' by grace (apparently a mediaeval accretion to St Paul's stages in the work of grace, calling, correcting and glorifying) and will be glorified hereafter.

He speaks in the manner recounted by Julian in the experience of her *Showings*, of the 'proficient' receiving infusions and withdrawals of grace without warning[39]. He suggests that the full gift of contemplation may be equated with full reformation in feeling. The fully reformed soul becomes master of itself in love of Christ in the constant beholding of him.

---

36 This theme is first announced in *Scale 1* chaps 4 and 5, 79-81, where the distinction is drawn
     between the simple and the learned. It is taken up again in *Scale 2* chap. 27, 242-247. There the
     emphasis is placed on different degrees of grace. He seems in the later context to be drawing
     the distinction between a genuine liberty of spirit (242) which reflects 'the grace-given feeling'
     of a 'spiritual sight of Jesus' (243) and one which is yet imperfect and may give 'scandal or
     harm' to fellow Christians. Such people have faith but they are yet unreformed.
37 *Scale 2* chap. 29, 249-52.
38 *Scale 2* chap. 29, 251.
39 *Ibid.*, 252.

Spiritual Knowledge

The overlapping nature of Hilton's concepts of reformation in faith and feeling, and their meaning in his discourse is explained in his discussion of spiritual knowledge. The soul must first come to a knowledge of itself[40]. This turning inwards in introspection seems to be a common Augustinian influence in all three of the fourteenth-century English mystics we have been discussing[41]. The soul gains knowledge of itself by reflecting on itself separated from consideration of all earthly things and all bodily senses. It 'feels' itself as it is in its own nature without a body. Hilton says the soul is not a body but a 'life invisible'[42]. It is not found within the body as one would find a heart or a smaller thing within a greater but as that which holds 'the greater' or 'the body' and gives it life. One thinks as one reads chapter thirty of *Scale II* of Julian's image of the hazelnut held in her hand which she receives in the first of her *Showings*. Hilton however wants to get away from the physical analogy[43]. Think of the soul, he suggests, as a virtue in the sense of the knowledge of a non-physical concept such as truth or humility for example. Like Plato's 'ideas' they are deathless and invisible. But in contrast to them these concepts of virtue enable the pilgrim to see and know the supreme truth and to love the supreme goodness that is God. This is the way for the human being to see itself. All spiritual things are seen by the understanding of the soul not by physical images. Just as a soul sees by understanding that the virtue of justice is to yield to each thing what it ought to have (a canon lawyer's example perhaps), so the soul can see itself by understanding the nature of virtue[44]. Like Augustine in *De Trinitate* perhaps it can reason from the notion of the trinitarian nature of God held in faith, to that of the trinitarian nature of the soul[45].

However, the soul cannot rest in knowledge of itself. As he has previously suggested it sees itself in the darkness, but it seeks a higher knowledge above itself and that is the nature of God. The soul, he suggests, is only a mirror in which one may see God

---

40 *Scale 2* chap. 30, 252-57; *Scale 1* chap. 42, 112, emphasises both 'its fairness and its foulness'.
41 The Augustinian influence derives not so much from particularities but from the impact of the *Confessions* as a genre in spiritual literature and from *De Trinitate* as a starting point for theological reflection.
42 *Scale 2* chap. 30, 252 and 253 and n.194, 315, on the notion of the Soul as 'a life invisible'. Suggested source Augustine's *De Quantitate Animae* 13.22. The idea is also reproduced by William of St Thierry; see the *Golden Epistle*, trans. T. Berkeley O.C.S.O., Kalamazoo, Michigan: Cistercian Publications Inc., 1980, Bk Two, IV., 79.
43 *Scale 2* chap. 33, 262.
44 It is probable, though not certain, that Hilton was a canon lawyer. See Appendix. To select the virtue of 'justice' in particular perhaps reflects a familiarity with the notion of justice which again, perhaps, might have been in the forefront of his mind as a consequence of being involved in the examination of people suspected of Lollard persuasions.
45 Hilton is familiar with the idea of the trinitarian nature of the soul. See for example *Scale 1* chap. 43, 113 and n.107, 172, and *Scale 2* chap. 31, 258.

spiritually. Find the mirror, keep it bright and clean (from earthly filth and vanity) and hold it well up from the earth so that it can be seen and the Lord also seen in it[46].

Nevertheless, while God is recognised only in the sensible imagination and not in the understanding, the human being has not arrived at a perfect love or at contemplation[47]. And this thought leads Hilton into a reflection on the nature of love.

Degrees of Love

There are three kinds of love of God[48]. The lowest degree of charity is faith; it is a condition in which the soul is without the grace of imagination or the spiritual knowledge of God. This seems to be the condition in which the Christian lives by faith and does what faith requires but has no lively consciousness of Christ in the imagination. The imagination he seems to say is not stirred by the degree or kind of grace that will be experienced by those in the second degree of love. In this second condition the image of Jesus in his humanity penetrates the consciousness. Hilton suggests the 'eye of the Spirit' is opened to behold the Lord's manhood.

The third degree of love is our present concern. A soul cannot feel this love until it is 'reformed in feeling' for it is concerned not so much with the image of the manhood of God as the invisible divinity within the manhood, the spirit which is united with the manhood and gives it life. Hilton refers to this feeling as understanding or insight. It places the soul on another plane of being because it is infused with understanding and love of the divine will, the creative and life-giving spirit which activates its being. The human being, it would seem, having reached this plane of spiritual insight, acts according to the infused understanding it receives. It does not understand the fullness of the divine will, only that which is necessary for it to act in accordance with it. But it remains fully conscious of its natural being as it is of its supernatural inspiration.

The distinction Hilton is wishing to draw between the second and third degrees of love is that between love for the Man-God and that for the God-Man[49]. In neither case is the divinity and the manhood separated. In the first case he is suggesting that the man, Christ, is loved because he is God and behaves as the perfect human being.

---

46 *Scale 2* chap. 30, 253.
47 *Ibid.* The distinction is similar to that drawn in *Scale 1* chap. 9 between the second and third parts of contemplation where the mirror image is contrasted with the sight of God face to face in heaven. So the devotion of the second part of contemplation is contrasted with the 'inward, more spiritual' devotion of the third.
48 *Scale 2* chap. 30, 253.
49 *Scale 2* chap. 30, 254 'Our Lord does not show himself as he is, or that he is'; when the soul is reformed in feeling it sees 'that he is an unchangeable being' but neither 'as he is' nor 'what he is'. See *Scale 2* chap. 32, 259.

In the second he is perhaps saying that God is loved because he has made himself intelligible as man and shown the perfection of God, which is a blinding revelation which the human being unless reformed in feeling is unable to bear.

He illustrates the distinction he is attempting to make with the biblical example of Mary Magdalene's encounter with the risen Christ[50]. She recognises his manhood when he speaks and attempts to embrace him. But the risen Christ says to her, *Noli me tangere; nondum enim ascendi ad Patrem meum*. Do not touch me; I have not yet ascended to my Father. Hilton interprets Christ's intentions in the following way. Mary Magdalene ardently loved the Lord Jesus before the time of his passion, but her love was much in the body, little in the spirit. She well believed that he was God, but she loved him little as God, for at that time she did not know how; and therefore she allowed all her affection and all her thought to go to him as he was, in the form of man; and the Lord praised her for that. But when after the Resurrection she would have honoured him with the same kind of love as she did before, the Lord said "Do not touch me" which is interpreted, do not set the rest or love of your heart upon that human form you see with your bodily eye alone, to rest in it, because in that form I have not ascended to my Father, that is, I am not equal to the Father. For in human form I am less than he. Set yourself to love me in the form in which I am equal to the Father - that is, the form of the divinity. Make me a God in your heart and in your love, and worship me in your understanding as Jesus, God in man - supreme truth, supreme goodness and blessed life - for that is what I am.

Even at this stage Mary Magdalene did not know how to love Christ as God, because at that time the divine purpose had not been fully accomplished. Hilton then goes on to illustrate what he means by an exegesis of the happenings at Pentecost when tongues of fire were seen to rest on the heads of the Apostles. He says it is true that the Holy Spirit, who is God invisible in himself, was neither that fire nor those tongues that were seen, nor that burning which was felt in the body, but he was felt invisibly in the powers of their souls, for he enlightened their reason and kindled their affection through the blessed presence so clearly and so ardently that they suddenly had the spiritual knowledge of truth and the perfection of love, as promised, *Spiritus Sanctus docebit vos omnem veritatem*[51].

This third degree of love, Hilton believes, is divinely infused as and when God wills. The soul is prepared to bear this infusion of divine love gradually by progressive stages. However he makes the point that he in no way wishes to give the impression that divine action is limited by his interpretation. He speaks according to his own experience and states that others have had different experiences[52]. He may even have

---

50 *Scale 2* chap. 30, 255 and n.200, 315.
51 *Scale 2* chap. 30, 255; cf. John 16.13.
52 *Ibid.*, 254 and *Scale 2* chap. 31, 257.

had the *Cloud* Author and Julian in mind when he says this. He says he fully expects that God works in other ways, beyond his understanding and feeling.

Recognising the infusion of Grace

Despite the differences in their respective approaches to the contemplative experience, Julian, the *Cloud* Author and Hilton, have a common understanding that contemplation is a divinely infused grace which the human being can hope and long for but not appropriate by an act of will. Nevertheless they all believe that the 'hoping' and 'longing' can be turned to preparation so that the grace may be recognised and appropriated when it is received, as they believe it always will be, to some degree, to all who seek it with sincerity. Hilton, in particular, sets out to assist those whom he addresses in the *Scale* about what 'reforming in feeling' is and how it is made and what are the spiritual feelings that a soul receives by which it may be recognised.

He bases himself on St Paul *Nolite conformari huic saeculo, sed reformari in novitate sensus vestri*[53]. He translates this to mean 'You who are through grace reformed in faith, do not henceforth conform yourselves to the manners of the world in pride and so on but be reformed in newness of feeling'. The newness of feeling in Paul's words are to be filled with knowledge of God's will in understanding and every kind of spiritual wisdom. This is to be reformed in feeling; to feel with the 'immediacy' of divine love.

He believes there are two kinds of feelings; 'outward' ones which are recognised through the bodily senses and 'inward' through the powers of the soul which are described by the Augustinian notion of mind, reason and will. The one is lower, that is, bodily and imaginative; the other higher is reason which is properly the image of God, and is to be clothed in a new light of truth, holiness and righteousness. Then it is reformed in feeling; - that is cast off from the love of the world which is fuelled by the senses and imagination - and renewed in the likeness of God in the perfect knowledge of God[54].

'Knowing' God

There are two ways of knowing God also in Hilton's discourse[55]. He illustrates them with a Pauline metaphor. The first form of knowledge is derived from the imagination mainly with little understanding. It is the way of beginners and proficients with bodily affections and in bodily likeness. It is like milk. The other kind is like whole

---

53 *Scale 2* chap. 31, 257, 258.
54 *Scale 2* chap. 31, 258, 259.
55 *Ibid.*, 258.

bread and is mainly in the understanding. Understanding, he says, is the lady and imagination the serving maid introduced when there is a need[56]. The difference is one of emphasis between the imagination and the understanding. He is not suggesting that understanding may wholly dispense with imagination but that the imagination is subsumed in an understanding which temporarily suspends the need for imagery in this kind of unitive 'feeling'.

It is a difficult notion to express for expression depends upon the analogies which the imagination provides. In chapter thirty-two of *Scale II* he attempts a fuller explanation of what he means. The Holy Spirit opens the inner eye of the soul 'little by little at different times' with the 'touch and shining' of light in the reason. The soul does not perceive the Spirit *as* he is but only *that* he is. He uses the language of extremity to express the inexpressible of the understanding *that* he is; unchangeable being, supreme power, supreme truth, supreme goodness, a blessed life, an endless beatitude. This boundlessness is what the soul sees and much more. Not, he suggests, in the manner of the scholar who sees him by his learning, only through the power of naked reason, blindly, nakedly and without savour but with understanding. The feature of this understanding is the reverence and burning love which accompanies the light of the Holy Spirit. This light gives 'spiritual savour' and 'heavenly delight' so that the understanding is clearer and fuller than 'may be written or told'. This paradox of a clarity and fullness which remains inexpressible suggests that the experience is without analogy, beyond anything in the experience with which it might be illustrated. It is the kind of experience to which the *Cloud* Author refers when he says a person who has it will run miles to find someone who has also experienced something similar in order to share the feeling with someone who can understand it.

The effect of this experience although it may only be brief in duration and substance, is such that it grounds all 'inward practice' in the affections[57]. He seems to mean that henceforward the sight and knowledge of Jesus is, as it were, associated with the experience of love which accompanied the illumination of the understanding. This is the condition which he refers to as reformation in faith and feeling, because the knowledge of faith is henceforth accompanied by the feeling of love. Knowledge, *scientia*, becomes as it were *sapientia*, wisdom. Wisdom seems to be that condition which unites all the faculties of the soul on a new plane of vision outside space and time. This new plane of vision is dark still to the extent that it is a vision *that* God is not *as* God is. It is a vision similar, perhaps, in its fullness, and blinding clarity, to that which the *Cloud* Author refuses to attempt to describe because his 'blabbering tongue' will be inadequate to the task. Julian also seems to recognise an incomprehensible joy which accompanies her infused insights of the meaning of the showing of the Lord and Servant parable. It is not so much a tempo-

---

56   *Ibid.*, n.210, 315.
57   *Scale 2* chap. 32, 259, n.214, 316.

ral joy which passes but a joy which is sustained whenever she meditates on her *Showings* and intensifies as the insights accumulate and are extended.

Relationships between Feeling, Faith and Darkness

Hilton uses the example of three men standing in the sun to illustrate the distinctions between faith, feeling and the relationship to darkness which he is drawing[58]. The one man is blind; the second has his eyes shut; the third has full sight. The blind man doesn't know he is in the sun but only believes because he is told that the warmth he feels is not that of a fire but of the sun. He is like the man who is reformed only in faith. The second man is aware of the sun but has closed his eyes, signifying the consciousness of bodily feeling of the sun but also of the human incapacity to gaze upon it. He sees, as it were, through grace. Yet his sight is so powerful that were no-one in the world to believe in and love God, he would do so. The third man has full vision as in heaven where God will be seen as he is in his full radiance. It is as if Hilton is led from his story of the men in the sun to a consideration of 'fire'. It is said, he remarks, that God is fire[59]. This is not to be interpreted as elemental fire but the burning sensation of love and charity. God is a purifying fire in the soul. Metaphors of this kind must be understood in a spiritual or anagogic sense if they are to have any savour. It is not possible to speak of God except through words of this kind, when through grace, as the interior light of the man with his eyes shut, we have some sight of God as Jesus. When we have such sight material things are easily understood in a spiritual sense. Just as when we think of the third man's full vision of God in heaven, we think only of Jesus as God.

Contemplation and Distraction

There are a number of similarities between Hilton's understanding of the contemplative moment and that of the *Cloud* Author. There is also one substantial dissimilarity. The similarity relates to 'forgetting'. Hilton suggests that to search for God 'within' it is first necessary to forget all material things - all that is outside - and one's own body[60]. This includes forgetting one's own soul. This would seem to conform to the *Cloud* Author's discussion of the 'cloud of forgetting' and being 'naked'. However, the dissimilarity arises in Hilton's emphasis on Jesus. Rather than think of 'nothing' and becoming internally as well as externally naked and blind,

---

58 *Scale 2* chap. 32, 260.
59 *Scale 2* chap. 33, 262. Note also the *Cloud* Author's use of 'fire' to illustrate the nature of an ejaculatory prayer.
60 *Scale 2* chap. 35, 268 'For then love is master and works in the soul, making it forget itself and see and consider only how love acts and then the soul is more passive than active: and that is pure love'.

Hilton suggests that the attention should be concentrated on the uncreated nature which is Jesus, by whom the individual was made, given life, held and given reason, memory and will[61]. The *Cloud* Author believes that concentration even on Jesus will lead to distraction, one thought leading to another. Hilton, on the other hand, relies on St John the Evangelist's description of God; God is light. This he understands to mean that God is both faith and truth. If we cannot trust God to fulfil his promises even in prayer, then there is little chance that one can learn to love him. Hilton, like Julian who vividly describes the nature of her distractions, does not deny that distractions will arise. This is a feature of the formation and reformation process; to learn about distractions, and how to overcome them by persistent effort. Not only distractions either but also the discouragement of unfulfilled prayer which Julian believes is the more serious threat to one's trust in God. Hilton does not abandon, even in the last stages of the approach to his Jerusalem, the belief that discursive reason applied to one's experience will enable the pilgrim to recover the ground lost by distraction[62]. With the help of the God who is 'light', the mind may be enlightened and helped to regain the ground that it has lost through distraction or mistrust of the instructions it has been given in its Christian formation.

Prospective Audiences

There is a difference in perspective between Hilton and the *Cloud* Author rather than a theological difference. The difference in perspective arises perhaps from their purpose which is influenced by their prospective audiences. There is a good deal of uncertainty about their respective perspectives but it seems clear that the *Cloud* Author is addressing prospective contemplatives from within an enclosed environment. They would be people drawn to the enclosed, undistracted life of worship away from the distractions of the world. To fulfil their vocation they would need to concentrate on the elimination of distractions. They wish perhaps like Mary of the Martha/Mary story to do nothing more than gaze upon the face of the Godhead because Christ has indicated that this is the most perfect life. Hilton, on the other hand, has a much wider readership in mind, it would seem. In the last period of his life in which he served as an Augustinian Canon and in which most of his writing seems to have been undertaken, he addresses not only those about to consider or undertake an

---

61 *Scale 2* chap. 33, 263.
62 See for example *Scale 2* chaps 25 and 26, where 'the desire to love Jesus ... kills all sins, all carnal affections and all unclean thoughts *for the time* and then you are fast drawing near to Jerusalem' but 'beware the false light' and *Scale 2* chap. 34, 263-67. This seems a pivotal discourse:
'The sight of Jesus is the full glory of a soul, and that is not only for the sight, but also for the blessed love that comes from that light. (263) ... and that love is not the love that a soul has in itself for God; but the love that our Lord has for a sinful soul that knows nothing at all about loving him is the cause why this soul comes to this knowledge, and to this love that comes out of it'. [etc.]

enclosed life, but also lay people and those concerned with the religious needs of lay people. He lives what has been termed a 'mixed life' in which the service of God in meditation and worship is combined with the service of his creatures in their manifold callings[63]. Thus dealing with and living with distractions rather than eliminating them is his perspective. He does not write from the perspective of a Mary happy to sit at the feet of Christ and allow Martha to deal with the business of the household. He writes from the perspective of an apostle, whose work is not only to draw strength and wisdom from Christ by being with him but also to do his bidding in the evangelisation of the world. This perspective may explain not only his insistence that Christ remain the focal point of contemplative prayer but also that distractions are inevitable as one tries to be Christ-like in the world.

The Virtue of Discernment

As Hilton recognises, the experiences of God may be manifold, but in the Christian ethos, they seem at least in this period of history, to derive from a long meditation upon the Christian revelation as recorded in the Scriptures and experienced in grace by earlier generations of Christians. The experiences of Scripture and grace evolved into a common theological infrastructure of thought affirming the utter goodness of God which is experienced as 'love'. Most Christians are said to have experienced this 'love' as 'faith', but relatively few have recognised it in their lives on a habitual basis as 'feeling'[64]. The progressive capacity to recognise divine love may be regarded as the development of the virtue of discernment.

As Hilton well knew, and his contemporary mystics too, it is one thing to recognise that there are manifold experiences of God within the Christian dispensation and another to recognise that all claims of a grace-given special insight are genuine.

3. 'THE ANAGOGIC VISION OF JERUSALEM': HILTON'S MODE OF DISCERNMENT

The 'Jerusalem' image which Hilton uses to symbolise the fulfilment of Christian spiritual development was also used by Cassian to illustrate the four ways in which the 'unity' of Scripture, 'the one Jerusalem', might be interpreted. One of these ways was the 'anagogic' which we have suggested is the imaginative mode in which Hilton envisages Christians who have emerged from the 'darkness', reformed in 'faith

---

63 His short treatise on the 'mixed life' written to a devout layman seems intended to encourage a man who while not appearing to have a contemplative vocation in the 'vowed' life, nevertheless should develop the graces received to the full extent possible while fulfilling his responsibilities in the world. - See Clark's Introduction, 20, for the relationship between *Mixed Life* and *Scale 1*.

64 See for example *Scale 2* chap. 18, 220-22 for a discussion of why relatively few have been reformed in both faith and feeling.

and feeling', might look at their fellow Christians and the world around them. The first stage of his dichotomy, 'reformation in faith', might be regarded as the analogical mode of imaginative operation. The two stages also reflect a degree of tension between imaging God as Christ and as Trinitarian, which perhaps Hilton is trying to resolve, between the active and contemplative notions of Christian love.

Hilton did not seem to have Julian of Norwich's perception of 'a great event' which would finally resolve the 'paradox' of divine 'love' reflected in the fate of the damned and the fears of 'Hell' among the living. Hilton's 'great event' was perhaps confined to the revealed parameters of Christ's sacrifice. 'Reformation in faith' was founded upon trust in the efficacy of that sacrifice. Like Augustine he found it difficult to understand why Christians would not accept this gift on trust and like Augustine he was conscious of the dilemma of original sin which led him and others to forfeit this gift while yet realising the nature of divine love from which it proceeded. Hilton's theme is 'reformation' but his emphasis ultimately, like Julian's, is on the way to appropriate divine love rather than on the consequences of failing to do so. Hell remains in the background, unlike in Dante's *Divine Comedy*, its torments remain unexplored. The focus is on a total transformation which follows that 'reformation in feeling' which complements the 'reformation in faith' and which is the work of divine grace. Hilton's emphasis is the same profound 'faith' in the abundance and efficacy of divine grace as Augustine of Hippo projected[65]. His purpose is to assist his readers and correspondents to appropriate this insight for themselves by recognising the signs and meaning of the presence of grace in their lives.

Unlike the *Cloud* Author, he did not suggest that the human being's 'fallen' nature, in the form of an unresolved 'lump of sin', should be ignored; that prospective contemplatives should offer themselves to God 'as they are', quite 'unresolved'. He advocates an ascesis which will reveal the 'lump of sin' for what it is. It is the realisation of the enormity of sin, which is uncovered by a traditional ascesis, which induces the 'darkness', the sense of the gulf which lies between 'persons reformed in faith', who are conscious of their sinful nature and totally contrite as a result, and the divine nature. Hilton and the *Cloud* Author are as one about the helplessness of the human condition. The *Cloud* Author suggests that the contemplative concentrate on calling for help, forgetful of all else. Hilton suggests that his readers concentrate on Christ, wearing his livery, with patience and humility, sorrowful but yet hopeful. Hilton wants Christ to lead to the Father by transformation effected in the feeling through the spirit in a hidden way in darkness. The *Cloud* Author expects the 'longing darts of love' to open up the 'cloud of unknowing' and enable contemplatives to be drawn into a divine union so ineffable that it is also unspeakable.

Hilton's account of the journey to Jerusalem is much more in the imaginative mode of Cassian than the Pseudo-Dionysius. It is based on 'reform' as a 'purifying' proc-

---

65   Clark/Dorward ed. *Scale*, Introduction, 43, 44.

ess but it recognises perhaps more clearly than Cassian did that Christ mediates the graces which begin the journey and ultimately bring it to a conclusion. There is 'mystery' in the process by which grace operates in the sense that its operation is 'hidden', but Christ's incarnation and life, as revealed in Scripture and the Church's teaching, is both the source of the mystery and its resolution. Christ is the stimulus for the analogical imagination which mediates the process of 'reformation in faith' and for the anagogical imagination which mediates the process of 'reformation in feeling'. Christ is transformed, it seems, into the Trinitarian God in the 'imaginative vision' and changes its focus to 'within' the individual rather than, as it were, from 'outside'.

One senses that Hilton is carrying the analogy of the 'purification' process beyond Cassian's explanation. Cassian's purification develops the virtues, Hilton's develops both the virtues and the imagination. The *Cloud* Author seems to reject the imagination in a deliberate cultivation of blindness and darkness because the God whom he seeks is essentially unknowable. Hilton seems to suggest that individuals may recognise God in the transformation of their feelings and this process is progressive as they recognise the twinkling lights of Jerusalem as they approach the end of the journey and dawn breaks to reveal its splendour.

Hilton like Augustine may have felt that the full splendour of Jerusalem would not be revealed in this life. He suggests his own experience may be of the twinkling lights and that dawn does not break until the pilgrim arrives within its walls[66]. It is left to John of the Cross to guide the pilgrim through the 'city' as the new day dawns.

There is another aspect of Hilton's teaching, however, which points forward to Ignatius of Loyola. Hilton seems to be making the insights of the contemplative tradition available to all conditions of people[67]. He is not suggesting as Ignatius will that contemplation may have a conscious purpose which has as its end 'making an election' to do 'more' for Christ. But he is suggesting, particularly in the second part of the *Scale*, that all Christians may deepen their spiritual awareness, and that the graces of contemplation are not reserved to an elite group of religious. In the first part of the *Scale*, he seems to think it is unlikely that someone who has mundane responsibilities will be able to proceed to the higher degrees of contemplation. Contemplation requires disengagement and solitude he seems to suggest. The change perhaps reflects those that have taken place in Hilton's own experience in the interval between the writing of the two parts of the *Scale*. He remains cautious about

---

66 *Scale 2* chap. 21, 227, 228. See J.P.H. Clark, 'The Cloud of Unknowing. Walter Hilton and St John of the Cross: A Comparison' in *Downside Review*, vol. 97, 1978, 281-98 and Andrew Ryder, 'The English and Spanish Mystics', Diss. University of Lancaster U.K., 1976 for a discussion of the link with John of the Cross and the other Spanish mystics.

67 Compare *Scale 1* chap. 9, 83 with *Scale 2* chap. 27, 245 and *Scale 2* chap. 41, 287, 288.

unguided attempts to extend the reformation process to the contemplative stage, no doubt because many enthusiasts had been led astray[68]. Hilton encouraged the practice of 'contemplation' with supervision but he was unspecific about the nature of the supervision. Ignatius, of course, was the architect of a highly supervised medium of contemplation which yet allowed for individuality and the personal 'call', as we shall see. Hilton's caution may have been confirmed from the experience of examining those suspected of holding Lollard views while Ignatius', paradoxically, from the experience of being suspected of Alumbrado sympathies and himself being examined on several occasions.

---

68 'I speak of those seculars who do not fear to set out on the way of the spiritual life without a director or capable guide, whether man or book, obeying their own impulse'. Quoted by J. Russell-Smith in 'Walter Hilton' in *Pre-Reformation English Spirituality*, ed. James Walsh S.J. New York: Fordham University Press, 1966, 193. Source is the Latin letter to Adam Horsley on the religious state (Bod. Lat. th. e.26, fol.127). Miss Russell-Smith's translation.

Appendix

HILTON'S LIFE IN THE CONTEXT OF THE *SCALE OF PERFECTION*

Hilton died in 1396. This seems to be the least conjectural fact about his life. *Scale 2* was perhaps written towards the end of his life and thus is approximately contemporaneous with the longer version of Julian's *Showings*. There is some doubt about whether *Scale 2* was addressed to the same person as *Scale 1* (Clark, Introduction, 19). This also raises the question we have encountered before in this study (see Prologue, 20 above) about whether the addressee of *Scale 1* is a distinct person or a convenient literary fiction representing a class of readers. The most substantial evidence that *Scale 2* is a later work and addressed to a class of reader is provided by the change in emphasis and depth of insight compared with *Scale 1*. In *Scale 2* 'contemplation' is regarded as the goal of spiritual development for all Christians whereas in *Scale 1* he seems to confine 'contemplation' to those in the religious life. The insights of *Scale 2* suggest the maturing of his experience as a spiritual director which he would have gained as an Augustinian canon and is perhaps reflected in the range of his correspondents and the other translations and exegetical work. The best estimate is that he entered the Augustinian priory at Thurgarton, between Nottingham and Newark, in 1386 or soon after. This estimate is based on evidence provided by his Latin letter (*De Utilitate et Prerogativis Religionis*) addressed to Adam Horsley, who in 1376 had been appointed Controller of the Great Roll, and eventually entered the Carthusian Community at Beauvale (where it is thought the *Cloud* Author may have resided), not far distant from Thurgarton. In this letter Hilton says he is himself thinking of joining a religious community and encourages Horsley in his purpose by providing a reasoned defence for the vowed religious life. It is therefore possible that Hilton joined the Augustinians shortly before or after Horsley joined the Carthusians. In an earlier letter, *De Imagine Peccati*, which he addressed to a solitary, Hilton had inferred that at the time of writing he too was living the life of a solitary. He had apparently found the life unsatisfactory; he had renounced the world but was being of little practical service to God and to the Church (perhaps Thomas Arundel had sought his assistance as a trained lawyer with a strong spiritual background, see below). It seems Hilton had entered the solitary state after giving up a promising legal career as a civil or canon lawyer (see *Walter Hilton's Latin Writings*, ed. J.P.H. Clark and C. Taylor, Salzburg, 1987, 262). The pieces of evidence on which our knowledge of Hilton's legal qualifications and career is based are circumstantial but sufficiently focussed to be regarded as more than suggestive. First of all, a Walter de Hilton Bachelor of Civil Law who at the time was a Clerk of the Lincoln diocese, was granted the reservation of a canonry and prebend of Abergwili, Camarthen in January 1371. See A.B. Emden, *Biographical Register of the University of Cambridge to 1500*. Cambridge, 1963, s.v. Hilton. Secondly there is a reference to a Walter Hilton, who was present at the Ely Consistory Court in 1375. At this time Hilton was probably still a Bachelor of Civil Law. It was usual to graduate first in Civil Law before studying Canon Law. In 1375 he was therefore probably studying Canon Law. This assumes, of course, that the Walter Hilton both of the Lincoln diocese and who was present in the Ely Consistory Court was our Walter Hilton. The third strand of evidence concerns his education and patronage. It has been suggested by Jonathan Hughes in his *Pastors and Visionaries: Religion and Secular Life in Late Mediaeval Yorkshire*, Woodbridge, Suffolk: Boydell Press, 1988, that there may be a link between Hilton and a circle of northern clerks retained in his administration at Ely by Thomas Arundel who became Bishop of Ely in 1374 and, later in 1388, Archbishop of York and finally Archbishop of Canterbury in 1396. Arundel was twice Chancellor under Richard II. He was evidently a man with patronage to bestow even in Hilton's lifetime. The circle of clerks were given preferment at Peterhouse, a Cambridge College with a strong bias towards canon law. See also J.P.H. Clark's 'Late Fourteenth Century Cambridge Theology and the English Contemplative Tradition' in *M.M.T. in Eng.*, 1992, 1-16. If Hilton was of this circle, and it tends to be supported by his presence at the Ely Consistory in 1375, it would seem he probably continued his studies at Cambridge beyond 1375 and would have been ready to incept as a Master or Doctor of Canon Law in 1381/82. There is in fact a manuscript tradition that Hilton was an Inceptor of Canon Law. Working back from the date of 1371 and taking account of age limitations on entry to Cambridge University and the average length of time it took to gain the bachelor of Civil Law degree, it has been conjectured that Hilton may have been born in the early 1340's, about the same time as Julian of Norwich. The connection with Arundel and his efforts at renewal within the archdiocese after his elevation to York in 1388, is at least supported by the internal evidence of Hilton's writings. At Thurgarton as a canon lawyer he may have become involved in the examination of Lollards against whom Arundel moved with increasing determination since the priory was authorised to examine those suspected of Lollard sympathies. (See K.B. McFarlane, *John Wycliffe and the Beginnings of English Non-Conformity*, London: English Universities Press Ltd, 1952, 150-55 and 161-65.) This is particularly evident in what Hilton says about the interpretation of Scripture which was a prominent issue in the examination of Lollards. Moreover, Hilton also warns against over-enthusiasm and reliance on sensual manifestations of the presence of the Holy Spirit which Richard Rolle had seemed to advocate. Rolle's intentions had apparently been misinterpreted and led to unruliness among certain advocates of charismatic renewal in the form of the 'liberty of spirit', associated with mystical experience.

PART II

FROM CHAUCER'S ENGLAND TO CERVANTES' SPAIN

Allegories of the 'Quixotic' Poetic

INTRODUCTION

Cervantes in *Don Quixote* did for his contemporaries towards the close of Spain's 'Golden Age' what Chaucer did for late fourteenth-century England with the *Canterbury Tales*. He enabled them to see themselves in a way that was at once pleasurable, recognisable and enigmatic. In this he captured the mood and tensions of the times. For the historian the works of Cervantes and Chaucer display societies which express the trials and enjoyments of life, yet seem to sense, if only dimly, the 'mystical' significance of the world around them which ultimately may shape their destiny. The people displayed seem to emerge from their canvasses as real and the relationships, particularly as displayed by Cervantes in dialogue, are those which we can in part identify from our own experiences. The societies of the fourteenth and sixteenth centuries within which the mystics of our study live, are different. But they have some common characteristics; the pervasive presence of the 'Church', for example, and a sense of life as an adventure, full of wonderment and sorrow, but especially full of mystery.

The sense of Spanish nationhood came into being gradually in the sixteenth century, after the way had been prepared by the union of the crowns of Castile and Aragon under Ferdinand and Isabella in 1469 and the completion of the Reconquista in 1492. The energies hitherto employed in the long struggle with the Moors, were redeployed in attempting to realise the synergies which might result from unifying its disparate but complementary parts. It was perhaps natural, though in some respects unfortunate, that the alliance of Church and State which had been forged in repelling and then defeating the Moorish infiltration of the peninsula, should become the cornerstone of the new unity. It was symbolised by the creation of the institution of the Spanish Inquisition in 1479 to pursue recalcitrant *Marranos*, oversee the conversion of the *Moriscos* and ultimately the extirpation of *Alumbrados* and Protestants. 'Unity' in this age implied both uniformity and conformity, though as Cervantes' work illustrates, the conformity was to be perhaps negative in the sense that it discouraged dissent rather than promoting ideals[1].

---

1 The peace of Augsburg of 1555 which the dictum 'cuius regio, eius religio' summarises, though it does not occur in the recess of the Diet (see G.R. Elton, *Reformation Europe, 1517-1559*, London: Collins, 1967, 266, n.1), enshrined the principle on which religious peace in the period was to be based. As Elton suggests, within the State, religious dissent seemed tanta-

However, despite the apparent intensity of an ancient and well-tried commitment to the 'Catholic' faith as the basis of Spanish culture, Spain was little different from other parts of Europe in displaying some religious indifference and moral laxity. For example, Philip Caraman in his biography of Ignatius Loyola recounts how Ignatius, while studying at Barcelona on his return from the pilgrimage to Jerusalem, attempted 'to bring back the nuns in the Convent of the Angels to a regular life' which 'ended in a severe beating by young gallants who frequented the place to satisfy their lusts'. It was apparently 'a thrashing he never forgot'[2]. Beneath the surface of society there lurked all the moral *peccadillos* which the reforming 'ascetic' or 'puritan' spirit both Catholic and Protestant, found so unauthentic about the inheritance of the mediaeval church, at once so spiritual and yet evidently and inconveniently corporeal[3].

The Spanish society we meet in the pages of Cervantes' *Don Quixote*, even at the turn of the century, suggests the ambivalent relationship of the spiritual and carnal, has not disappeared[4]. The spirituality which El Greco's canvasses display may represent an ideal to which his patrons aspired. The elongated images and subdued but phosphorescent colours convey perhaps the commitment of his patrons to a disciplined life of the spirit. The aura of sadness perhaps captures the melancholy which may accompany the longing to explore the 'inter-stellar' space of their imaginations restrained by the rack of temporal and corporeal circumstance[5].

---

mount to sedition, 280; and perhaps his notion that toleration grew out of weariness with extremes and religious indifference rather than Christian charity is not altogether wide of the mark in this period.

2   Philip Caraman, Ignatius Loyola, 57, 58.

3   Erasmus' life and writings perhaps illustrate this point. See for example, *The Praise of Folly*, trans. Leonard F. Dean, Chicago, 1946, 79-82, 95, 104, 109-13.

4   See for example the encounter with the 'strolling wenches' in Riley, ed. *Don Quixote*, Pt I, chap. 2, 31, in the 'first sally' made by Don Quixote from his village. See also James A. Parr, *Don Quixote: An Anatomy of Subversive Discourse*, Newark Del., 1988.

5   Paul Guinard, *El Greco; Biographical and Critical Study*, trans. J. Emmons, Lausanne: Skira, 1956, 26, remarks 'his [El Greco's] painting is a window on an inter-stellar world beyond the sluggishness of gravity. All these distinctive qualities of his, destined to scandalise the classical-minded 18th century, seem to have been accepted almost as a matter of course by the contemporaries of Santa Teresa and Cervantes'.

An Allegory of 'Love' in the Tradition of 'Quixotic' Spirituality

The composition of this work is similar to that of Figure 2. However, it is painted after El Greco's arrival in Spain. The mood has changed. Christ is represented as a symbol like a sun hidden behind storm clouds. In the foreground, Philip II surrounded by members of the church militant has replaced the three beautiful maidens as if he alone, the 'Quixotic' hero, stands between the pilgrims, seen making their way to Heaven and Hell depicted as in Figure 2. See the detail in Figure 1.

El Greco, Adoration of the Name of Jesus (Dream of Philip II), ca. 1580.

The Spain of the sixteenth century which saw the emergence of saints of the stature of Ignatius of Loyola, Teresa of Avila and John of the Cross[6], displayed the range between heroic and picaresque extremes which the literary heroes and anti-heroes of the period reflected[7]. It has been suggested that soon after his 'history' appeared in 1605, the character of 'Don Quixote', as the parodic image of the chivalrous hidalgo, had displaced the former favourite Amadis of Gaul in the 'national' imagination[8]. In the time of conquistadors and Ignatius of Loyola, Amadis of Gaul seemed to symbolise the aspirations of the Spanish hidalgo. The tapestries which adorned the walls of the hall in the house of the Treasurer of Spain where Ignatius spent his early manhood, contained images of the exploits of Amadis of Gaul and other literary heroes[9]. However the image of Don Quixote began to appear in pageants in Spain and other parts of Europe soon after the publication of Cervantes' story[10]. The exploits of the new 'hero' were comic in the realism of the delusions, which they displayed. The immediate popularity of Cervantes' story suggests it captured a sense of 'picaresque' disillusionment in his readers about the dream of realising the heroic denouement which characterised stories of the chivalrous knight-errant, but also a sense of a deep affection for the ideals and sense of adventure, which inspired the quest. Perhaps Spain's heroic age had passed by 1615 when part two of *Don Quixote* appeared, but its passing may have been regarded with the sadness, even melancholy reflected in El Greco's pictorial images, as the increasing burdens of the Spanish involvement in the European political and religious imbroglio came to be recognised[11].

---

6   While Ignatius of Loyola, Teresa of Avila and John of the Cross are well known for their profound influence on the development of Christian spirituality, they were not alone. They were preceded by an earlier generation of distinguished reforming and spiritual teachers in Jiminez de Cisneros (1436-1517), Francisco de Osuna, author of *The Third Spiritual Alphabet* (1537) and Bernardino de Laredo, author of *The Ascent of Mt Sion*. The latter two were recognised as powerful influences by Teresa of Avila in her autobiography chaps 4 and 23 respectively. See also M. Bataillon, *Erasme et l'Espagne: recherches sur l'histoire spirituelle du XVIe siècle*, Paris, 1937 and E. Allison Peers, 'The Historical Problem of Spanish Mysticism' in *St Teresa of Jesus and Other Essays and Addresses*, London, 1953, 139-152.

7   Cervantes had contributed to the wave of picaresque novels with a story 'Rinconete y Cortadillo' which was written before 1604 and later revised and published as one of the *Exemplary Novels* (1613). Riley ed., *Don Quixote*, viii.

8   See Caraman, *Ignatius Loyola*, 14.

9   *Ibid.*, 12.

10 Riley ed. *Don Quixote*, vii. By 1621 the figure of Don Quixote had appeared at least ten times in pageants as widely dispersed as Cuzco in Peru and Heidelberg.

11 See H.A.L. Fisher, *A History of Europe*, 2 vols. London: Eyre & Spottiswoode, 1949 (first publ. 1935), Vol. 1, 608. He sums up the Spanish experience thus: 'A long succession of reverses experienced by a religious people may either shake or confirm them in the faith. In the agony of the great Channel fight [1588] the Spanish sailors exclaimed, 'God has deserted us'. Later the nation was brought to believe that it was punished because it had deserted God'. This may be a somewhat colourful view but it perhaps in part explains the act of self-flagellation which led to the expulsion of the Moriscos by Phillip III.

We suggest that the Christian tradition of 'discernment of spirits' reached some sort of apogee in this period in the spiritual teaching of Ignatius of Loyola and John of the Cross. While we do not wish to suggest that either social conditions or some orthogeneous characteristics in the tradition itself led inevitably, as it were, to this development, nevertheless the intensity of Spanish spirituality was perhaps focussed in a special way in response to some of the tensions between suppression and adventure which the circumstances of the society generated. We have already referred in passing to the 'inquisitorial spirit' which was reflected institutionally in the Spanish Inquisition. This spirit not only led the orthodox reformers to be cautious but also impressed upon them the need to be precise and articulate about their intentions.

There was also a 'creative humanist spirit' abroad which is reflected, of course, in Cervantes' achievement with *Don Quixote*, a literary masterpiece which emerged after a long gestation period of observation, extensive experience - which included five years as a captive of the Moors and presence in the Spanish squadron at the battle of Lepanto - and several vain earlier attempts to achieve literary and dramatic success. The poetry of John of the Cross shared this creative and humanist spirit[12]. And Ignatius has been called a 'logothete' by Roland Barthes[13]. We would dispute the claim in part that Ignatius invented a 'new language' of spiritual discourse as Barthes argues. On the other hand, the development of his spirituality did owe a great deal to the 'spirit of adventure' among young hidalgos in the first half of the century which perhaps endowed with its dynamism the creative spirit whose achievements in the last part of the century were so notable.

Our thesis is that rather than containing orthogeneous characteristics which inevitably evolve to some apotheosis, the tradition of 'discernment of spirits' responds in a symbiotic relationship to the mystical character of the Christian spiritual tradition itself. There is little doubt that the manner in which the tradition of discernment of spirits displays itself in the two Spanish mystics seems to reflect a different spiritual climate from that of the late fourteenth-century English mystics. The Protestant challenge which emerged in the sixteenth century to the mystical nature of the 'faith' seemed to heighten the consciousness of its 'mystery' for the Spanish mystics[14].

---

12 See Kieran Kavanaugh's introduction to the writings of John of the Cross, New York: Paulist Press, Classics of Western Spirituality series, 1987, 24-34 and in particular page 27, where he refers to Dámaso Alonso's judgement that John of the Cross is 'the loftiest poet of Spain'.

13 Roland Barthes, *Sade/Fourier/Loyola*, trans. Richard Miller, New York: Hill and Wang, 1976, 3.

14 Luther's early encounter with the 'mystic way' and Staupitz seems to have led to a distrust and fear of the human response to the divine mystery which is reflected in his theology. See Roland H. Bainton, *'Here I Stand', a Life of Martin Luther*, New York: The New American Library, 1950, 42-45. See also Roger Haight S.J., *The Experience and Language of Grace*, New York: Paulist Press, 1979, chap. 4, 79-104 on 'Luther: Sin and Grace', particularly 99-101.

In England in the late fourteenth century, the mystics were not faced with the extensive challenge to the 'mystery' of their inherited faith as the Spanish mystics of the sixteenth century were to experience. It is true that in Wycliffe and the Lollards a challenge was beginning to emerge but it received only passing political support from the secular arm[15]. In Europe in the sixteenth century not only had 'the mystery' of the faith been challenged in its doctrinal basis, but the challenge had been championed by the secular arm in a number of states[16] and had become engulfed in the political tensions of the period rather in the manner that the Donatist controversy had evolved by the time of Augustine of Hippo[17]. On the one hand a doctrine apparently inimical to the idea of 'mystery' was being rapidly developed under powerful patronage. On the other hand, religious 'enthusiasm' had developed in a form which did not recognise the 'legitimacy' of the traditional constraints of spiritual discernment. The unbounded behaviour resulting from 'freedom of the spirit' focussed attention on the need for 'discernment' in much the same way as similar internal and external developments had in late fourteenth-century England[18].

The spiritual challenge in the late fourteenth century in England, however, was perhaps to revive the traditional spirit of 'faith, hope and love' in a society dispirited by the effects of 'post-plague shock' and enervated by a long, indecisive war[19]. In the sixteenth century in those parts of Europe which remained in communion with

---

15 See K.B. McFarlane, *John Wycliffe and the Beginnings of English Non-Conformity*, 58-88, 'Wycliffe in Politics, 1371-78'. He sums up (p.86): 'His aristocratic employers [Wycliffe's]... were soon doing their best to silence him and to nullify his work'.

16 See for example G.R. Elton, *Reformation Europe*. He asks the question (297-304) in what sense did the Reformation assist the political development of the age, acknowledging the importance of politics in the progress of the Reformation.

17 The religious issues which underlay the controversy were by Augustine's day overlaid by nationalistic and political considerations.

18 The situation in 14th-century England is well summed up in J.P.H. Clark's article 'Walter Hilton and 'Liberty of Spirit'' in the *Downside Review*, Vol. 96, 1978, 61-78, particularly page 63. See also Beryl Smalley *Studies in Mediaeval Thought and Learning: From Abelard to Wyclif*, London: Hambledon Press, 1981. In Spain 'Alumbrados' were already in detention awaiting trial at Alcala when Ignatius of Loyola arrived there in 1526. At their head was Francesca Hernandez who believed she had been granted a mystical union with God that made it impossible for her to commit sin. Others went further believing they might indulge their lusts without scruple. See Caraman, *Ignatius Loyola*, 62.

19 Jonathan Hughes, *Pastors and Visionaries. Religion and Secular Life in Late Mediaeval Yorkshire*, describes the pastoral programme carried through by a series of reforming Archbishops at York. 'Lollardy' seems to have been as much a social as a religious movement. K.B. McFarlane, *John Wycliffe and the Beginnings of English Non-Conformity*, suggests that after 1414 the lower middle class monopolised it completely (187) and it remained a non-conformist undercurrent unconnected with the Reformation in England. For the Black Death see A.R. Bridbury's articles: 'The Black Death' in *Econ. H.R.*, xxvi, 1973, 577-592 and 'Before the Black Death', *Econ. H.R.*, xxx, 1977, 393-410.

Rome, the challenge appeared to be to articulate and defend the mystical character of the faith itself, as well as renew it[20].

In the last resort we must say the challenge to the spiritual and mystical nature of Christianity was much stronger in the sixteenth century than in the late fourteenth. The stronger spiritual response which the situation called forth in Spain as perhaps the strongest stakeholder in the counter-reformation, also called forth a more focussed articulation of the tradition of 'discernment of spirits' which the defense of the 'spiritual mystery' required to legitimise it.

In the two following chapters we will attempt to trace how Ignatius of Loyola and John of the Cross in their different ways responded to the challenges which faced them and explored and re-articulated the tradition of 'discernment of spirits' as an integral part of a mystically inspired religion.

---

20 See Desiderius Erasmus, *Christian Humanism and the Reformation. Selected Writings*, ed. John C. Olin, New York: Harper Torchbooks, 1965, 20-21. Olin cites French scholar, Gentian Hervet, who in the Preface of his 1526 translation of a Sermon of Erasmus into English, writes: 'The clear springs of Holy Scripture that the Philistines had so troubled, so marred, and so defiled, that no man could drink or have the true taste of the water, they be now by his labor and diligence to their old pureness and clearness so restored that no spot nor earthly filth in them remaineth'.
There is a suggestion here that that is all that needed to be done. The mystics of Spain were concerned as we shall see, with recognising purity, keeping the waters pure and persuading others to enjoy drinking from them regularly.

Chapter 5

IGNATIUS OF LOYOLA

On his return from the Holy Land, Ignatius began to display the kind of self-effacing, evangelical life-style which reflected the change in orientation which we outlined in the Prologue. His commitment and orthodoxy were recognised by those who, suspicious of his zeal, examined him and his *Spiritual Exercises* at Alcala and Salamanca in the period in which he was developing and testing the early drafts[1]. However, in the *Spiritual Exercises* his quixotic zeal was tempered by the influence of Thomas a Kempis' *Imitation of Christ* which remained a source of spiritual insight for Ignatius throughout his life[2]. The influence perhaps led him to cultivate a compassionate detachment in his guidance of those whom he introduced to the *Spiritual Exercises*. It was a key quality he was to recommend that Spiritual Directors develop in administering the *Exercises*[3].

No doubt his gifts of 'quixotic' leadership, apostolic fervour and self-denial all played their part in attracting a following of men of the calibre of the first compan-

---

1   The *Spiritual Exercises* were not completed in final written form until 1541 and were not approved by Pope Paul III until 31st July 1548. See the *Autobiography*, Appendix II, 132 and 155; Appendix I, Preface of Father Nadal, n.2. Ignatius was pursuing his studies at Alcala 1526-27 and Salamanca 1527, and in both places the authorities were suspicious that in his pastoral work he might be spreading 'Illuminist' ideas. The suspicion of illuminism persistently dogged Ignatius and the Jesuits in Spain. See N.20 below. For illuminism and the 'Alumbrados' see E. Colunga O.P., 'Intellectualistas y mysticos en la Teologia espagnola in el siglo XVI' in *Ciencia Tomista* X, 1914-15, 223-42 and G. Constant in *D.H.G.E.*, II, 1914, s.v., 'Alumbrados', cols 849-853 with bibliography; G. Leff, *Heresy in the Later Middle Ages*, Manchester: Manchester University Press, 1967; R.E. Lerner, *The Heresy of the Free Spirit in the Later Middle Ages*, Berkeley: University of California Press, 1972; R. Guerniera, 'Frères du Libre Esprit' in *Dict. Sp.*, Vol. 5, 1964, cols 1241-68; B. Llorca, *Die Spanische Inquisition und die Alumbrados*, Berlin-Bonn, 1934, 159.

2   Caraman, *Ignatius Loyola*, 77, suggests it was during his time at the Montaigu that Ignatius was introduced to the *Imitation of Christ*. However, it seems more probable he first read the *Imitation* while at Manresa. See Tylenda's commentary on the *Autobiography* 26, 34, in which he records that Ignatius referred to the *Imitation* as 'Gerçonzita', n.7, 142, refers to F.N.I, 1943, 584, where Gonçalves also records that Ignatius read a chapter of the *Imitation* every day of his life.

3   *Exercises* 15, 6 and 23, 12: 'Therefore, we must make ourselves indifferent to all created things...' is the essence of Ignatian detachment in order, in the case of the Spiritual Director, to allow God to work directly in the Soul of the exercitant and 'inflame' it.

ions during his time at the University of Paris[4]. But it was that gift of compassionate objectivity which made the *Spiritual Exercises* such an effective instrument in mediating their personal conversions to the ideals on which the *Exercises* were based.

The text of the *Spiritual Exercises* was a set of stage directions, not a spiritual treatise. The text was a new genre; a manual of instructions to guide the Spiritual Director. It presupposed a range of qualities in the Director, not only of compassion and objectivity but also intellectual and imaginative without which the effectiveness of the *Exercises* would be diminished. Ignatius had initially perceived that education was an essential need for himself to enable him to pursue his vocation as he perceived it on his return to Barcelona after his pilgrimage. His subsequent experience had reinforced this perception. First, his brushes with church authorities had convinced him that it was not possible in the conditions of his day to play an evangelical role without the sanction of the Church. Second, that sanction would not be forthcoming unless it was possible to convince the authorities that one was both theologically literate and obedient to the tenets of faith which theology helped one to understand. Third, and most importantly, theological instruction enabled one to understand and recognise divine activity and requirements in the world. Education opened the mind and extended the understanding; theological education directed the mind and understanding to the role of the divinity in the world and in one's own life. In other words, theology was a study about the meaning of life and of all the situations encountered in life. This notion was largely unchallenged in Ignatius' day. Theology was the 'queen' of the sciences, to which all other disciplines pointed[5].

Thus the *Spiritual Exercises*, while in accord with and reflecting theological propositions, were not a mode of theological enquiry in themselves. They were designed to facilitate a participation in theological truths by prayer and reflection to bring about an intimate understanding of one's own role in the furtherance of God's kingdom, and having understood that role, to elect to fulfil it with the assistance of the divine grace which had already made the seeking participant aware of the origin of the calling.

---

4   Short curricula vitae of the first companions are included as nn.19-24, 149-150 in Tylenda's edition of the *Autobiography*. Earlier in his sojourn in Paris his influence over Juan Castro, Pedro de Peralta and Amador de Elduayen led to Ignatius being investigated yet again. *Autobiography* 77-78 and Tylenda's commentary pages 77, 78 and 81.
5   Most of the universities in Christendom were ecclesiastical foundations concerned with teaching the understanding of Ignatius' first principle and foundation at 23 of the *Exercises*: 'Man is created to praise, reverence and serve God our Lord, and by this means to save his soul'.
     The theory and the practice are one; and 'The other things on the face of the earth are created for man to help him in attaining the end for which he is created'.
     It is perhaps not surprising that those people who were particularly attracted to Ignatius personally were university students or people trained at universities seeking a clearer idea of their vocation in life.

The *Spiritual Exercises* were designed as a beginning not an end. However, they were a most important beginning because they would, it was hoped, make the participant aware by experience, by feeling, by reasoning, by willing of the authenticity of the call. Two singular features of this experience were the processes of discernment and election. However they, in Ignatius' concept, were processes based respectively on the reason and the will as we shall see. The exercises were also designed to stimulate the senses to experience the call more profoundly. The exercises concerned with the Application of Senses[6] seem to have been designed for this purpose and it is to these we must first turn because they were to make the spirit present to all the senses, so that it might be discerned in the depths of one's being and followed with self-sacrificing love.

1. THE APPLICATION OF THE SENSES

Ignatius evidently considered the 'Application of Senses' exercises to be an important element in the *Spiritual Exercises*. He specified that each day's meditations should conclude with a systematic review in the imagination of the gospel scenes with which the day's meditations had been concerned. The exercitant was instructed to apply each of the senses in turn to the scenes in order to evoke a holistic impression of them; not only the senses of hearing and seeing but also smelling, touching and tasting. There has been some debate about what Ignatius actually meant[7]; whether he intended the exercitants to confine themselves to the senses relevant to a simple reconstruction of the scenes in the imagination, so that tasting, smelling and touching would only be relevant to those situations in which they played a part; where ointments of great fragrance were used, or where food was cooked or eaten, or where Christ or one of the participants actually touched people as in healing. This interpretation of Ignatius' meaning might be regarded as simplistic, both as an interpretation and as a reflection on this aspect of Ignatian prayer.

The alternative interpretation is that Ignatius intended the 'Application of Senses' exercises to relate both to the physical and spiritual senses. It is impossible to draw the distinction without reference to the physical senses. The spiritual senses refer not to an application which reconstructs an imaginative impression of the scene but to a real presence in spirit, anagogically, which can only be described in physical terms[8].

---

6   I am particularly indebted to Hugo Rahner's essay on 'The Application of the Senses' and his other essays in *Ignatius the Theologian*, trans. Michael Barry, London: Geoffrey Chapman, 1990, 181-213, for what follows. See also Antonio T. de Nicolas, *Ignatius de Loyola: Powers of Imagining* (A philosophical hermeneutic of Imagining through the Collected Works), State University of New York Press, 1986.

7   Hugo Rahner, *Ignatius the Theologian*, 190, 191.

8   *Ibid.*, 194, cites A. Brou, *Saint Ignace, Maître d'Oraison*, Paris, 1925, 188: 'Aux images succède quelque chose de beaucoup plus intime, ce que les psychologues appellent le sentiment de présence'.

However, it is recognised that by analogy with the physical one cannot convey the sense of real presence which derives from an apparent detachment of the spirit. It is as if one were experiencing the most vivid of dreams but yet is convinced it is not a dream. We might here recall the experience of Julian of Norwich. This interpretation of the 'Application of Senses' exercises of course suggests a spiritual experience occurs not just an imagined physical experience. The emphasis which Ignatius placed upon the exercitants' emotional reaction to the experience suggests that he expected the simple physical reconstruction of biblical scenes to lead into a spiritual experience which went beyond the simple reconstruction. The prayerful attempt at reconstruction of a scene might be rewarded with a divine or diabolic supernatural presence which would console or terrify, evoke joy or sorrow, peace or distress, depending on whether the presence was of divine origin or diabolic; the experience of sorrow might perhaps denote a divine presence as in some reflection on the circumstances of the crucifixion, whereas an experience of distress or terror would almost certainly denote a diabolic presence. These are comparatively straight forward emotional reactions to interpret. However in practice Ignatius recognised, apparently deriving from his own experiences at Manresa and subsequently confirmed in the remaining fragments of the *Spiritual Diary*, that the emotional reactions might be mixed or clouded and less easily interpreted.

It is through the link which the 'Application of Senses' create with the processes of discernment of spirits and election that these exercises come to assume such importance in the *Spiritual Exercises*. In the context of an election the transition from an imaginative use of the physical senses to a spiritual experience seems to be expected to take place. The exercitant is praying for divine guidance and Ignatius expects in such circumstances a divine response, or perhaps a diabolic response, will be forthcoming. None of these processes were novel in themselves; neither the meditations, nor the 'Application of Senses', nor the processes of discernment of spirits and election. What was perhaps novel was the systematic manner in which all these activities were brought together and integrated within a meditative framework for the purpose of recognising and following the divine will. For those who received particular divine graces, during the spiritual exercises, it was perhaps expected that this process of prayer, of seeking guidance and choosing what would do more for the establishment of Christ's kingdom, would become habitual, almost a way of life, as it was to become for Ignatius and the first companions. The way of life was one of continuing spiritual contact with the spirit of Christ derived from an initial sensual assimilation of his life as revealed in the Gospels. In this respect we may recall John Cassian's understanding of the fruits of the meditative process. The exercises related to the 'Application of Senses' were to be the foundation on which discernment and election strategies were to be built. They were a way of recognising the spirit of Christ and how it differed from that of 'the enemy of human nature'.

The centrality which the celebration of the Eucharist later assumed in Ignatian spirituality illustrates how the 'Application of Senses' might assume a fundamental role in liturgical prayer. The manner in which Ignatius relied on the Eucharist to mediate the gift of discernment is well illustrated by the fragments which remain of his *Spiritual Diary*[9]. In them are recorded the manner in which Ignatius both prayed for guidance in framing those *Constitutions* of the Society of Jesus which deal with poverty and how he interpreted the movements within him which arose before, during and after the Eucharistic celebration. The Eucharistic celebration itself draws together for the participants the central mysteries of the Christian faith in a re-enactment of Christ's sacrifice. The symbolism of the liturgy leads into a spiritual event. A transposition occurs, for those who believe, which is unseen. The faith of the participant that Christ is really present in the bread and wine and enters the soul to feed it, is like the faith of exercitants in the *Exercises* who believe in the reality of the mysteries on which they are meditating and that the meditation and reflection through the 'Application of Senses' will lead them into the scene spiritually.

None of the commentators who interpret the exercises utilising the 'Application of Senses' as a means of developing the spiritual senses, regard these exercises as simple and easy[10]. Historians may reflect on their own difficulties of assimilating all that has been written and produced on or in a period in the past, of evaluating it and entering into the spirit of the period. This is what the *Spiritual Exercises* is asking of exercitants in meditating on the biblical scenes which record the mysteries of their faith. Perhaps the primary documents are accepted in faith, a concession which may not be allowed to the historian in a professional capacity, but the task of bringing a period to life in their own imaginations is somewhat similar. They try to live with those they write about; to enter into the spirit of the people and the age; to understand what is happening, how it is happening and why. Historians like exercitants, are attempting to bring the past into the present to help illuminate and influence the future as an evolving present.

We have suggested that exercises in the 'Application of Senses' were not novel. It would perhaps be not going too far to suggest that Christian piety was grounded in attempts to touch the imaginations of the Christians in liturgy and in morality plays for example; to enliven the central mysteries so that they might become a way of life by opening the imagination and understanding so that the heart might in turn be touched by the grace of the divine spirit which the mysteries embodied. The disembodiment of the spirit or its awakening was thought to take place within the human heart, at the point of the spirit as the *Cloud* Author had told his readers. In the case of Ignatius it is unlikely that he was conscious of this tradition directly when he initially arrived at Loyola suffering from wounds which had almost proved fatal.

As we know Ignatius was steeped in the hidalgo tradition. His imagination and his conduct had been formed by its ideals. The ideals were perhaps Christian in origin

9   Caraman, *Ignatius Loyola*, 157-65, who quotes from *The Spiritual Diary*, 99, 121, 123 and 145.
10 See for example the discussion in Hugo Rahner, *Ignatius the Theologian*, 194ff.

but in application they were concerned with the kind of 'court and camp' life the hidalgo was expected to lead in sixteenth-century Spain[11]. Although Christian beliefs defined the purpose of life and the Christian *reconquista* mission had directed the way of life and perhaps in spirit continued to do so throughout the century, they did not, perhaps, dominate the consciousness of the hidalgo. We have suggested that Cervantes at the end of the century was perhaps not questioning this spirit and the ideals but the ambivalent behaviour which it had bred in his countrymen, in at once parodying and sentimentalising Don Quixote's spirit.

Ignatius at Loyola was confronted with the origins of the sacrificial ideals which had once informed the 'courtly' tradition, in Ludolph of Saxony's *Life of Christ*, when he read it while convalescing at Loyola from the wounds received at Pamplona. There he found an account written in the style of the courtly romances with which he was already familiar[12]. The object of the romance was different but the qualities of character, and particularly determination against all odds, were similar. However, Christ's was a type of kingship with which he was totally unfamiliar. The ambition, the richness, the livery, were absent; only the service was the same. However, the kind of love which this service called for was apparently quite different.

We have already considered Ignatius' conversion, as it were, to a new loyalty[13]. In Ludolph's book he also found a style with which to express the change of role. There is a reference in Ludolph to the technique, as it were, of the 'application of the

---

11 Ignatius' Christian heritage should not be underestimated. Saint John the Baptist and Saint Peter were two of Ignatius' patrons; the former was the patron of the Onaz side of the family, and the latter was the patron of the Loyola side. It was to St Peter that Ignatius prayed at Loyola when he was thought to be at the point of death from his wounds. See Tylenda's commentary in the *Autobiography* 3, 10 and n.5, 140. Moreoever, it was on the feast of Saint John the Baptist that he received the last sacraments and at midnight as the vigil of Sts Peter and Paul began the first signs of his recovery were noticed. It may be, of course, that such coincidences owe something to the hagiographical spirit of Gonçalves da Câmera in interpreting Ignatius' account of his recovery.

12 Tylenda's Commentary on the *Autobiography* 5, 11, 12 and 140 n.8. According to the *Autobiography* 12, Ignatius considered entering the Carthusian Monastery at Seville after his return from the pilgrimage to Jerusalem and had requested a servant who was going to Burgos to gather information about the Carthusian rule from the foundation there. The connection with *Amadis de Gaula* is suggested in Tylenda's Commentary, 18. See also Caraman, *Ignatius Loyola*, 31. It has to be borne in mind that Ignatius' purpose in the *Autobiography* was to emphasise his realisation of the need to practise self-effacement as an antidote to the temptation to vainglory, hence his reference to the Carthusian foundation at Seville, where, if he entered it, his rank and connections would be unknown. His interest in the Carthusian rule might have been awakened by reading about King Lisuarte's choice of a Carthusian foundation with royal connections as a place of retirement after he had abdicated the English throne in favour of Amadis of Gaul. The Monastery at Burgos, known as La Real Cartuja de Miraflores, was originally a royal hunting lodge.

13 See Prologue N.108.

senses' as a means of assimilating the life of Christ and appropriating its spirit[14]. It was in many respects the same technique with which he had perhaps meditated on Amadis of Gaul. Through it he might have quite naturally come to assume the spirit of service which the new master required. As reflected in the lives of the Saints, the bedrock qualities for this service were not so different from those already strongly present and developed in his personality; the qualities of courage, determination, loyalty, steadfastness, imagination; they were the qualities required by a good military strategist no less than an apostle or saint. His immediate response to conversion was to undertake a pilgrimage to the Holy Land. The pilgrimage not only symbolised the desire to serve in a quixotic gesture, it also offered an opportunity to become fully immersed in the locations of Christ's life; to actually see and kiss the imprints of Christ's feet, as they had been sketched in *Flos Sanctorum* on the rock on the Mount of Olives, where he was believed to have stood before the Ascension[15].

Before Ignatius left the Holy Land and against the expressed wishes of the Franciscan Superior, he made a visit to the Mount of Olives[16]. As he was led down under restraint, he believed he experienced a sense of being accompanied down the Mount by Christ. He later reflected that this sense of presence was an endorsement of his daring enterprise and perhaps also of the wish to assimilate the atmosphere and terrain in which Christ had lived. As is well known the desire to return to the Holy Land remained with him and his first companions until circumstances finally convinced them that their mission lay elsewhere.

An aspect of the 'Application of Senses' was the exercise known as the 'composition of place'. The mediaeval tradition of making pilgrimages to the Holy Land[17] was in part perhaps a reflection of the prayerful need to be able to visualise the actual scenario in which Christ lived and died. Like all pilgrimages, no doubt, that to the Holy Land was undertaken in search of the special graces which might be obtained after such an arduous and dangerous mission of penance. One of these graces was perhaps a spiritual sense of place which would form a backdrop throughout the

---

14 See Hugo Rahner, *Ignatius the Theologian*, 192, 193.
15 Caraman, *Ignatius Loyola*, 51, asterisked footnote. In the *Autobiography* it is noted 47, 55:
    'While there [at Bethphage] he remembered that on the Mount of Olives he had not taken full notice of the direction in which the right foot was pointing and which way the left'.
    He gave away his scissors to the guard to let him reenter the Mount of Olives. On the first occasion he had given the guard his penknife.
16 Tylenda's Commentary on the *Autobiography* 46-48, 54.
17 Margery Kempe the contemporary of Julian of Norwich in her *Book* records such a pilgrimage undertaken in 1413 in chapters 26-30. B.A. Windeatt in the introduction to his modern English version published by Penguin Books, 1983, 12, notes that unlike other pilgrims who have described their experiences she seems to have recalled in the main the visions and spiritual experiences she received and her difficulties in getting along with fellow pilgrims. See n.6, 298, for other works dealing with other accounts of pilgrimages to Jerusalem.

pilgrim's life for an evocation of Christ's life and a remembrance of the reality of the places in which his life unfolded. It is perhaps not too great a liberty to wonder whether Ignatius began to regard himself as a type of crusader; not one who bore arms and attempted to drive out the Muslims by force but a spiritual crusader who would persuade the Muslims to become Christians with the help of the spirit which the significance of the scenario would evoke.

When therefore we say that Ignatius was probably unconscious of the long tradition which had formed itself around the notion of 'spiritual senses' and their development from the utilisation of the physical senses, we have immediately to qualify the statement. The manner in which the 'spirit' of mediaeval Christian culture itself formed the unconscious mind of those who were born into it, is perhaps impossible to trace. But it seems reasonable to assume that particular events in Ignatius' life which appear as if they are particular calls of grace, trigger or release some unconsciously absorbed memories which have powerful emotional associations. Again we might recall the three wishes of Julian of Norwich when she was a child which were suddenly brought to mind by the *Showings*. His decision to undertake the pilgrimage to the Holy Land is perhaps an illustration of this deeply entrenched association from his Basque childhood. The vision of the Lady Mary was the event which was perhaps responsible for triggering the reaction which led to his decision. It perhaps brought together two powerful streams of piety which impregnated the cultural life of his childhood; the devotion to Our Lady and the penitential efficacy of the pilgrimage. We know that Ignatius had undertaken the pilgrimage to Compostella as a child and had visited some of the shrines to our Lady which seemed to link the contemporary society with an ancient Christian past[18]. The outward signs of devotion may sometimes seem infertile and appear to have died, having become overlayed with more immediate impressions; yet they may take root surreptitiously and blossom unexpectedly.

The second generation of Jesuits had no difficulty in justifying the 'Application of Senses' exercises as part of a long tradition of Christian piety[19]. Ignatius, during his own lifetime was charged with 'meddling' with spirits. The charge was not perhaps quite so crudely expressed[20]. Nevertheless, the possible association with the 'Alumbrado' tendency, with which he was suspected, seems to have made him very cautious about being too explicit in speaking about 'spiritual' senses or indeed about referring to the 'Holy Spirit'. This suspicion continued to surround the Jesuits and

---

18 Caraman, *Ignatius Loyola*, 7.
19 Hugo Rahner, *Ignatius the Theologian*, 204, 205. For example he says 'the men close to Ignatius who knew him best and were the first authoritative commentators on the *Exercises*, rediscovered in these words [*de arriba*] the doctrine of the spiritual senses as found in Bonaventure (and thus forming part of a genuine tradition going back to Augustine and Origen)'.
20 *Ibid.*, 158. The Bishop of Valencia, Thomas de Villanueva, referred to the *Exercises* given in his city in 1535 by Ignatius as 'mystery-mongering'.

the *Exercises* after Ignatius' death. Ignatius' close associate, Juan de Polanco, was well read in the Church Fathers[21]. He was able to demonstrate how the 'Application of Senses' exercises were but a reflection of a well-documented tradition. For Ignatius they may have seemed a natural and practical approach to meditative prayer, but for his followers they also had a theoretical, theological, justification. The notion of 'spiritual senses' has been traced back to Origen and through his influence upon the theology of 'contemplative prayer' came to permeate contemplative thought as practised by the Desert Fathers and the ascetic movement[22]. There is one famous passage in the *Confessions* of St Augustine of Hippo, which alone might ensure, through its poetry, that the 'application of the senses' remained in the forefront of the practice of prayer. The passage from book x.6 of the *Confessions*, which we have previously quoted, is about 'what do I love when I love my God':

> A light of a certain kind, a voice, a perfume, a food, an embrace ... of the kind I love in my inner self, when my soul is bathed in light that is *not bound* by space; when it listens to sound that *never dies away*; when it breathes fragrance that is *not borne* away on the wind; when it tastes food that is *never consumed*; when it clings to an embrace from which it is *not severed* by *fulfilment of desire*. That is what I love when I love my God[23].

Augustine is describing an experience, the infinite beauty of which can only be described by negating the finiteness of any experience which relies purely on physical sensual perception. The soul, it seems, transcends the physical universe to dwell, at least for a moment, in the creative source of all the beauty it perceives.

The passage from the *Confessions* may be compared with one from Origen's commentary on the *Song of Songs*:

> He [Christ] is something for each particular sense of the soul. He is called Light so that the soul may have eyes. Word, so that it may have ears to hear. Bread, so that it may savour him. Oil of anointing so that it may breathe in the fragrance of the Word. And he has become flesh, so that the *inward* hand of the soul may be able to touch something of the Word of life which fashions itself to correspond

---

21 See N.19 above. Nadal and Polanco are singled out as close associates of Ignatius. For Polanco's role see for example, Caraman, *Ignatius Loyola*, 149, and Nadal, 158, where he is referred to as 'perhaps his [Ignatius'] most intimate confidant'. See also pages 204, 205.
22 See N.19 above and Hugo Rahner, *Ignatius the Theologian*, 201, 202, with reference to Bonaventure's *Itinerarium mentis in Deum*, ed. Quaracchi, V, 306, C 4, 3 and in particular 202, n.23, for the most important texts on this teaching.
23 Hugo Rahner, *Ignatius the Theologian*, 200, quotes from the English translation of R.S. Pine-Coffin, Penguin Books, 1961 [my italics].

with the various manifestations of prayer and which leaves no sense of the soul untouched by his grace[24].

In this passage Origen seems to suggest the outward manifestations of Christ's life perceived through the physical senses have counterparts inwardly where the spiritual senses absorb and transform them into what Augustine would term 'love', a total manifestation of the spiritual sense reflected outwardly.

When Ignatius read in the preface to Ludolph's *Life of Christ* the following passage, he is unlikely to have recognised its antecedents, though he and his followers in later years came to appreciate the continuity. That appreciation probably only reinforced their perception that the spiritual insights he built into the *Spiritual Exercises* were of divine origin. The passage probably was taken from the *Meditationes Vitae Christi*, now thought to have been written by a fourteenth-century Franciscan rather than Bonaventure[25]:

> If you wish to draw profit from these meditations [on the life of Christ] set aside all cares and anxieties. Lovingly and contemplatively with all the feelings of your heart, make everything that the Lord Jesus said and did present to yourself, just as though you were hearing it with your ears and seeing it with your eyes. And they all will become sweet to you, because you are reflecting upon it with longing and savouring it yet more. And even when it is related in the *past* tense you should contemplate it all as though *present* today. *Go into the Holy Land, kiss with fervent spirit the earth on which the good Jesus stood*. Make present to yourself how he spoke and went about with his disciples, with sinners; how he speaks and preaches, how he walks and rests, sleeps and wakes, eats and performs miracles. *Write* down *in your heart* (*describens tibi in corde tuo*) his demeanour and his actions[26].

It would seem as if Ignatius almost took this passage to heart literally with his pilgrimage and visit to the Mount of Olives. The physical experience became as it were a spiritual experience as the past seemed to become present and he felt himself walking down the mountain with Christ beside him.

Ignatius' commitment to this form of prayer experience of Christ was complemented by an equally intense commitment to the spiritual presence of evil. Consider his Dantesque suggestions in the *Exercises* for reflecting on the inconceivable mystery of eternal loss which the notion of 'Hell' represents:

---

24 Quoted by Hugo Rahner, *Ignatius the Theologian*, 200. Source at n.20, *Commentary on the Canticle*, 2 (GCS, *Origen*, VIII, 167f.) [my italics].

25 Hugo Rahner, *Ignatius the Theologian*, 192, 193.

26 *Ibid.*, 193 and N.7 identifies source as *Vita Christi* per Ludolfum Saxonium excerpta, Lyons, 1554, 5 [my italics].

With the gaze of the imagination, to *see* the immense fires. With the *ears*, to *hear* wailings, howls and cries. With the smell, to *smell* the smoke, the burning sulphur, the sewer and putrid matter. With the taste *to taste* bitter things, such as tears, sadness, and the worm of conscience. With the touch, to *feel* how the fires touch and burn and burn the souls[27].

This is balanced by a counterpart as his directions for reflecting on the Incarnation illustrate:

With the gaze of the imagination, see the people concerned. With the hearing, hear what they say or might be saying. With the sense of smell and the taste, smell and taste the infinite suavity and sweetness of the divinity. With the touch, to embrace and kiss the places where these people walk or sit[28].

During his pilgrimage to the Holy Land, he had perhaps smelt and tasted the infinite suavity and sweetness of the divinity. At Manresa, where thoughts of suicide had come to him, he had perhaps faced the possibility of eternal loss and the repelling force of its consequences. It might be thought that this pictorial juxtaposition of images of the divinity and of evil was perhaps a little naive in that in life the choice would rarely seem so clear-cut. However, for someone who had experienced at Manresa first the joy which the feeling of commitment to the divine had created and then faced the feelings of suicidal depression which his scruples had aroused, and made a deliberate choice between the two, it might seem realistic rather than naive. He had overcome the depression by electing to live and experienced not only the return of equanimity, but also the architectonic illuminations, the faith and the deepening of his own faith which followed the election. It was a choice he was confident perhaps every exercitant would make if they could but experience, first through the imagination and then through feelings aroused by the alternative life strategies presented in the meditations.

2. ELECTION: 'LABOR ET GLORIA'

The objective of the *Spiritual Exercises* was to enable those who felt drawn towards Christ to make an election about how to respond to his call. The *Exercises* were the process, so carefully designed by Ignatius, by which the exercitant might arrive at the nature of the election. All the special features of the *Exercises*, the prayers, the meditations and their sequence, the application of senses, 'the rules for the discernment of spirits', 'the rules for thinking with the Church', the directions for the Spiritual Director, were all subordinate to the end of making an election in the spirit of

---

27 As quoted by Hugo Rahner, *Ignatius the Theologian*, 186. See also *Exercises* 66-70, 32, 33. El Greco's representation of Hell in Figs 1, 2 and 3 perhaps evoke a similar revulsion.

28 Hugo Rahner, *Ignatius the Theologian*, 186. See also *Exercises* 122-125, 54, 55.

serving Christ better[29]. The process is one in which individuals come to a reaffirmation of their allegiance to God, their creator; and in considering what that allegiance means how individuals may do more to strengthen their own commitment to Christ, the King and further his cause.

Those undertaking the *Spiritual Exercises* were understood to be answering a particular call to serve Christ more fully. The nature of the service to which they were called was perhaps not perceived clearly. The *Exercises* presupposed a willingness on the part of the exercitants to serve how best they might and to accept whatever service was called for[30].

The *Exercises* seem to reflect Ignatius' personal experience of the paradox of *labor* and *gloria* in the choice of service not only at Loyola, Montserrat and Manresa but also in his earlier life. The metaphors he uses to explain his understanding of the paradox were those of his early experience of a feudal society in which military service was the basis of allegiance between a Lord and his Vassal. The call to serve was the call of the King. The glory of the ideal of military service was its privileged status rather than its *labor*. It was an ideal which remained very dear to Ignatius. The vassal was on terms of privileged intimacy with the Lord and shared his fortunes for better or for worse. The honour of the vassal was intimately associated with the honour of the livery which was worn. Livery was the symbol, no less in sixteenth-century Spain than in fourteenth-century England, which evoked the meaning of allegiance, both its obligations and its privileges and power[31].

The labour was represented by the no less powerful symbol of the Lord's standard around which the companions rallied in battle. The King's call was to join the battle. The exercises concerned with the two standards enable the vassal to recognise not only the defensive rallying point of his own Lord's standard but also that of the enemy so that in the heat and smoke of battle the vassal would recognise them at once and know where to carry the fight.

These images of allegiance were the ones to which the senses were to be applied in a christological transformation of the metaphors. Christ's enemy was the enemy of human nature whose objective was to destroy Christ and all his followers. Just as it might be in military terms, the fight was to be a fight to the death for the honour of the Lord if so called on. The *Spiritual Exercises* were designed to evoke the intensity of this conflict and test the mettle of the exercitant to the full. The elections the exercitant was called on to make would sometimes be made in the heat of battle, the

---

29 *Exercises* 1: 'so we call Spiritual Exercises every way of preparing and disposing the soul to rid itself of all inordinate attachments, and, after their removal, of *seeking and finding* the will of God in the disposition of our life for the salvation of our soul'.
30 *Exercises* 5.
31 Hilton refers to the 'livery' of Christ.

first time of election, or in the glow of victory, the second time of election, or finally in the peace of his estates, the third time of election. Ignatius did not perhaps extend his use of the metaphors quite this far but it is not difficult to feel where the images were leading.

Moreover, though the battle between Christ and the devil had been fought and won, once and for all, the devil's forces although now inferior were still capable of mounting further attacks, and disturbing the peace of the kingdom. The election process might possibly seem to be a personally recurrent process for those who had answered the call and engaged in the spiritual battle which the *Exercises* had staged. However, the experience of the *Exercises* themselves might be sufficiently powerful to make it unnecessary for the exercises to be repeated every time an election loomed. The process had been learnt and the signs recognised. If this interpretation of the Ignatian 'Election' process might seem a little too contrived and theatrical, we might recall Fr. Davila's Spanish text in which the call of the King is expressed in a typically Ignatian way:

Llamar a los hombres a que le ayuden en esta empresa[32].

'Empresa' was the classical word used by the Spanish knight for an armed enterprise. It was the word Ignatius used when sending Francis Xavier on his mission to India, 'Esta es vuestra empresa'. The Navarese knight would have known immediately what that meant. But it was not a call to a knightly *messianisme de prestige* but to *labor et gloria* in the spirit of obedience and sacrifice in the service of his crucified Lord, whose standard was the cross[33]. The language of military service had been appropriated by them for a more glorious service.

For Ignatius and for Francis Xavier the metaphor was far from theatrical. The original objective of Ignatius and his companions following the Montmartre vows was a mission to the Holy Land in which they were to undertake, as it were, a spiritual crusade. After the companions had come to abandon this choice and he was on his way to Rome to seek a different apostolic challenge, Ignatius stopped to pray at a chapel at La Storta[34]. It had always been the intention of the companions to offer their services to the Pope, to be directed by him, if their original intention was frustrated by circumstances. Ignatius at La Storta was perhaps still doubtful how this change of course would do 'more' for Christ. While at prayer at La Storta he received a vision in which he was addressed by Christ bearing his cross in the pres-

---

32 [The call to render assistance in that undertaking.] Hugo Rahner, *Ignatius the Theologian*, 107.
33 *Ibid.*, 107, N.75.
34 November 1537. The village of La Storta is about eight miles outside Rome according to Tylenda, 113, and the chapel some twelve miles according to Caraman, *Ignatius Loyola*, 112.

ence of his heavenly Father[35]. Christ, Ignatius recorded, said to him in the vision, 'It is my wish that you should serve us'. The experience confirmed for Ignatius that the course the companions had adopted was in accordance with the divine will and although the nature of their service was still unclear, the manner or spirit in which it was to be performed was quite clear. It was to be in a manner like that of Christ in a sacrificial spirit of obedience, 'free of self-love, self-will and self-interest'[36].

The criterion for choosing the nature of service was also quite clear and already reflected in the *Exercises*. The choice should be the course which corresponds better to the intentions and example of Christ in conformity with either his counsels or his commandments according to personal circumstances. The supreme end, according to Fr. Davila in his commentary on the *Exercises* was:

> to find the heart of Christ in the midst of the turmoils of his passion, and to rouse ourselves to enter into community with the crucified Christ, so that we may say: 'amore meus crucifixus est'[37].

The battle was not so much a knightly *empresa* but a battle to overcome one's own self-love, self-will, and self-interest. This interpretation of the electoral battle is very much in the ascetic tradition of contemplative Christian life. To be able to enter into the heart of Christ and understand his will it was necessary to enter the spirit of his conflict with evil in the Passion in abandonment of self-interest and in detachment from self-love and self-will.

The meditations of the *Exercises*, particularly those of the third and fourth weeks, were intended to draw the exercitant into the immediacy of the Passion of Christ. Fr. Davila refers to the words which the Pseudo-Dionysius put into the mouth of Christ:

> I am ready to give my life again for you[38].

It is an idea which, as we saw, impressed Julian of Norwich in her *Showings* where Christ says to her, in effect, 'what more could I have done than give my life'[39]. In Davila's view it is in these meditations that one discovers the endlessness of Christ's love and enters into the intimacy of it.

---

35 *Autobiography* 96. Ignatius had been praying to our Lady to place him with her Son. Gonçalves da Câmera records that while praying Ignatius 'felt a great change in his soul and so clearly did he see God the Father place him with Christ, His son, that he had no doubts that God the Father did place him with His Son'. See also Tylenda's commentary on 96-97 at page 113, and n.23 on page 154, which records the source as Lainez. See also Caraman, *Ignatius Loyola*, 113, 114.
36 *Exercises* 189, quoted in this form by Hugo Rahner, *Ignatius the Theologian*, 128. See also his *The Vision of St Ignatius in the Chapel of La Storta*, Rome: CIS, 1979.
37 Quoted by Hugo Rahner, *Ignatius the Theologian*, 132 and N.120.
38 *Ibid.*, N.119.
39 See Chapter 2, N.30 above.

In paragraph 236 of the *Exercises* Ignatius expresses that aspect of the life and passion of Christ which had so impressed him. 'Consider', he says, 'how God works and labors for me [the exercitant] in all creatures upon the face of the earth, that is *he conducts himself as one who labours...*'[40]. Christ spent himself totally for humanity and to imitate him humanity must also spend itself. Ignatius brought out the profoundest sacrificial meaning of the ideal of kingship in his words about the passion of Christ:

> The divine Majesty stripped himself of all these riches of his eternal glory in order to give us a share in them. He took all our wretchedness upon himself in order to free us from it, he desired to be sold in order to redeem us, to be abused in order to glorify us, to become poor in order to make us rich to be led in pain and ignominy to his death in order to bestow upon us a life of eternal bliss[41].

Christ provides the example of the servant in a service to which his revered friends are called. It is as if Ignatius were saying compare this example with that of a human Lord who we are prepared to follow and lay down our lives for. The contrast between the imperfections of human lordship and the perfection of divine lordship could not be greater. How much more therefore should the exercitant be prepared to follow Christ and abandon himself to work for his cause; to make Christ's cause his own. It is in this frame of mind that the exercitant is invited to make his election.

Everard Mercurian[42], a General of the Society of Jesus, summed up the significance of the Election in the following terms:

> In the matter of the Election our Spiritual Exercises combine everything which can be found on the subject in the writings of the doctors and all the Saints; but a great deal is new and unheard of (*nova et inaudita*) and especially the passage concerning the Three Times for making an Election, where the third Time of discursive reasoning in a state of calm is so admirable and full of true wisdom[43].

We may feel this perhaps underestimates the vitality of the ideal of 'election' in the contemplative tradition, rather than discerning the particular contribution of the *Exercises* to it. However, the *Exercises* bring together a number of streams of thought which have been featured in other authors in an integrated focus on election as a commitment of heart and mind to do 'more' for Christ with one's life.

---

40 *Exercises* 236, 103.
41 Quoted by Hugo Rahner, *Ignatius the Theologian*, 133 and N.124.
42 Fourth General of the Society of Jesus 1573-1580. Hugo Rahner, *Ignatius the Theologian*, 148, implies that Mercurian was 'anti-affective'.
43 Quoted by Hugo Rahner, *Ignatius the Theologian*, 139 and N.8.

Ignatius describes three types of situation of varying degrees of emotional intensity in which an election in conformity with divine will may be made[44]. The first was characterised by a reaction when the individual is so moved and attracted that there is no possibility of hesitation in understanding what has been indicated. St Paul's and St Mathew's decisions to follow Christ are of this kind. We have suggested earlier the analogy with a commitment in the heat of battle which corresponds with an entry into the heart of the passion. The second stage is when 'much light and understanding' are derived from the experience of emotional desolations and consolations and of the 'attractions and repulsions felt in the discernment of diverse spirits'. Again, we have suggested an analogy with the after-glow of battle when mourning for those who have perhaps died in it alternates with the joy of victory. The third, which Mercurian found to be 'so admirable', is at a time of tranquillity - a time when individuals are not conscious of agitation and have the free and peaceful use of their reasoning powers. We have suggested the analogy with vassals who return to their estates and reflect on the nature of their allegiance to their Lord. This reflection in the context of the *Spiritual Exercises* might consider how a particular decision would conform to their renewed understanding of Christ's life and passion.

In the context of the *Exercises* the third time of election may either be an occasion where a previous insight is confirmed by careful reflection or when an insight is first obtained without accompanying emotional reactions[45]. Ignatius suggests several possible ways of going about making a choice in this third situation. The first involves a conscious weighing of the benefits and disadvantages of alternative courses for the end in mind. The second is to use the imagination and undertake some role-playing: how would a particular choice look if one was a third party - not just any third party but one who was revered or perfect, or again at the moment of death, or on the judgement day. It is not suggested by the first commentators on the *Exercises* that the 'third' time of election should override or supersede elections made at the 'first' or 'second' times[46]. It was clear that Ignatius regarded an election made in response to what both exercitant and the Spiritual Director believed were direct divine interventions in the form of powerful emotional and spiritual reactions, was not to be revoked in response to the discursive reasoning of the 'third' time of election. It was always possible that the human reasoning of the third time of election was fallible, because human reason was not always privy to the divine purpose. A conflict between discursive reasoning limited by human foresight and 'divine' illumination was perhaps unusual but Ignatius himself frequently pressed ahead with

---

44 *Exercises* 175, 176, 177 refer to the 'three times when a correct and good choice of a way of life may be made'.
45 *Exercises* 177 emphasises this is a time of 'tranquillity' by which Ignatius means 'a time when the soul is not agitated by different spirits, and has free and peaceful use of its natural powers' and in 169 he emphasises 'whatever I choose must help me to this end for which I am created'. He goes on in 178 through 188 to suggest ways of making 'a choice of life in the third time'.
46 Hugo Rahner, *Ignatius the Theologian*, 145.

projects of whose outcome he was uncertain because he had recognised they were divinely authenticated[47]. Ultimately, the criterion he used to resolve his doubts was the success or failure of the project itself.

Whatever the situation, the decision of the exercitant in the exercises is always to be related to the purpose of life. The *Exercises* are there to make this purpose a living reality for the individual. The reality is brought to life by what is hoped will be a dramatic experience of God and the alternative, Mammon. There is no middle course available on this battlefield. If one hesitates, it is only to be cut down by the enemy of human nature. The choice is always to seek how one may do 'more' to ensure a divine victory and in doing so save one's own soul. There is no room for fear in the *Exercises*, the battle is already joined. Bravery translates itself into action not simply bravado. Don Quixote at the end of the sixteenth century and in a secular context perhaps struggled with the distinction which to Ignatius in a spiritual context was clear.

3. DISCERNMENT OF SPIRITS

Ignatius' 'Rules for the Discernment of Spirits' have been regarded, and rightly so, as a significant benefit or product of the 'making' of the *Exercises*[48]. This is meant in two senses. Firstly, it equips those who 'make' the exercises with a means of discerning spirits both during them and in their future lives. Secondly, the rules emerged from Ignatius' own experiences on which the *Exercises* themselves were founded. In both cases they mediate the meaning of experience and election.

This is perhaps to say no more than that the 'rules' guide an iterative learning process in which success is reinforced and unsuccessful practice avoided by monitoring performance against specific criteria. Ignatius interposed the mediating process of 'discernment' between the meditative experience which the *Spiritual Exercises* provided, by making the nerves of consciousness raw and vulnerable, and the election which was to be their outcome or objective. The rules were formulated to guide

---

47 See for example Ribadeneira, *Vita Ignatii*, V, II ed. Cologne 1602, 649. Quoted by Hugo Rahner, *Ignatius the Theologian*, 223/224. The fate of the plan of the first companions to go to the Holy Land also exemplifies how practical difficulties were interpreted as indicative of the divine will.

48 As Herbert F. Smith S.J. suggests in his article 'Discernment of Spirits' in *Notes on the Spiritual Exercises of St Ignatius of Loyola*, ed. David L. Fleming S.J., St Louis, Mo.: Review for Religious, 1985, 229, the 'rules' are meant 'to ward off' a 'mistaken concept of living in the Spirit'. There are a number of accounts of the Ignatian concept of Discernment of Spirits. See Piet Penning de Vries S.J., *Discernment of Spirits According to the Life and Teachings of St Ignatius of Loyola*, trans. W. Dudok van Heel, New York: Exposition Press; Eng. trans. 1973, and Gerard Hughes, *God of Surprises*, London: Darton, Longman and Todd, 1985, repr. 1986, for two different approaches.

not only the exercitant but also the Spiritual Director whose task was to assist the exercitants to understand what was happening to them.

Ignatius seems to have drawn primarily on his own spiritual experiences in drawing up the guidelines rather than on traditional practice with which at this stage of his life he was little acquainted. Their purpose was to enable exercitants to distinguish the divine will, *de arriba*, working in their consciousness through their emotional reactions to the *Exercises*[49]. Ignatius believed that various 'spirits' would be at work within the exercitants' consciousness during the exercises as they had been within his own at Loyola and Manresa. The rules were intended to assist the exercitants to recognise the various spirits and in particular the divine spirit amid the babel produced by the spiritual conflict which he thought the *Exercises* would arouse within the exercitants' consciousness[50].

The meditations, as we have seen, were designed to awaken in those who undertook them a spontaneous reaction from deep within their emotional/intellectual matrix. The meditations were carefully calibrated so that the 'spiritual movements' they awakened would register and be sharpened in terms both of understanding of Christ's life and emotional reactions to it such as consolation and joy or sorrow and desolation. The rules of discernment were devised to assist in the recognition of the origin of the response which the meditations evoked, not only to the particular scenes of Christ's life but also to the spontaneous thoughts which arose of how he might be better served by the exercitant. Ignatius believed that the meditations would stimulate thoughts and dreams of how Christ might be better served, similar to those which his own reflections about the life of Christ and the Saints had evoked. The question to be answered was whether such thoughts and dreams were divinely inspired, whether they were in accord with the divine will and met with divine approval, the sign for which was a sense of peace and tranquillity. Or alternately were inspired by the enemy of human nature and therefore contrary to the divine will producing a sense of disquiet and restlessness[51].

Not all thoughts aroused by the meditations, of course, originated 'outside' the individual. There were, according to Ignatius, so-called 'free' thoughts which originated

---

49 *Autobiography* 19-31 provides an account of Ignatius' spiritual experiences at Manresa. *De arriba*, 'from above', as Hugo Rahner, *Ignatius the Theologian*, 3-10, suggests was a 'key word' in Ignatius' theology. In *Exercises* 338 Ignatius suggests that 'love' derives from God and God is the cause through his revelation (his descent among us) which moves the love to a lesser or greater extent. In other words, the charity we display is not 'ours' but 'God's'; it is a revelation of His love acting within us. See also *Exercises* 322, the third reason we suffer from desolation.

50 See for example the exercises associated with the Three Classes of Men, 149ff. There is a conflict for example between the attachment to what one has and the attachment to God as reflected in the choice presented to the 'rich young man' of the Gospel story (Mt. 19:16).

51 *Exercises* 336 and 329.

'within' the individual[52]. It was not always straight-forward to distinguish between them. The context in which they were recognised was a useful guide, particularly how they developed and what occasioned them. However, thoughts which were of divine or diabolic origin appeared to have no origin. They took the consciousness unawares in the form of sudden illuminations, insights or inspirations if of divine origin and in the form, perhaps, of temptations, confusions or distractions if diabolic[53].

Thoughts of diabolic origin might be particularly difficult to recognise for they were often disguised. The traditional notion of Satan's appearance was, of course, as an angel of light dissembling as if to promote the individual's well-being and interests rather than destruction. The notion of the 'midday devil' was a commonplace among the mystics and referred to by Hilton and the *Cloud* Author[54]. The celebrated gospel account of Christ's temptations in the wilderness seemed to take this form. The three temptations appeared to be designed to exploit human tendencies towards self-love, self-will and self-interest. The christological focus of the *Exercises* was designed to promote a Christ-like response of detachment from self and replace it with attachment to Christ. The purpose is similar to the objective of traditional ascetic practice designed to achieve purity and a likeness to Christ in virtue as a *sine qua non* to participation in the divine union[55]. However, the emphasis in the *Exercises* is upon service and abandonment to the divine will in order to discover how to serve more efficaciously in the establishment of Christ's kingdom. Compared with the tradition, there is an emphasis upon continuing Christ's mission on earth rather than enjoying its fruition in heaven[56]. The image of Christ labouring and carrying his cross which Ignatius received at La Storta is very much the livery which those participating in the *Exercises* are encouraged to adopt. As we have suggested, the emphasis in the *Exercises* is an election 'here and now' to do something more for Christ with one's life.

The most difficult aspect of an election was to discover what that 'more' should be not from a standpoint of personal preference but from recognising Christ's call and

---

52 The notion of 'without previous cause' is explained in *Exercises* 330. It corresponds to something which arises from a source 'outside' the individual. Free thoughts tend to be prompted by 'a previous cause', whatever that may be, within the individual as a natural reaction to it.

53 *Exercises* 331.

54 *Exercises* 332. See Hilton Scale 2, chap. 26 and n.148, 239 and 312 and the *Cloud* Author, *ST* H.114.23 and Commentary 186.

55 See for example references to Cassian and Climacus in Chapter 1.5 above. See also Hugo Rahner, *The Spirituality of St Ignatius Loyola. An Account of its Historical Development*, trans. F.J. Smith S.J., Westminster, Maryland: The Newman Press, 1953.

56 However, see for example the account of Julian's temptation to look up to the heavenly father rather than at suffering Christ on the cross, Chapter 2.3 and N.53 above. This suggests *labor* must precede *gloria*. *Gloria* of 'divinisation' might be regarded as the objective of the contemplative tradition.

what it asked of the individual. The enemy of human nature, it could be expected would do his utmost to frustrate the recognition of the call by 'aping' it with one of his own; thus the emphasis placed upon the meditations concerned with the two kingdoms and the standards of Christ and Mammon and their respective characteristics[57].

It was thought that those who undertook the *Exercises* were already predisposed by grace in the form of an orientation to seek the will of Christ concerning their lives. Hence the reaction to the forays of the enemy of human nature would be to produce feelings of unease, confusion and disturbance like 'desolation' and hopelessness in the rational/emotional matrix of the individual. On the other hand, the 'call' of the divine king would produce reactions of consolation, peace and joy. A feeling of consolation was always likely to be an unequivocal indication of divine presence and encouragement.

Feelings of desolation by contrast might be regarded as discouraging or encouraging depending on whether they inferred sharing in the divine suffering or a diabolic attempt to encourage the exercitant to believe that divine light had been withdrawn by interposing some intrusive 'smoke' or 'shadow'. The desperation which Ignatius experienced at Manresa when he contemplated suicide was perhaps an example of the diabolic attempt to thwart the divine consolations which had accompanied his conversion and decision to undertake the pilgrimage to the Holy Land. Desolations of the encouraging kind which indicated divine sorrow deeply experienced were perhaps enlivening; being found worthy to follow Christ in carrying his cross and in his crucifixion. An example of this type of desolation was perhaps experienced by Ignatius at La Storta. However, the effect was not to produce a sense of despair or lethargy and impoverishment, such as that induced by diabolic activity, but of renewed vitality[58].

In the context of the *Exercises*, an exercitant's reaction to the meditations on Christ's crucifixion was regarded as being of a particular significance. It was ex-

---

57 *Exercises* 136-146. The Colloquies at *Exercises* 147 are very much in the spirit in which Ignatius prayed prior to the vision he received at La Storta.

58 In his account of the La Storta experience in the *Autobiography* 96, as recorded by Gonçalves da Câmera, Ignatius simply recorded the facts of the vision. Those who were with Ignatius, however, Favre and Lainez, gave a more complete account of what had happened as suggested by Tylenda in his commentary on 96 drawn from *FN* 2:133. Ignatius seems to have realised that they were called to share something of Christ's desolation on the way to the cross and experience the renewal for which that desolation was the prelude. Unlike the revulsion he experienced at Manresa when reflecting that St Honofrio had spent his whole life as a hermit in the desert with its concomitant hardship, the hardships and rejection which he recognised as his future lot from the call he received at La Storta, produced the opposite effect. His wish to serve had been accepted by the Father, and the realisation produced a sense of peace and a great increase in faith, hope and love.

pected that sorrow would be felt, but whether the exercitant was drawn towards contrition and participating in the sorrow or fleeing from it in horror and distaste was critical. We might recall Julian of Norwich's temptation to look away from the crucifix at the foot of her bed. To follow Christ was to participate in his suffering. If exercitants drew back from this participation, it was indicative that they were being called to follow Christ in some other way by, perhaps, obeying 'the commandments' and reforming their life-style rather than in a way suggested by 'the counsels'. From the exercitant's point of view, it was not a rejection of Christ but only a disinclination to follow his example to give up life itself. The rich young man in the gospel story had asked Christ what he must do to have 'eternal life'. Christ replied that he should follow the commandments. The young man, it appears, had assiduously obeyed the commandments since childhood. Christ had then said, 'give away all your possessions to the poor and follow me'. The rich young man in the gospel account felt he could not go that extra step. The story perhaps illustrates not only the difference between following 'the commandments' and 'counsels' of Christ but also the nature of a divinely induced form of desolation, the awful realisation that one must be willing to suffer as Christ did in the garden of Gethsemane before the crucifixion; to be able quite rationally to give up all to find the only real treasure, that which ought to be enjoyed eternally[59].

Perhaps it was the rational approach to the movements of the heart produced by the *Exercises* which so impressed Mercurian in the passage quoted previously. The Ignatian election process relied on discernment in the form of recognition and understanding but it was also dependent on alertness and watchfulness. The context in which the movement of the heart was experienced was as important as the movement itself in the understanding of its import. The processes of examination of conscience which the *Exercises* require the exercitant to undertake regularly were perhaps designed to develop the sense of alertness and watchfulness. Examinations of conscience were by no means *nova et inaudita*. They were part of the contemplative tradition which, as Mercurian pointed out, were embedded in the *Exercises*. The 'discernment of spirits', however, perhaps added a different emphasis; it was not primarily concerned with the identification of sinful thoughts and actions, though this process remained important, but with the relationship of the responses of the heart to the context of meditation; not so much with sin as with the interpretation of the responses to particular meditations, particularly those concerned with Christ's passion and death. Ignatius' instructions for the Spiritual Director make this point clear. The Spiritual Director is not a confessor but rather a 'sounding board'[60].

59 See Mt. 19:16.

60 *Exercises* 17. The Spiritual Director 'should not seek to investigate and know the private thoughts and sins of the exercitant...'. In the context of the judgement Ignatius received at Salamanca forbidding him and his companions to discuss venial and mortal sin, and Ignatius' reaction to that restriction, the 'notes concerning scruples' appended to the *Exercises*, 346-351, indicate his recognition of the link between the discussion of sin and discernment of spirits.

As we have seen the earliest Church Fathers had expected the reading of and meditation upon Scripture to be accompanied by spiritually induced movements of the
heart and mind. The Ignatian *Exercises* were designed to heighten such movements
by the concentration of the meditative process on the drama and reality of Christ's
life and suffering. To follow the movements these meditations induced, it was necessary to remember them within the context in which they occurred. The movements
consisted of a stimulus and a responsive movement of the heart, almost like a series
of Pavlovian electric shocks. Both stimuli and responsive movements were important. The exercitant's role initially was to record them faithfully and relate them to
the Spiritual Director. The Spiritual Director's role was then to assist the exercitants
to come to an understanding by applying their own experience of the meaning of the
movements in relation to the divine will and as a cumulative experience[61]. The expression of the divine will was not expected to be something that would change
frequently or come and go; there was no fear that if some aspect or stimulus was
missed, the opportunity for understanding and election would be lost. A divinely
induced stimulus was expected to be steady and insistent, if in the gentlest of ways,
like a rain drop. Ignatius' use of the metaphor of the rain drop belies our more radical metaphor of an electric shock, like those which Pavlov used to condition his
dogs[62]. Yet it is the quality of penetrative insistence of water rather than the impact
of a rain drop which seems to be important. Those who have listened at night to the
drip of rain will recognise the impact of its insistence as Pavlov's dogs came to
recognise and be conditioned by a consistently applied system of stimuli associated
with particular behaviours. The objective of Ignatian discernment is to recognise the
different stimuli which the divine and malign spirits use. The choice to follow the
lead of the divine stimuli is however not the result of instinctual conditioning to
avoid pain and suffering. It is rather a matter of rational decision to accept *labor* and
the pain associated with it, the results of which will reinforce the correctness of the
decision, its contribution to the *gloria*, both in the heart of the exercitant and in the
successful outcome of the events which flow from the decision.

The experience of joy which subsumes and overrides pain and suffering is the principal lesson which Ignatius hoped the making of the *Exercises* would promote. The
experience of consolation might be felt with more consistency than desolation.
'Desolation', even that occasioned by sorrow and contrition, may ultimately give
way to consolation. 'Desolation' is not a condition to wallow in. Pain and suffering
which do not lead to consolation and renewed activity may not be of divine origin.
The distinction between the two forms of suffering is one of the discernments to be
experienced and understood.

---

61 See for example Judith Roemer O.S.F. in 'Discernment in the Director' in Fleming ed., *Notes
on the Spiritual Exercises, op.cit.*, 249.

62 *Exercises* 335. The electric shock seems more like the action of the evil spirit.

There is a form of suffering which must be accepted in the Ignatian view and one which must be eliminated[63]. Those forms of suffering which are occasioned by actions which contravene the commandments are of the latter kind. The source of suffering is the target for action, the suffering itself may be turned to some good purpose. It is clear that Ignatius did not believe that suffering was an end in itself bringing with it some masochistic satisfaction. Self-denial was not masochistic, its purpose was to eliminate inordinate desires.

Ignatius seems to have believed in an ordered existence which inordinate desires disrupted. 'Ordered' for him suggested a recognition that the human being needed the resources to maintain his being as human and rational in the light of his salvation and eternal destiny. Christ's life provided an example of a properly ordered life-style and his counsels suggested the basis on which 'ordering' should be developed. The rational and dispassionate assessment of alternatives facing the individual who undertook the *Exercises* in the 'third time of election' assumed a providentially ordered creation such as Ignatius had experienced in the insights he received at Manresa. The providential order presupposed that individual human beings had the potential to assume specific roles within it[64]. The *Exercises* were designed to reveal not only the potential but the manner in which it might be developed. The necessary skill to assist in this task was an ability to discern the spirits which promoted or denied the realisation of the potential. They were active among the thoughts and moods which surrounded everyday life. Ignatius had begun to experience them and recognise their characteristics while closeted and confined during his convalescence from the wounds he had received at Pamplona. Here was a form of suffering which, he believed, the Holy Spirit had turned to good purpose without any need to condone the situation which produced the wounds in the first place. Yet he had only come to turn the suffering to good purpose by being forced, as it were, to concentrate his attention on the thoughts and moods which various stimuli from his reading had occasioned. The characteristics of the *Exercises*, - their emphasis on the concentration of attention, the dramatic impact of a carefully selected and ordered series of meditations, the 'application of senses' exercises to transfer attention to the scenario in which the drama takes place, the intuitive response to the drama, the training of the memory to

---

63 *Ibid.*, 322, outlines the 'principal reasons' why we suffer from desolation, the third of which is to enable us to recognise that 'consolation' is a gift and that by suffering desolation we learn to avoid spiritual pride. Moreover, in accordance with 23 the 'first principle and foundation', we need to learn to become indifferent to whether we are in consolation or desolation in the same way as we should be indifferent to whether we are in health or sickness, etc. Accept what is given and be thankful.

64 The emphasis on 'election' in the *Exercises* presupposes that each individual has a divine purpose which 'discernment of spirits' is designed to help find. In this regard we may recall both the Pseudo-Dionysius and the words which Dante puts in the mouth of Piccarda about the individual's role in the divine thearchy. See Chapter 1.3, N.23 above. See also D.T. Asselin S.J., 'Christian Maturity and Spiritual Discernment' in *Notes on the Spiritual Exercises of St Ignatius Loyola, op.cit.*, 201-213, esp. 211.

absorb the context of the response, the recital of the response to a third party, the Spiritual Director, and the establishment of its meaning by rational process and colloquy and above all the constant prayer for guidance which a beneficient creator would not deny - all these characteristics are applied by Ignatius to a process of rational election based ultimately for the exercitant on faith but which for Ignatius, their designer, seems to have originated from the revelations, and the illuminations, which accompanied them, at Manresa.

Ignatius believed it was inevitable that exercitants, whether their elections were in accord with the divine counsels or commandments, would be faced with an encounter with the evil spirit in their lives. Indeed their election might well lead them to seek out the evil spirit in order to expose it. In doing so they would place themselves in extreme danger as Christ had done in confronting and overcoming the devil in his own day and, as Ignatius had read, the Saints had done[65]. The ability to recognise the characteristics of the enemies of human nature and understand their menace as well as those of the divine spirit and its welcome, was at the heart of the discernment process and an essential skill to be exercised in life after the election. Ignatius and the companions, for example, would have recognised at Montmartre when deciding to undertake a mission to the Holy Land to convert the Muslims, that they would probably lose their lives in the *empresa*. Ignatius from his earlier experience on his pilgrimage to the Holy Land would certainly have done so and would have made the dangers known to his companions. The vision he received at La Storta, to which we have already referred, indicated or confirmed for Ignatius that he and his companions were not called to follow Christ in his crucifixion but to assist him in carrying his cross. The imagery in which this confirmation was conveyed is biblical and the understanding of its meaning would probably have depended on what 'carrying the cross' implied. Ignatius interpreted it as 'labour'. The companions, he inferred, were called on to work to overcome evil as Christ laboured in carrying his cross to the site where the enemy of human nature was finally defeated.

4. 'UNCTIO' AND 'RATIO': A REFLECTION ON IGNATIAN 'DISCERNMENT'

We earlier made the observation that the tradition of 'discernment of spirits' seemed to reach some sort of 'apogee' in the teaching of Ignatius of Loyola and John of the Cross. In the next chapter we will consider this observation in relation to John of the Cross and the contemplative life. In the present chapter we have considered how Ignatius of Loyola appropriated the tradition and in what sense the tradition might be regarded as reaching some sort of apogee for the 'active' life in his life and teaching. While this consideration has been the main purpose of this chapter, it is perhaps

---

65 Climacus, in particular was aware that the confrontation with the devil was an inevitable part of spiritual growth. Ignatius makes the same point in the 'meditations on two standards'. *Exercises*, 141 and 142. See also Hugo Rahner, *Ignatius the Theologian*, 85.

pertinent to recall that within the context of the wider scope of our study, the purpose of our discourse is to consider what light the treatment of 'discernment' by Ignatius throws on the role of 'discernment of spirits' in mediating the interlocking nature of the Christian 'Tradition' and the manner of its appropriation not only by the Spanish mystics but also by the fourteenth-century English mystics whose lives and teaching we have treated in Part One of this study. We propose to consider those two objectives as separate issues for the moment. First of all, let us review the reasons why we might regard Ignatius' appropriation and application of the tradition of 'discernment of spirits' as representing some sort of apogee in its development.

The first observation is that he sought perhaps to apply the practice of discernment of spirits developed in the *Spiritual Exercises* to the whole Church and its direction. He emphasises that there is but one spirit guiding the mission of the Christian community and each individual within it. He believes the purpose of the guidance is the same for both community and individual to further the establishment of Christ's Kingdom and in doing so for each individual to secure their own salvation and that of all other Christians in accordance with the divine will. The Pope as head of the Church, was perhaps as much responsible as each individual Christian, to search for the way, at each moment of their lives, to do 'more' to establish Christ's Kingdom. This seems to be what Nadal meant when he wrote to Lainez that the 'men of the Society' although they were 'papists', were only so to the extent 'they absolutely had to be'[66]. That is because they are Christians and working to the same ends. This does not, in Nadal's interpretation, absolve the Society of Jesus from making its own discernments, nor does it absolve each individual member from doing so. There is also an implication in this teaching that the Pope's discernments which guide his initiatives, are subject to rational explanation. Obedience is not blind in the Ignatian view. On the other hand, where conflict arises in the interpretation of Scripture and the Fathers, the Church and the Pope, who are the 'visible' mediators of the spirit, are to be obeyed[67].

The circumstances of the day were largely responsible for recognition of the need to distinguish between individual discernment and community discernment as exercised by the visible Church. There is an implicit recognition by Ignatius, the soldier and strategist, that a church leader is concerned with apostolic strategy. It is the function of the local commander, on the spot as it were, to translate a general strategy of apostolic mission into local plans and tactics according to the local circumstances of the church and the same kind of devolution of responsibility should apply in the case of each individual Christian. Ignatius' recognition that the application of the military paradigm in the war against the 'evil chieftain' was relevant to the circumstances of his day, was based first on a recognition of the Muslim threat to Christendom and subsequently on the recognition of the threat posed by an unre-

---

66 Quoted by Hugo Rahner, *Ignatius the Theologian*, 237 and N.96.

67 See *Exercises*, 352-370. Rules for Thinking with the Church.

formed Church and militant schismatics seeking to transcend what they supposed to be a church in which the anti-Christ was enthroned.

The second point which Ignatius made explicit, which had perhaps always been implicitly recognised, was that 'spirit' while remaining hidden in essence was 'visible' in its effects on the lives of Christians. There had always been recognition that the note of the presence of the divine spirit was humility. 'Enthusiasm' which expressed itself in conflict, self-righteousness, and a spirit of aggression, was contrary to 'Christ's mind'. Ignatius emphasised that elections made with the assistance of his guidelines for the 'discernment of spirits', should be seen to be rationally based and in accordance with Scripture and Church doctrine. Perhaps neglecting this teaching some Jesuits had been led astray[68]. Yet, on the other hand, Ignatius recognised, as his letter to the Duke of Alba illustrates, divine providential purpose was not always rational in a human way[69]. When the indications were present in the form of strong emotional responses to some election, as in the 'second time' of election, that the course elected was in accordance with the divine will, Ignatius believed that those indications should be allowed to override considerations of human prudence. There were sufficient checks and balances in the administration of the *Exercises* and in the Society of Jesus to ensure that strong emotional responses were monitored in an environment of personal detachment. The tension between *unctio* and *ratio* was always present, in Ignatius' view. The tension would always exist because *unctio* resulted from the uncreated mind operating in an anagogical mode, whereas *ratio* was a power of the created mind operating perhaps in the analogical mode. The created mind might never 'know' more than the uncreated mind out of which it received its being. Nevertheless if *unctio* and *ratio* seemed to be in conflict in relation to an election and the circumstances surrounding it, the conflict should be 'visible', openly recognised and an adjudication made. In this way it would be possible for divinely inspired new initiatives to germinate within individuals and the Church. Ultimately the growth and health of the initiatives would verify whether or not they were of divine inspiration.

A third aspect of the Ignatian 'discernment' process which perhaps took it beyond earlier practices, was the absence of some prior or parallel programme of asceticism which would restore 'purity'. The precondition for undertaking the *Exercises* was the desire, the commitment, to seek the divine will with regard to lifestyle or vocation. Thus we see the first account of the making of the *Spiritual Exercises* en-

---

68 See for example Hugo Rahner, *Ignatius the Theologian*, 226/227 for the case of the Jesuits in Gaudia, Onfroy and Oviedo.

69 'For it may often be that those things which do not seem to fit in at all with human prudence are perfectly compatible with divine prudence: for this cannot be bounded by the laws of our reasonings (*no se ata á las leyes de nuestras razones*)'. Quoted by Hugo Rahner, *Ignatius the Theologian*, 225.

shrined in the testimony of a reformed prostitute at Alcala[70]. Ignatius seems to recognise what was again implicit in the tradition, that a change in human will, a 'turning' in Augustinian terms, resulted from *unctio*, the divine gift of grace, rather than
ratio. As his own experience indicated, the action of such a grace might be quite
sudden. Yet Ignatius was careful to create in the context of the *Spiritual Exercises*
and the care with which he designed the sequence of meditations, a scenario in
which the exercitant might avoid all external distraction and concentrate on the divine will as revealed in Christ. He was seeking to create what Hilton would have
referred to as the 'darkness' in which the divine presence and affirmation might be
'felt' and also the antithesis reflected in either 'divine absence' or the presence of
the 'evil chieftain'. The presence of the 'evil chieftain' generated fear and distress
rather than the sorrow which accompanied the absence of a divine presence. The
insights on which Ignatius crafted the *Spiritual Exercises* and the relationship between election and discernment, seem to reflect initially the unique circumstances of
his own spiritual conversion, and further the pastoral challenges which he recognised in Spanish society from his experiences at Manresa, Barcelona, Alcala and
Salamanca. The English mystics, even Walter Hilton, did not seem to have the peri-
patetic Pauline active lifestyle, nor opportunity for it, which characterised Ignatius',
though we know so little about their lives and circumstances that such a statement
has to be made with caution.

The claim that Ignatius of Loyola's teaching on 'discernment of spirits' may represent some sort of apogee in the tradition is supported by Mercurian's observation
that he seems to incorporate in his approach, with various emphases, all the insights
which the earlier tradition reveals. However, perhaps what was *nova and inaudita*
rather than Mercurian's observations about the rationality of the third time of election, was the manner in which the insights were so succinctly blended together to
support an 'active' apostolic tradition in the spirit of St Paul. But more than this their
apostolic effectiveness which Ignatius was able to demonstrate to his immediate
companions and a wide circle of Christians from so varied a background of national-
ity and circumstance gave his *Spiritual Exercises* and rules for 'discernment of spirits' in different circumstances the kind of prestige which the achievements of scien-
tists in our own day, give to the scientific method.

In a way the Ignatian approach to the 'discernment of spirits' which seems to em-
body the Pauline missionary spirit within mediaeval Christian spirituality, illuminates the uniqueness and individuality of the approaches of the English mystics. The
English mystics were dependent on the earlier tradition as we have attempted to
show. Yet in each case the application expressed the individuality of their experiences which, for those reading their works in a later period, create the impression
that they are based on an authentic 'turning' experience of unspeakable joy and awe.

70 Maria de la Flor in her deposition to the examiners of Ignatius at Salamanca in 1527. Caraman,
    Ignatius Loyola, 64 and *MHSJ Fontes Documentales de S. Ignatio*, Rome, 1977, 335-6.

Their attempts to put their experiences and the insights derived from them at the disposal of others provide the tradition with that characteristic of 'diversity within unity' which suggests the manner in which the analogical and anagogical imaginations are related. The unity of the godhead may only be 'felt' in the soul anagogically as '*unctio*' as in the darkness of a cloud; the godhead is only visible analogically in the light of its diversity as '*ratio*' in Christian lives. This is an observation with which Ignatius would surely have agreed, since the 'success' of the *Spiritual Exercises* was to a very large extent based on their applicability to the whole spectrum of diversity in human being.

Chapter 6

ST JOHN OF THE CROSS

1. A 'QUIXOTIC' SPIRIT

Philip Caraman referred to Ignatius of Loyola as a 'Quixotic' character[1]. He meant there was a touch of impulsive 'madness' about the dedicated manner in which his ideals informed his life's work. To the onlooker, 'reality' and 'illusion' might have seemed to lose their polarity; for example, in his decision to undertake the pilgrimage to Jerusalem in the manner he proposed so soon after recovering from wounds that proved almost fatal. His capacity to 'discern spirits' perhaps enabled him to walk a tightrope of personal choices throughout his life in a way which to others might have seemed, at best, foolhardy. John of the Cross was no less 'Quixotic' but his touch of 'madness' seemed to manifest itself in a different form of 'discernment'. Whereas Ignatius' discernment was about 'elections' inspired by love, John's seemed to be about the nature of 'love' itself as a unity of faith, hope and charity. Both Ignatius and John exemplify in their lives as well as in their teaching the tradition of 'discernment of spirits' as applied respectively in the 'active' and 'contemplative' 'poles' of Christian life. Their lives are case studies in which they illustrated their teaching, and that of the mediaeval Christian tradition of spirituality, for future generations. There are two aspects, therefore, of their use of the instrument of 'discernment'; in the immediacy of the unfolding of their own lives and in the mediatory process of reflecting upon their experience in their writing.

In the Prologue we suggested that John of the Cross' capacity to withstand the pressures to which he was subjected in the dungeon at Toledo, may have derived from the stability of character which the love he experienced as a child established. After his father's death when John was three years old, 'love', 'faith' and 'hope' were perhaps the only assets which the family possessed. His father had been disowned by his own family when he had married against their wishes. They may have considered that marrying a 'weaver' who appeared to be beneath his station in life, was a form of 'madness'. They were apparently a well-established merchant family with a sense of family honour and a position in society to uphold. 'Love', they may have felt, was a romantic notion based on 'feeling' which was notoriously fickle. John's father, however, held to his intention despite the threatened loss of his patrimony.

---

1   Caraman, *Ignatius Loyola*, viii.

His decision to marry for 'love' was spontaneous and intuitive but something more than a 'quixotic' gesture; it derived, perhaps, from a genuinely 'quixotic spirit' which manifested the 'amour courtois' ideal in its purest form as spontaneous, persevering, loyal and self-sacrificial rather than as socially and culturally 'conventional'. John of the Cross seems to have inherited that 'spirit' of spontaneity and integrity and recognised its value despite the poverty which befell the family on his father's death.

From an early age, therefore, John of the Cross experienced in the heart of his family life the nexus which links the spontaneity of sacrificial love and poverty. He did not seem to compensate for his smallness of stature and straightened material circumstances by an aggressive demeanour. On the contrary, he was by nature a sensitive child. It was a sensitivity which developed into an aesthetic sensibility and spontaneous recognition of natural beauty. It was a characteristic which later caused him to be dubbed 'God's archives' by Teresa's nuns because they were much impressed by his feeling for the beauty of nature and, in particular, the night sky which he displayed on a journey he undertook with them in 1568 to Valladolid[2]. His natural intelligence had enabled him to take advantage of the limited educational opportunities available to him in his youth. He was encouraged to develop an artistic talent which enabled him to extend his powers of observation and to discover and express the poetry within him[3].

---

[2]   *John of the Cross. Selected Writings*, ed. and introduction by Kieran Kavanaugh O.C.D., New York, Mahwah: Paulist Press, 1987, 13-14. It is referred to as *S.W.* hereafter. The translation is based on the *Collected Works of St John of the Cross*, trans. Kiernan Kavanaugh and Otilio Rodriguez. 2nd ed. Washington D.C.: ICS Publications 1979 and incorporates a number of changes 'for the sake of clarity' (2). Quotations from and references to St John's works are taken from this source and the page number indicated. The references to the works will follow the form set out below:

ASC = The Ascent of Mount Carmel which will be followed by book number, chapter and paragraph number.

D.N. = The Dark Night, followed by the book number, chapter and paragraph number.

S.C. = The Spiritual Canticle, followed by the stanza and paragraph number.

L.F. = The Living Flame of Love, followed by the stanza and paragraph number.

My confidence in using these selections for the references is based on the editor's scholarly reputation and his purpose to 'concentrate on the core message and main spiritual situation found in the individual work' (1). Furthermore, this work offers a convenient entry into a canon in which it is not always easy to identify and relate the parts to the whole experience of spiritual development which St John's works provide. This arises from the circumstances and purpose which prompted St John to write and the richness of the spiritual experience he was describing.

[3]   While working at the hospital at Medina del Campo, he found the opportunity to study Latin and Rhetoric at a nearby Jesuit school. *S.W.*, 8. It was here interestingly enough that his intellectual and poetic potential was aroused by Fr. Bonifacio S.J., a novice at the time. See Bruno de Jésus-Marie, *Saint John of the Cross*, ed. by Benedict Zimmerman, New York: Sheed and Ward, 1932, 11.

For John the beauty of creation seems to have illuminated by contrast the impoverishment of human existence. In poverty, perhaps, he began to recognise the potential
for beauty in human existence through his own response to the beauty of creation
and the reflection of his Mother's love. The 'night' was 'dark' but it was also 'tranquil' and 'serene'; images which his most sublime poetry subsequently explored[4].
Poverty, moreover, directed him towards the Church and so to the source of beauty,
the divine Creator. The hospital at Medina del Campo in which as a youth he gained
employment was a charitable foundation governed by a former 'caballero'[5]. Part of
John's work was to seek alms to sustain it. The other part was to care for its inmates.
He apparently displayed the qualities of dedication and competence since he was
offered holy orders, a benefice, and the security which this might bring[6]. He chose
instead to join the novitiate in the 'mendicant' Carmelite Monastery at Medina del
Campo through which he subsequently obtained a Thomist orientated theological
education at the University of Salamanca and developed an interest in the possibility
of the contemplative life[7]. As Ignatius of Loyola had before him, he considered
joining the Carthusians[8]. It was after his ordination when he was thinking about the
direction of his vocation that he met Teresa of Avila and was introduced to her ideas
for the restoration of the contemplative tradition in which the Carmelite order had
been founded before its expulsion from the Holy Land and reestablishment in
Europe as a mendicant order[9].

The association with Teresa of Avila seemed to focus the direction of John's subsequent vocation for it provided the opportunity to draw together his 'contemplative'

---

4   In *S.C.* 15 and 19 the night was both 'tranquil' and 'serene' respectively. In the poem 'The
     Dark Night' which provides the basis for both *ASC* and *D.N.* he refers to the night as 'dark',
     stanza 1, but in 3 it is also 'glad'. See Georges Morel, *Le Sens de l'Existence selon S. Jean de
     la Croix*, 3 vols, Paris: Aubier, 1960-1.
5   Bruno de Jésus-Marie, *Saint John of the Cross*, 9. The hospital warden was Don Alonso Alva-
     rez de Toledo. See Richard Hardy, *Search for Nothing: The Life of St John of the Cross*, New
     York: Crossroad, 1982.
6   *Ibid.* - John was twenty-one when the offer was made.
7   Ross Collings O.C.D., *John of the Cross*, Collegeville, Minnesota: Liturgical Press, 1990,
     Appendix, 162, for a curriculum vitae. John entered the Carmelite novitiate at St Anne's, 1563,
     taking the name Juan de Santo Matia. From 1564 he attended the University of Salamanca
     where he undertook a course in philosophy and theology. It is not known which lectures he at-
     tended (*S.W.*, 10). His intellectual ability was recognised as he was made prefect of studies at
     the Carmelite College of San Andrés in Salamanca. The University was a centre of Thomist
     scholarship as later evidenced by the production there of the *Cursus Theologicus Summam d.
     Thomae Complectens* from 1631-1701 by a group of discalced Carmelites. In the words of the
     Oxford Dictionary of the Christian Church, 1229, it 'is a gigantic commentary on the *Summa*
     of St Thomas Aquinas undertaken to provide a sound basis of theological teaching for friars of
     the Teresian reform'.
8   *S.W.*, 10. For Ignatius, see *Autobiography* 12, and Chapter 5.1, N.12 above.
9   *Ibid.* He first met Teresa at Medina del Campo in 1567, when she was fifty-two. He had re-
     turned there to say his first Mass.

aspirations and his 'poetic' sensitivity in a role of spiritual direction at Avila. Contemplative discipline, like personal crucifixion, which he had experienced at Duruelo in the first of the discalced foundations for monks in 1568[10], enabled him to combine an anagogic vision of Christian faith with its analogical expression in which he was able subsequently to translate his own 'unitive' contemplative experiences into poetry and prose.

We have suggested in the Prologue that his imprisonment at Toledo as the unwitting victim of the 'imbroglio' of ecclesiastical and secular politics in Spain became the pivotal experience in his life[11]. It was in this intolerant and harsh environment that he apparently underwent the contemplative experiences which tempered his spirituality and 'coloured' its discernment as at once forbidding and ecstatic. His escape from captivity was 'quixotic' in its daring and, perhaps, miraculous in its success[12].

2. THE POETRY OF 'THE NIGHT'

Edith Stein in her study of John of the Cross has characterised his œuvre as '*The Science of the Cross*'[13]. And so it is. But if it is left at that we gain a very one-sided view of his mystical genius. His experience of the Cross, like that of St John the Evangelist who did not flinch from its agony as he watched at its foot as Christ died[14], opened up for him a vision of the love of God which found expression in the lyricism of his poetry. In the image of 'night' he found a potent symbol to contain both aspects of his experience; the cross as symbolised by darkness and the love by tranquillity and serenity.

It sometimes takes another poet's imagery to provide a language which will mediate the vision of a fellow poet. John Keats in his *Ode to a Nightingale*, for example, in a very different age and circumstance from John of the Cross, uses the images of the 'tender night' and the 'embalmed darkness' to capture the sweetness which the

---

10 *Ibid.*, 14/15. Duruelo is a lonely spot in Castile mid-way between Avila and Salamanca. The former prior of Medina, Antonio de Heredia, became the first superior of the foundation established in 1568. John took the name of Juan de la Cruz at this time and became the first novice master.

11 *Ibid.*, 15-20, for a narrative account of the 'imbroglio'.

12 *Ibid.*, 19. See also Crisogno de Jésus Sacramentado O.C.D., *The Life of St John of the Cross*, trans. Kathleen Pond, London: Longmans, Green & Co., 1958.

13 Edith Stein, *The Science of the Cross. A study of St John of the Cross*, ed. Dr. L. Gelber and Fr. Romaeus Leuven O.C.D., trans. Hilda Graef. London: Burns and Oates, 1960. See also E.W. Trueman Dicken, '*The Crucible of Love'. A Study of the Mysticism of St Teresa and St John of the Cross*, London: Darton, Longman & Todd, 1963 and E. Allison Peers, *Spirit of Flame. A Study of St John of the Cross*, London: SCM Press, 1943.

14 John 19:25-27.

darkness preserves and makes the 'night' tender[15]. The darkness which is terrifying to those unaccustomed to it yet contains all the beauty and potentiality of the dawn[16]. But the darkness has to be experienced before its qualities of tenderness, tranquillity and serenity can be appreciated. One of the achievements of John of the Cross was to find a medium through which to express what other contemplatives apparently experienced anagogically in its immediacy but felt unable to articulate analogically[17]. John of the Cross apparently felt the same difficulty when he found himself having to move from the poetic to the prose medium. His poetry managed, as it were, to 'embalm' the immediacy of the 'unitive' moment in which he shared the divine love and the divine agony in the dungeon at Toledo.

The symbol of 'night' also characterised the nature of John of the Cross' ideal of the 'contemplative' vocation in opposition to the 'active'. The 'active' seeks to do more for Christ's kingdom in the daylight where the midday devil roams. The 'contemplative' by contrast according to John seeks the divine being itself in order to offer its own 'purified' being as a sacrifice of love and praise. 'Contemplatives' set out on their journey in the 'night' of 'faith', 'hope' and 'love'; their heroic task is to purify their 'faith', 'hope' and 'love' by abandoning not only the world but themselves[18].

This type of journey requires a different form of discernment from that which Ignatius of Loyola brought to some form of apogee in the active life. The kataphatic approach of Ignatius in which the spiritual senses are developed through experiencing the anagogic reality of the analogical images of the Gospel, is reversed for John of the Cross. In the 'night' the analogical images are systematically stripped away as so many 'veils' which conceal the 'anagoge' itself, the divine spirit, the potentiality from which all 'act' originates. John's discernment is concerned, in part, with the purity of the apophatic emptying approach to the divine in which *all* that is not God is rejected. It is also concerned with recognising the immediacy of the divine reality

---

15 J. Keats (1795-1821), 'Ode to a Nightingale' in *The Golden Treasury* arranged by F.T. Palgrave, London & Glasgow: Collins, 1861, 244, fourth and fifth stanzas, 236. St John of the Cross in *S.C.*, 39, also refers to the 'sweet nightingale' as well as the 'serene' night.

16 Commenting in *S.C.* 39.12 and 13 St John compares the serenity which is the medium of contemplation when all bodily and spiritual faculties are stilled with the phantasies and apprehensions which are present when the intellectual and corporal faculties are active at night (*S.W.*, 281).

17 Chapter 3.1 and N.16 above for the *Cloud Author*. John of the Cross refers in *S.C.* 39.12 to 'some spiritual persons call this contemplation knowing by unknowing' (*S.W.*, 281).

18 Collings, *John of the Cross*, 102, comments 'the perfection of our powers of action is wrought in a kind of emptying of their natural energy' about the passage in *ASC* 2.6.2 in which John says:
   'These three virtues all cause emptiness in the faculties: faith in the intellect causes an emptiness and darkness with respect to understanding; hope in the memory causes emptiness of all possessions; and charity causes emptiness in the will and detachment from all affliction and from rejoicing in all that is not God (trans. by E. Allison Peers)'.

itself in the union of the Spiritual Marriage and the mediating process by which the love of this reality is passed on to others.

The stages of discernment are not easily separated in John's 'night' because the circumstances of his life seem to have determined the form and order in which his works were written. Nevertheless, the *Spiritual Canticle* seems to provide the most complete insight into his notion of 'discernment'.

3. THE SPIRITUAL CANTICLE

John's *Spiritual Canticle*, which is arguably one of the greatest mystical works in the genre, was largely composed while he underwent the greatest of deprivations in prison. The form follows that of the *Song of Songs* of the Old Testament and relives its spirit as John's personal testament to his own spiritual journey. He knew the *Song of Songs* by heart before his imprisonment and it provided a model for the expression of his own poetic gifts[19]. He owed his knowledge and understanding of Scripture to his theological education at Medina del Campo and at Salamanca. This education also provided an intellectual model in the Thomist synthesis and interpretation of Aristotelian philosophic insights[20].

John's natural love of the beauty of creation seems to have found intellectual confirmation in his theological and philosophical studies. The quality of his scholarship was recognised while he was still at Salamanca where he became Prefect of Studies at the Carmelite College of San Andreas. Moreover, it was confirmed in 1571, when after his participation in the foundation of the first 'discalced' house for monks at Duruelo, he was appointed Rector of the Carmelite College at Alcala. It was while in this post, which he occupied only briefly, that Teresa of Avila secured his services as Confessor at the Convent of the Incarnation at Avila to which she had recently been appointed Prioress with a brief to institute its reform. Teresa evidently recog-

---

19 *S.W.*, 213. He was also familiar with contemporary poets such as Boscán and Garcilaso, *S.W.*, 25.

20 For John of the Cross' knowledge and use of Scripture see *S.W.*, 28-31. Federico Ruiz in the general introduction in *San Juan de la Cruz: Obras Completas*, introducciones y notas doctrinales Federico Ruiz, Madrid: Editorial de Espiritualidad, 1980, 34, regards John as perhaps the most original and vigorous of Spanish theologians, *S.W.*, 32. See also *S.W.*, 33:
'In his academic studies, John learned the categories and theological priorities of his time. But at stake for him was the spiritual development of the human person, the creation of a doctrinal synthesis in which all these converging realities of the process of divinization would acquire unity and cohesion'.
For John's use and dependence on Scripture see Barnabas Ahern, 'The Use of Scripture in the Spiritual Theology of St John of the Cross', in *Catholic Biblical Quarterly* 14, Jan. 1952, 6-17; Henri de Lubac, *Exégèse médiévale. Les quatre sens de l'écriture*, 4 vols. Paris: Aubier, 1959-64, esp. 4, 500-505; Jean Vilnet, *Bible et mystique chez Saint Jean de la Croix*, Bruges: Desclée de Brouwer, 1949.

nised the value of John's gifts in which his love of beauty and remarkable sensitivity were allied to an intellectual integrity and profound theological and philosophical understanding of the contemplative vocation[21].

In the *Spiritual Canticle* John of the Cross seems to harness the love of the beauty of creation and the search for its source in the creator. He links, on the one hand, the Aristotelian and Thomist notion of the potentiality of all beauty in the mind of the creator, who as prime-mover makes possible its enactment on the stage of creation, with, on the other, the search in the *Canticle* for the bridegroom who will bring the creative process to fruition in his own life.

The *Spiritual Canticle* begins with the bride's plaintive question left alone in the creation

> Where have you hidden
> Beloved, and left me moaning?[22].

The 'Beloved' has 'hidden' not departed. So the bride sorrowfully begins her search for him in the creation:

> O woods and thickets
> Planted by the hand of my beloved!
> O green meadow coated, bright with flowers
> Tell me, has he passed by you?

She recognises his image in all things:

> With his image alone
> Clothed them in beauty.

But only He and not his creatures has the power to heal:

> Do not send me
> Any more messengers,
> They cannot tell me what I must hear.

---

21 *S.W.*, 14. While he was with Teresa at Valladolid, John underwent a brief novitiate to gain a better notion of how to initiate the Teresian life among the friars. Teresa in the *Foundations* wrote of this time that Fray Juan was so good that she could have learned more from him than he from her. See chap. 13 of *The Foundations* in *The Collected Works of St Teresa of Avila*, Vol. 3, trans. Kieran Kavanaugh and Otilio Rodriguez, Washington D.C.: I.C.S. Publications, 1985.

22 *S.C.* 1 (*S.W.*, 221). The quotations which follow are taken from the same source.

The autobiographical tone is maintained with the sense of deprivation only heightening the desire for that which is hidden:

> How do you endure
> O life, not living where you live?
> And being brought near death
> By the arrows you receive
> From that which you conceive of your beloved.

The longing breaks out again:

> Why, since you wounded
> This heart don't you heal it?

The faith with which the beloved has wounded her heart has exposed the bride to all this agony; to what purpose if not to heal her again?

The bridegroom returns, 'cooled by the breeze' of the bride's flight. The bride is ecstatic:

> The tranquil night
> At the time of the rising dawn,
> Silent music,
> Sounding solitude
> The supper that refreshes, and deepens love.

The 'night' takes on a different appearance when the bridegroom is present; 'And she rests in delight'. The bridegroom's speech reminds us that the experience is not autobiographical only but the experience of humanity:

> Beneath the apple tree:
> There I took you for my own,
> There I offered you for my own,
> And restored you,
> Where your mother was corrupted.

The bride recalls the experience:

> When you looked at me
> Your eyes imprinted your grace in me;
> For this you loved me ardently;
> And thus my eyes deserved
> To adore what they beheld in you.

And the bridegroom responds:

> She [the small white dove or the Spirit] lived in solitude
> And now in solitude has built her nest:
> And in solitude he guides her,
> He alone, who also bears
> In solitude [the crucifixion] the wound of love.

So the happy bride:

> Let us rejoice, Beloved,
> And let us go forth to behold ourselves in your beauty...

> There you will show me
> What my soul has been seeking,
> And then you will give me,
> You, my life, will give me there
> What you gave me on that other day;

it was given there in that dungeon -

> In the serene night,
> With a flame that is consuming and painless.

And his escape from prison is likened to the escape of Israel from the Egyptians as the Red Sea parted to facilitate their flight, opening up new visions of glory[23].

Most of the *Spiritual Canticle*, is believed to have been composed in the dungeon and provides some insight into John's state of mind and how that image of 'night' came to dominate his writing, as the image of the hidden bridegroom; not absent; only hidden in the depths of his being, 'in solitude'[24]. The *via negativa* for John of the Cross was this sort of night where longing heightens the pain of deprivation. Discernment in John of the Cross' exposition of spiritual development becomes almost synonymous with faith; faith that the divine is only hidden, never absent. The

---

23 *S.C.* 40. This is a rather different interpretation from that given by John himself. See *S.W.*, 283.
    He relates the last two lines of stanza 40 to the purification which takes place when the sensory
    and lower part [of the soul] is reformed and brought into conformity with the spiritual part
    which enables the spiritual marriage to be consummated. Nevertheless, the analogy we have
    suggested seems apposite.

24 *S.W.*, 213-16 outlines the genesis of the *Spiritual Canticle*. Stanzas 32-34 were added in 1577-8
    while John of the Cross was at El Calvario after his escape from prison in Toledo. Stanzas 35-
    39 were added at Granada. Stanza 11 during the second redaction of the poem. See Colin P.
    Thompson, *The Poet and the Mystic: A study of the Cantico Espiritual of San Juan de la Cruz*,
    Oxford: Oxford University Press, 1977, on the critical questions surrounding the Canticle.

bride must wait patiently, but with mounting longing, for the beloved to show Himself. The paradox of a longing contained in patience is suggested by the metaphor of night as the bride waits for the dawn to see her beloved.

The prose explanation of the poem was written later at the request of Madre Ana de Jésus as the Prologue states[25]. John takes the opportunity to avoid any autobiographical reference and puts his experience in a wider context of general spiritual development. In the Prologue to the Commentary John makes clear the relationship between the poem and his explanation of it:

> Who can describe the understanding He [the Holy Spirit] gives to loving souls in whom He dwells? And who can express the experience He imparts to them? Who, finally, can explain the desires he gives them? Certainly no one can! Not even they who receive these communications. As a result these persons let something of their experiences overflow in figures and similes, and from the abundance of their spirit pour out secrets and mysteries rather than rational explanations[26].

In the Commentary he relates his experiences to the tradition of the Church and particularly to his background in Carmelite spirituality as reflected in the *Book of the First Monks*[27] and in the Teresian reform. The origins of the order were contemplative. That original contemplative existence on Mt Carmel is reflected in the metaphor of the 'night' as the *via negativa*. Here are found the conditions where God speaks and may be heard in the silence and solitude of the mountain top by the undistracted heart[28]. He tells Madre Ana:

---

25 *S.W.*, 219 and n.1. Madre Ana de Jésus was prioress of the Discalced Carmelite nuns of St Joseph's in Granada in 1584, having been hitherto prioress at Beas.

26 *S.W.*, 219/20.

27 *S.W.*, 9, n.2. The *Book of the First Monks*, trans. Michael Edwards, Boars Hill, Oxford: Teresian Press, 1985, would probably have been studied by John of the Cross during his novitiate. A critical edition of the *Liber de Institutione Primorum Monachorum*, a fourteenth century Carmelite work is under preparation by Dr Paul Chandler who suggests that 'by using both literal and allegorical/tropological exegeses of the biblical texts about Elijah and his disciples, the work created a myth for the Carmelite order which functioned both for institutional and ideological legitimation and as a handbook of spiritual formation'. See also Otger Steggink, *Experiencia y Realismo en Santa Teresa y San Juan de la Cruz*, Madrid: Editorial de Espiritualidad, 1974, 99-122.

28 The Order of Our Lady of Mount Carmel was founded in Palestine c.1154 by St Berthold d. c.1195, but it has claimed continuity with hermits settled on Mount Carmel in earlier times and even to be a direct descendent of Elijah (see 2. Kings 2 and N.27 above). The primitive rule as laid down by Albert of Vercelli, Latin Patriarch of Jerusalem was one of extreme asceticism, prescribing absolute poverty, total abstinence from flesh, and solitude. See Melchior de Ste-Marie O.C.D., 'Carmel (Ordre de Notre Dame du Mont-Carmel)' in *D.H. G.E.*, xi, 1949, Cols 1070-1104; T. Brandsma O.Carm., 'Carmes' in *Dict. Sp.* Vol. 2, 1953, Cols 156-71; Gabriel de Sainte-Marie-Madeleine O.C.D., 'Carmes Dechaussés' in *Dict. Sp.* Vol. 2, 1953, Cols 171-209;

I hope that, although some scholastic theology is used here in reference to the soul's *interior converse* with God, it will not prove vain to speak in such a manner to the pure of spirit. Even though Your Reverence lacks training in scholastic theology by which the divine truths are understood, you are not wanting in mystical theology, *which is known through love* and by which one not only knows but *at the same time* experiences[29].

Her faith is illuminated by love founded in the immediacy of experience, like John's. She may not understand what is happening to her but knows that it is happening. She is free to relate his images to her own experience:

There is no reason to be bound to this explanation [in his commentary]. For *mystical wisdom, which comes through love* and is the subject of these stanzas, need not be understood distinctly in order to cause love and affection in the soul, for it is given according to the mode of faith, through which we love God without understanding Him[30].

Faith, in this interpretation, is the gift of a love which persists despite not being understood clearly but which inspires the hope that one day it will when the Beloved is met face to face. John offers her this expression of his own experience of love as poetry first and only secondarily as the mind groping for some explanation of the inexplicable mystery of the divine love. Concentrate on the 'love', he tells her, and let the understanding take care of itself. 'Love' is for the 'night', understanding for the 'dawn'[31].

4. DISCERNMENT OF THE CONSUMMATION OF LOVE

In figures 4 and 5 we have displayed the sketch, one of several, which John of the Cross made to illustrate the ascent of Mt Carmel. His representation resembles in shape El Greco's representation of Mt Sinai displayed in our frontispiece. Mt Sinai was the traditional image of contemplation in the Judaeo-Christian tradition; its summit the place of God's self-revelation to Moses in the cloud.

From its foot, the mountain seems at first insurmountable. This is apparently the impression which many readers who approach the work of John of the Cross receive if they begin at the beginning with the *Ascent of Mt Carmel*[32].

---

and Fabrizio Foresti, *Sinai and Carmel: the Biblical Roots of the Doctrine of St John of the Cross*, Darlington, Carmel, 1981.

29 *S.C.* Prol.3 (*S.W.*, 220/21) [my italics].
30 *S.C.* Prol.2 (*S.W.*, 220) [my italics].
31 *S.C.* Prol.1 (*S.W.*, 219/20).
32 See *S.W.*, 46 for a discussion of the difficulties in approaching *The Ascent of Mt Carmel*.

Sketch of Mount Carmel by St John of the Cross

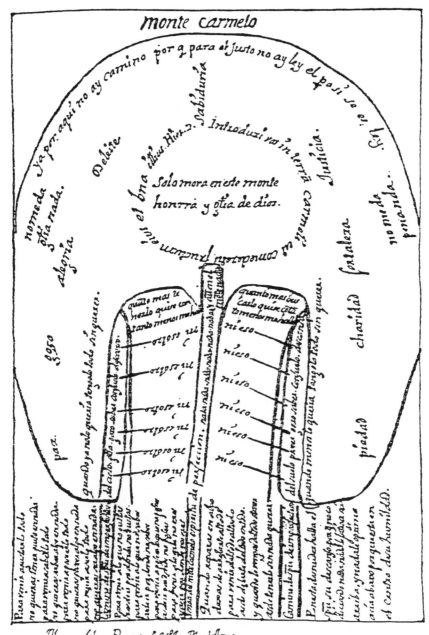

English Translation of Terms Used in St John's Original Drawing

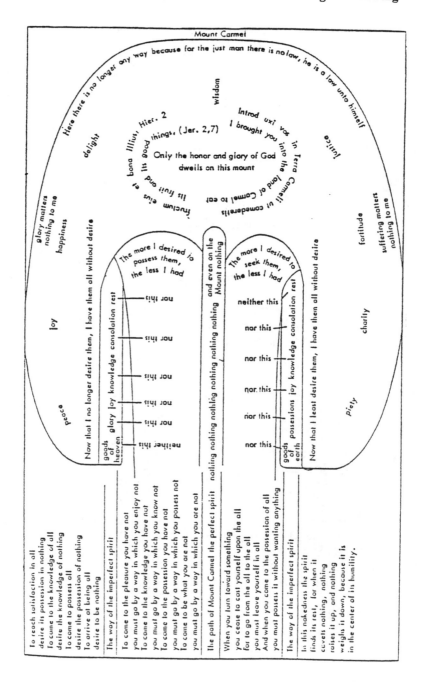

The ascent appears steep, even at the start, and the summit is shrouded in cloud. John himself seems to have realised that this might discourage people from attempting the climb. At the outset of the *Ascent* he sets out in full the stanzas of his poem *The Dark Night*. They are perhaps intended to encourage the reader to recognise that 'faith' is the inspiration needed to reach the goal which is only dimly perceived at the outset. So in the final stanza of *The Dark Night*, he records his own experience:

> I abandoned and forgot myself
> Laying my face on my beloved;
> All things ceased; I went out from myself,
> Leaving my cares
> Forgotten among the lilies[33].

Paradoxically, the guide for this spiritual journey, represented as an ascent but more akin to a descent into the depths of the psyche, is the beloved who is the object of the search. The guide only shows himself when longing is abandoned in trust and forgotten. Faith becomes transformed into love.

John appreciated, - if the Prologue to the *Ascent of Mt Carmel* is any guide, - that there are many paths to the top which may be followed and people find themselves lost on the mountain in the 'dark night' in various stages of the climb and in differing circumstances:

> A deeper enlightenment and wider experience than mine is necessary to explain the dark night through which a soul journeys toward that divine light of perfect union with God that is achieved, in so far as possible in this life, through love[34].

The path, the guide and the goal is love. He is not the only one who has trodden the path, found a guide, and reached the goal:

> The darknesses and trials, spiritual and temporal, that fortunate souls ordinarily undergo on their way to the high state of perfection are so numerous and profound that human science cannot understand them adequately[35].

The 'fortunate souls' are those, who in possession of the 'sheer grace' of faith, venture forth:

FIGURE 5

> On that glad night,
> In secret, for no one saw me,
> Nor did I look at anything

---

33   *D.N.* 8 (*S.W.*, 56).
34   *ASC* Prol. 1 (*S.W.*, 57).
35   *Ibid.*

> With no other light or guide
> Than the one that burned in my heart;
>
> This guided me
> More surely than the light of noon
> - him I knew so well - [36].

The 'invisible guide' who came to guide him appeared from nowhere, 'sheer grace', and yet was a surer guide from within the darkness of the soul than the 'light of noon' from without which he knew so well[37].

In the *Ascent*, however, he is not prepared to trust only in his own experience and he says,

> In discussing this dark night, therefore, I will not rely on experience or science, for these can fail and deceive us...[38].

Not only the Alumbrados perhaps can be deceived but those who profess to know, perhaps even the Church authorities who imprisoned him are included:

> Although I will not neglect whatever possible use I can make of them [experience and science], my help in all that, with God's favor, I shall say, will be Sacred Scripture, at least in the most important matters, or those that are difficult to understand[39]

for

> Taking Scripture as our guide we do not err since the Holy Spirit speaks to us through it.

He here endorses the belief reflected in contemplative tradition of the past in the power of Scripture to mediate the immediacy of divine love for the individual. On the other hand, the safeguards against misinterpretation are the same as those Ignatius of Loyola advocated so definitely:

> Should I misunderstand or be mistaken on some point, whether I deduce it from Scripture or not, I will not be intending to deviate from the true meaning of Sacred Scripture or from the doctrine of our Holy Mother the Catholic Church.

---

36 *D.N.* 3 and 4 (*S.W.*, 56/7).
37 *D.N.* 1 and 2 (*S.W.*, 56).
38 *ASC* Prol. 2 (*S.W.*, 57).
39 *ASC* Prol. 2 (*S.W.*, 57).

Should there be some mistake, I submit entirely to the Church, or even to anyone who judges more competently about the matter than I[40].

The Prologue to the *Ascent of Mt Carmel* was probably written about the time Pope Gregory XIII, in a brief dated June 22, 1580, allowed Teresa's friars and nuns to form a separate province and govern themselves[41]. John, perhaps, felt his stand during his imprisonment at Toledo against the detractors of the discalced reform had been justified when he wrote of 'judges more competent than I'. He perhaps shared Teresa's own view: 'Now we are all at peace, calced and discalced; no one can hinder us from serving our Lord'[42]. She might have added 'in the way we have taken'.

The papal brief which placed the discalced Carmelite reform on an officially approved footing, coupled with the help he perceived his own spiritual experiences might afford to others seeking to follow the same path, seemed to provide the occasion for the creativity which characterised his time at Baeza and Granada from 1579 to 1588. He was concerned initially with the problems of both beginners and proficients at the College at Baeza and with the spiritual direction of nuns for which Teresa had sought his help[43]. So in *The Ascent of Mt Carmel*:

We will discuss… how individuals should behave; what method the confessor should use in dealing with them: the signs for the recognition of this purification of the soul, which we call the dark night; whether it is purification of the senses or of the spirit; and how we can discern whether this affliction is caused by melancholia or some other deficiency of sense or spirit… We will also discuss many other experiences of those who walk along this road: joys, afflictions, hopes and sorrows - some of these originating from the spirit of perfection, others from the spirit of imperfection[44].

He is going to address beginners and proficients on the way to achieve perfection. But in order to recognise the working of the spirit of perfection it is necessary to weed out the imperfections of sense and spirit which have been seeded by the spirit of imperfection. The 'weeding out' is the purification process which may seem so daunting. This is conceived as the 'dark night'. The progress in the process is from darkness to the light of dawn; first in the senses and then in the spirit. As one becomes accustomed to the dark, one begins to recognise objects and move around. This is sensual recognition. Spiritual recognition is to recognise movements within;

---

40   *ASC* Prol. 2 (*S.W.*, 57).

41   *S.W.*, 20.

42   *Ibid.* and n.6. See Teresa of Avila, *The Foundations*, chap. 29.32.

43   *S.W.*, 20. He was only at El Calvario for a year. The appointments which followed were Rector at the College at Baeza 1579-82, Prior of Los Mártires at Granada, 1582-85, Vicar Provincial of Andalusia, 1585-87, based in Granada, and prior again 1587-88. While Madre Ana de Jésus was prioress at Beas and Granada (N.25 above) he also acted as spiritual director of the nuns.

44   *ASC* Prol. 6 (*S.W.*, 59).

not of objects but of spirits. Spirits work on the desires for objects, so sense and spirit are not entirely dissociated. The bride in the *Canticle* has to focus all her desire on the beloved object who created all the other good things she sees. The concentration of desires, gathered up into an exclusive longing and patiently sustained, brings the beloved object into vision. And when the beloved appears the pent-up desire explodes in an ecstasy of love which takes the individuals experiencing it not only outside themselves but into a crescendo of ecstasy which seems to have no end until the beloved withdraws.

Discernment in the above passage is represented as diagnosis. John is the diagnostician. He can recognise ill-health because he has experienced good health and has sensitively followed the path from the one to the other. Purification of the senses and the spirit, both active and passive, in the 'dark night' brings a progressive return to good health. However, the purpose of this mountain climb in the 'dark night' is not just to achieve good health but to meet with the beloved who alone can transform the good into the perfect in an ecstatic transformation. This meeting with the beloved is what the contemplative should long for and it is the thought of this meeting which John holds out as the incentive to motivate the contemplative to endure the hardships of the 'dark night'.

He broke off his discourse on the *Ascent of Mount Carmel* to comment on the *Spiritual Canticle* which, as we have seen, describes the search for the beloved, his appearance and the final surrender of the bride. In the *Living Flame of Love* he describes the ecstatic experience of love which followed the surrender of the bride to the beloved.

The major part of the poem of the *Canticle* and the poem of the *Dark Night* were both written down in the beautiful surroundings of El Calvario[45] which must have seemed to John after the experience of nine months in a Toledo dungeon which took toll of his health, like the realisation of the Beatific Vision which he had glimpsed through a 'thin veil' in his prison. He wrote both the poem and the *Commentary* of the *Living Flame of Love* for Doña Ana de Peñalosa while at Granada; the latter in just fifteen days[46]. Such an explosion of energy in writing about it suggest that the poem itself was deliberately brief to capture the concentrated nature of those ecstatic moments which make the endurance of the *Ascent* and the *Dark Night* so desirable.

Compared with the forty stanzas which ultimately comprised the *Spiritual Canticle*, the *Living Flame of Love* is brief. It has just four stanzas. They deal with an ecstasy which is unbounded but for the frail 'veil' which holds the spirit in the body. The

---

45 El Calvario is situated in a beautiful mountainous solitude near Beas in Andalusia near the head-waters of the river Guadalquivir.

46 *L.F.* Prol. (*S.W.*, 293). See also *S.W.*, 298.

'veil' is so frail that the bride can see through it so that it seems no longer to be there.

John of the Cross is not referring to sensual effects either in the *Canticle* or the *Flame*. The metaphors he uses relate to spiritual experiences and effects which may only be expressed by analogy with common experiences of objects. The metaphor he uses in the *Living Flame of Love* seeks to express an analogy between the ecstatic experience of love within the soul and the progress of the enkindling of a log which first heats to combustion point, then smoulders and suddenly sends out flames. The effect is to cauterise and wound the soul but also to heal it:

O sweet cautery
O delightful wound
O gentle hand! O delicate touch
That tastes of eternal life
And pays every debt!
In killing you changed death to life[47].

The first stanza was set out in the Prologue[48]. In discussing the second line, 'That tenderly wounds my soul', he says:

God's speech is the effect He produces in the soul[49].

The divinity is known by the effect it has upon the soul, but more than this, what is said, John believes, is known by those effects. The reason is that those effects are felt 'in its deepest center'[50]. 'This feast [of love] takes place in the substance of the soul' he explains, 'where neither the center of the senses nor the devil can reach'. The implication is that there are several 'centers'. The soul is 'centered' in God but in God there are many 'centers': 'The more degrees of love it has [the soul], the more deeply it enters into God and centers itself in Him'[51]. - 'A stronger love is a more unitive love, and we can understand in this manner the many dwelling places the Son of God declared were in His Father's house [Jn. 14:2]'. And so:

Hence, that the soul be in its center - which is God, as we have said - it is suffi- cient for it to possess one degree of love, for by one degree alone it is united with Him through grace. Should it have two degrees, it will become united and con- centrated in God in another deeper center [and so on]... But once it has attained

47 *L.F.* 2 (*S.W.*, 293/4).
48 See Prologue 6. and *S.W.*, 293.
49 *L.F.* 1.7 (*S.W.*, 297). See Lucien-Marie de Saint Joseph O.C.D., *L'Expérience de Dieu. Actuali- té du message de Saint Jean de la Croix*, Paris, 1968.
50 *L.F.* 1.9 (*S.W.*, 297).
51 *L.F.* 1.13 (*S.W.*, 298).

the final degree, God's love will have arrived at wounding the soul in its ultimate and deepest center, which is to transform and clarify it in its whole being, power and strength, and according to its capacity, until it appears to be God[52].

The soul seems, it appears, to become so transparent that God shines through. He uses the metaphor of a sparkling crystal to illustrate his meaning.

The notion of 'the degrees' of love is a commonplace among mediaeval spiritual writers. Walter Hilton refers to three degrees of love in Book One of the *Scale of Perfection*[53] and the Benedictine author, William of St Thierry, uses different words, 'voluntas', 'amor', 'caritas', 'sapientia' to express an ascending scale of love with different characteristics in the *On the Nature and Dignity of Love*[54]. John of the Cross, however, unlike these other authors is actually claiming to have experienced those degrees of love and he has the experience, as an objective observer, of Teresa of Avila to corroborate his own feelings[55].

When John comes to discuss the line

Tear through the veil of this sweet encounter[56]

he says it 'is easy to reach God when all the impediments are removed and the veils that separate the soul from union with Him are torn'. We may assume 'the veil' is also an allusion to the veils of the temple which mask the sanctuary. The significance of the apparent 'tearing' of the veil when Christ died would have been immediately recognised by contemplatives literally 'fed' on Scripture[57]. John recognises three 'veils'; the temporal 'veil', comprising all creatures; the natural, embodying the purely natural inclinations and operations of the human being; and the sensitive, which consists only of the union of the soul with the body. He suggests this third 'veil' is what St Paul is referring to in *2 Corinthians* 5:1: 'We know that if this our earthly house is dissolved, we have a building of God in heaven'[58]. The 'veils' mask the mystery of the sanctuary of God located in the depths of the psyche and in heaven.

---

52 *L.F.* 1.9 (*S.W.*, 297).

53 Walter Hilton, *The Scale of Perfection, op.cit.*, Bk 1, chap. 44, 117.

54 William of St Thierry, *De Natura et Dignitate Amoris*, P.L. 184, 382.B 'Primum enim ad Deum voluntas animam movet, amor promovet, caritas contemplatur, sapientia fruitur'.

55 As spiritual guide at the Convent of the Incarnation at Avila (*S.W.* Gen. Intro. 16) 'He was present when she reached the highest stage of her inward journey to the center of the soul where the Holy Trinity dwells, a stage she, and John himself, was later to refer to as 'spiritual marriage''.

56 *L.F.* 1.29 (*S.W.*, 300).

57 Mt. 27:51; Mk. 15:36; Lk. 23:45.

58 *L.F.* 1.29 (*S.W.*, 300/301).

The first two 'veils' are destroyed when 'all things of the world are renounced, all the natural appetites and affections mortified, and the natural operations of the soul divinised'[59]. These veils are the subject matter of the *Ascent of Mt Carmel* and the *Dark Night*. John does not wish these earlier operations to be forgotten where this 'flame' is felt in its 'oppressive' mode and the spiritual purgation is completed. When the third 'veil' encounters the 'flame', it is not 'harsh' but 'savorous and sweet' in its cauterising effect.

The third stanza refers to that 'sapientia' which both Augustine of Hippo and William of St Thierry described[60]:

> O lamps of fire!
> In whose *splendors*
> The deep caverns of feeling
> Once obscure and blind
> Now give forth, so rarely, so exquisitely,
> both warmth and light to their beloved[61].

The 'warmth' is the warmth of deep compassion generated by the fire which unites with the enlightenment of the understanding generated by the leaping flames to evoke the 'sapientia' which both knows and loves God, the beloved, at the same time. But the 'sapientia' is realised in a prayer of thanks for the beloved's gift of himself. The rare and exquisite quality of this divine wisdom which so harmoniously unites feeling and knowledge is recognised as it makes itself felt in the fourth stanza.

> How gently and lovingly
> You wake in my heart,
> Where in secret you dwell alone;
> And in your sweet breathing
> Filled with good and glory,
> How tenderly you swell my heart with love![62]

The essence of this awakening is also the essence of 'sapientia', wisdom. As John says, 'The soul knows creatures through God and not God through creatures'[63]. This amounts, he says, to knowing the effects through their cause and not the cause through its effects. The latter is knowledge *a posteriori*, and the former is 'essential knowledge'.

---

59 *Ibid.* (*S.W.*, 301).
60 St Augustine of Hippo. *Ep.* 140.45. P.L. 33:557, 'sapientia est caritas Dei'. William of St Thierry see N.54 above.
61 *L.F.* 3 (*S.W.*, 307) [my italics].
62 *L.F.* 4 (*S.W.*, 312/13).
63 *L.F.* 4.5 (*S.W.*, 314).

The center 'where in secret you dwell alone'[64] is true of all souls:

> Yet there is a difference, a great difference, in His dwelling in them. In some
> souls he dwells alone, and in others He does not dwell alone... He lives in some
> as though in His own house, commanding and ruling everything; and in others as
> though a stranger in a strange house, where they do not permit Him to give or-
> ders or to do anything.

He goes on to explain:

> Thus in this soul, in which neither appetite nor other images or forms nor any af-
> fections for created things dwell, the beloved dwells secretly with an embrace so
> much the closer, more intimate, and interior, the purer and more alone the soul is
> to everything other than God.

The soul which is gathered in the immediacy of this close embrace 'knows' what is
happening:

> Yet it is not secret to the soul itself that has attained this perfection, for within it-
> self it has the experience of this intimate embrace.

The stirring only occurs intermittently however. He uses the metaphor of 'sleep' to
explain; 'it seems to the soul that he is awakening in its heart, where before he remained as though asleep', and when still asleep 'knowledge and love are not communicated mutually'. Yet even while the beloved is resting there, the soul lives in
tranquillity which nothing can disturb. This seems to be that state of 'sapientia' of
the tradition. And were the beloved to be awake constantly John wonders what the
experience would be like for 'he has such an effect on the soul'.

In those souls that have not reached this state of perfection, 'the awakening is not of
this kind and high quality' but they are still able 'to understand something through
the movements of the senses'.

> For the senses are not fully annihilated until the soul reaches this union, and they
> still have some activity and movements concerning the spiritual, since they are
> not yet totally spiritual.

He does not wish to speak of the full awakening of the beloved in the heart because
he feels incapable of doing so other than what he has said in the last three lines of
the poem

> And in your sweet breathing

---

64 *L.F.* 4.14 (*S.W.*, 314).

Filled with good and glory,
How tenderly you swell my heart with love!

The discernment of this experience is a matter of recollection for while it is taking
place the soul is totally absorbed in it.

5. 'CRUCIFIXION' AND THE 'EMPTY TOMB': A REFLECTION ON 'DISCERNMENT'

We may now turn to consider firstly in what sense the life and teaching of John of
the Cross may represent some sort of apogee of the mediaeval tradition of 'discernment of spirits' and secondly how his achievement illuminates its role as mediating
the interlocking nature of the traditions within a living mystical tradition. At the
same time we may reflect, through John's experience, upon the manner in which the
late fourteenth-century mystics reflected a similar mediating role for the instrument
we have called 'discernment of spirits'.

We suggested that Ignatius of Loyola represented the apogee of the tradition of
'discernment of spirits' within an active, affirmative, perhaps evangelical, Pauline
spirituality. We wish now to suggest that John of the Cross represents the apogee of
the tradition of 'discernment' in the other wing of Christian spirituality, the Johannine. The Johannine experience underlies a tradition of contemplation which seems
to have influenced the *via negativa*. We do not wish to imply that the Ignatian 'kataphatic' way is not also 'contemplative'. Only that it is primarily concerned with
labour as an outcome of contemplation in the La Storta image of Christ carrying his
Cross as exemplified in St Paul's mission after his conversion. John of the Cross is
primarily concerned with *labour* in the sense of identifying with Christ in his crucifixion and death like St John the Evangelist at the foot of the Cross and later at the
empty tomb. The one is concerned with the experience of love as dying for the
world (John of the Cross), the other with that of enlivening it (Ignatius of Loyola).
Both are concerned with the resultant transfiguration as Christ mediated by the immediacy of his spirit reveals the 'unity', of Christ in his godhead and Christ in his
humanity, as divine love.

The Carmelite tradition in its discalced form is very much an extension of that of the
Desert Fathers which we saw exemplified in the lives and teaching of Cassian, the
Pseudo-Dionysius, and John Climacus[65]. It is interesting that we should identify the
via negativa as expounded by Pseudo-Dionysius, posing as the disciple of St Paul,
with an interpreter of Christian spirituality in the Johannine tradition. Yet of all
Christ's disciples, St John seems to be the one who dies with Christ as Mary, his
Mother, and Mary Magdalene did, experienced the empty tomb, and was transfig-
ured for a new life with him to manifest that in the unity of the godhead 'God is

---

65   See discussions in our Chap. I.

love'. By the same token, of course, St Paul dies to self in order to serve Christ actively in renewing the world. Yet the Pauline 'spirit' is very much a 'spirit' of selfless service in a world to be renewed 'actively' just as it had already been renewed mystically as, of course, Paul was well aware.

In their separate ways, therefore, Ignatius of Loyola and John of the Cross represent the Martha/Mary dichotomy in the biblical story. The one seeks out what must be done to 'win' the world while the other, John of the Cross, living in a world that is already mystically 'won', exemplifies the manner in which Mary's is the 'better part' by witnessing 'what God is' rather than 'what God wills', in the sense that the latter is subsumed in the former.

'Discernment of Spirits' has for John of the Cross almost an opposite meaning to that which it has for Ignatius. For him 'discernment' is about the abandonment of self in order to find the divinity and serve by proclaiming the nature of his presence within the community. For Ignatius 'discernment' is about finding oneself and how God wishes to be served in the gifts he has given each individual.

In the discerning relationship John of the Cross also exemplifies the Johannine tradition of spirituality which weaves its counterpoint through the mystical tradition. Knowing and experiencing are one in this relationship and the contemplative and the divinity are united in 'love' because in 'union' 'love' is the fulfilling experience of faith, that is 'knowing' without 'seeing'. It is the immediacy of the experience of 'being fulfilled in love', which John of the Cross expresses in the images and rhythms of poetry in the *Canticle* and the *Living Flame* as we have seen.

But John of the Cross also discerns that the ascesis which leads to love's fulfilment is a way of love. 'Love' in his interpretation of mystical theology begins as the gift of 'faith'. Faith grows in 'hope' into a fulfilment for those who are called into the relationship as 'betrothal' and 'spiritual marriage'. Without the extreme tempering of faith, similar to that which he himself experienced in the dungeon at Toledo which became for him, as it were, 'an empty tomb', the bridegroom will not recognise the trust which the intimacy of marriage requires. In a sense, therefore, John of the Cross married the spiritual experience of 'love' with its theological understanding as mystical knowledge similar to that experienced by those who remained with Christ as he died, for they later also experienced his resurrection as evidence of the creative life of love. The exposition of this growth in faith and its fulfilment in a new creative life is exemplified in John of the Cross' life and works. His testimony and witness particularly in 'spiritual direction' are his discernment of the spirit of unitive love in the contemplative tradition.

The *Cloud* Author, among the fourteenth-century mystics, is the one whose spirituality and discernment John of the Cross, as the apogee of the mediaeval contemplative tradition, most clearly illuminates. There are two particular ways in which the mystical experiences of the *Cloud* Author both resemble and differ from those of John of the Cross.

First of all John attempts to evoke the immediacy of the experience of divine union as 'love' which the *Cloud* Author cannot describe and is not even prepared to consider describing[66]. For the *Cloud* Author the experience is ineffable and by refusing to say more he emphasises its transcendent nature which his correspondents must experience for themselves. This seems to be his way of 'stirring' or encouraging those for whom he writes to persist in the 'work' of contemplation. They will 'know' when it is experienced. John of the Cross in the prose of the *Canticle* and the *Living Flame* attempts to satisfy the intellect of his readers as they seek a fuller explanation of his poetic images. In his other works, the *Ascent of Mount Carmel* and the *Dark Night*, he outlines the rigorous path to the summit of experience, of being lifted up on the cross, of the desolation represented by the empty tomb and of the resurrection. The *Cloud* Author leaves his readers in the clouds as Moses was on the Mountain. He perhaps does not know whether further revelations lie beyond his own experience. He is not prepared to compare his own experience with any other or with the spiritual betrothal and marriage like John of the Cross though he is aware of the traditional images of the *Song of Songs*[67]. There seems to be a contrast which perhaps reflects the circumstances of the times. The *Cloud* Author is aware that Rolle's attempts to describe the experience of the divine presence in the analogical terms of senses had been misunderstood by some of his admirers, who had been misled to seek physical signs of the divine presence. John of the Cross, on the other hand, seems to be overwhelmed by a sense of thanksgiving which he pours out in verse. His prose may be seen as corrective to avoid the type of misunderstanding which the *Cloud* Author feared, which the Alumbrados reflected and which the excesses of some Protestant reformers justified.

The second way in which the teaching of John of the Cross illuminates the work of the *Cloud* Author is the manner in which the process of ascesis is described. We have suggested that John of the Cross is concerned with burning away the 'veils' like cataracts obscuring the 'eye' of the soul which the world, the self and the senses interpose between the human spirit and the divine flame within the human soul. He regards the process as in part 'active' in the sense that it requires some human activity to enkindle the fire, like Mary Magdalene visiting Christ's tomb to find it empty,

---

66 See Chapter 3 and N.16 above. - However, John of the Cross explains in *ASC* 2. 26.1...3 in discussing 'spiritual visions':

'For an adequate exposition of this subject (the knowledge of naked truths), God would have to move my hand and pen. For you should know, beloved reader, that what they *in themselves* are for the soul is beyond words... People [however] are capable of describing [them] only through general expressions' (*S.W.*, 137) [my italics].

See also Nieva Constantino, 'The Cloud of Unknowing and St John of the Cross' in *Mt Carmel* 26, 1978, 79-89 and his *This Transcending God*, London: The Mitre Press, 1971.

67 See Chapter 3 and N.68 above.

and in part 'passive' requiring divine activity to fan the glowing embers into a flame. The final 'veil' of the body, though it may glow and become translucent in the heat of the flame in this life is not finally consumed until death. The human being, as it were, is gradually drawn into the flame which is the symbol of the God-head as the active and passive processes merge into one another, first the one pre-dominating and then the other. The 'veils', as it were, conceal the mysterious dark-ness of the soul as the bridal chamber which comes alight when penetrated by the flame of love. The contemplative proceeds from the false light of worldly and self-centred desires into the heart of the flame which cleanses it of falsehood but does not consume it in this life.

The *Cloud* Author plunges his correspondents into various intensities of darkness as they enter first the 'cloud of forgetting' in which they shed the clothing which has been besmirched by the mire of the world and become 'naked'. Then 'naked' they enter the 'cloud of unknowing' where they lose themselves in the impenetrable darkness, in the intensity of which they find themselves totally blind, groping to-wards the warmth of the 'dark ray' which draws them on to some unseen and inde-scribable consummation, where light dawns not revealing its source but purifying the world and the self in a new vision of faith. John recognises the bridegroom as the 'flame' and also sees the world anew in the light of his faith and love. For the *Cloud* Author, on the other hand, there is no bridegroom, no recognisable source of light, only the 'intense light' of total darkness which is blinding. There the *Cloud* Author leaves us at the sovereign point of the spirit where the loving creative process be-gins. He seems to wish to emphasise the passive nature of faith as the precursor of knowledge and love, rather than its active manifestation. The way of faith is a fol-lowing of the 'stirring' in darkness. The end is unknown until it is reached at the 'sovereign point'[68].

John of the Cross is totally committed to the transformation process which Teresa of Avila had initiated in the Carmelite order in Spain. That movement perhaps contin-ues the renewal process in the old Church which was reflected in earlier movements such as the *recogidos* within the Franciscans and that initiated in the *Devotio Mod-erna* by the Brethren of the Common Life in the Netherlands - where in fact the first Carmelite houses for nuns had been founded[69]. In John's lifetime in Spain the

---

68 See also J.P.H. Clark, 'The Cloud of Unknowing, Walter Hilton and St John of the Cross; a Comparison' in *Downside Review*, vol. 96, 1978.

69 *S.W.*, 10-13, concerning *recogidos* suggests a link between the Teresian reform and its empha-sis on smaller communities and the reaction against the anti-intellectual tone, especially among Franciscans, which emphasised community vocal prayer. The emphasis on 'recollection', from which *recogidos* derives, was one of those general reactions of which the *Devotio Moderna* it-self was an example. See for example Oliver Davies, *'God Within': The Mystical Tradition of Northern Europe*, London: Darton, Longman and Todd, 1988. Teresa, as noted, was influenced by Francisco de Osuna and others who espoused the *recogidos* 'Movement'. It was sometimes difficult to distinguish between *recogidos* and the more extreme *alumbrados*. The line of de-

movement towards the renewal process in religious orders was encouraged, as we have seen, by the belief which Phillip II and his father, Charles V, apparently shared, that the Reformation was brought about by the indiscipline of the religious orders[70]. For Teresa and John transformation did not mean 'reform' so much, as a return to the original inspiration of their order by reverting to the contemplative ideal rather than that of an 'active' mendicant order. The 'mendicant' rule had been adopted when the order was re-established in Europe after the failure of the Crusades to regain the Holy Land where the order had found its contemplative inspiration. In the sixteenth century the opposition which this change in the way of life faced within the Carmelite order stimulated, in a climate in which 'reformation' was an ambiguous process, as it were, a *creative articulation* not only of the contemplative way of life but also of its inspiration and theological basis.

The *Cloud* Author, from his asides, was evidently aware of some scepticism among his contemporaries ('actives! actives' he sighs) about the worth of the contemplative life as the most spiritual affirmation of Christian faith. Yet his inspiration does not seem to come from the opposition of sceptics. It seems to derive from a conviction bred by an experience and a tradition that faith must precede understanding, which leads him to articulate his understanding of the contemplative life, primarily at the request of others, drawn to him, perhaps, by his lifestyle, literacy, and witness. Unfortunately, we can only speculate about the background of his convictions since we know nothing of the *Cloud* Author's early life and little of his subsequent vocation.

For both John of the Cross and the *Cloud* Author 'discernment of spirits' seems indistinguishable from 'faith' in the last resort. Faith is experienced as 'hope' and 'love'. 'Discernment' recognises the spirit, in other words, experienced as faith and hope and love as progressive and cumulative stages of development. 'Discernment' is a reflective process, best perhaps evoked in its fulfilment by some lines of another poet, not Keats but T.S. Eliot:

> And what the dead had no speech for, when living,
> they can tell you, being dead; the communication
> of the dead is tongued with fire beyond the
>   language of the living.
> Here, the intersection of the timeless moment
> Is England and nowhere. Never and always[71].

Dying to the world and self in faith restores the anagogic vision of love and the *sapientia* of tradition which is stateless and ageless.

---

marcation between orthodoxy and heterodoxy was, and seems still to be, a fine one. See for foundation of Carmelite nuns *Oxford Dictionary of the Christian Church*, 'Carmelite Order', 240.

70 *S.W.*, 19.
71 T.S. Eliot, 'Four Quartets. Little Gidding I' in *Collected Poems 1909-1962*, London: Faber & Faber, ed. 1963, repr. 1983, 215.

EPILOGUE

Peter Brown concludes the Epilogue to his work *The Body and Society* which is about 'Men, Women and Sexual Renunciation in Early Christianity' with some observations which are instructive for us. He says:

> Early Christian themes of sexual renunciation ... carry with them 'icy overtones'[1].

He goes on to suggest that through the historical connection between the Roman Empire, the Middle Ages and our own times, 'these notions still crowd in upon us, as pale, forbidding presences'. The task of historians he suggests is to

> bring to them [these themes] their due measure of warm red blood. By studying their precise social and religious context, the scholar can give back to these ideas a little of the human weight that they once carried in their own time.

Furthermore, 'when such an offering is made':

> the chill shades may speak to us again, and perhaps more gently than we had thought they might, in the strange *tongue* of a long-lost Christianity.

Our own work has in part been concerned with similar ascetic themes to those of sexual renunciation which Peter Brown developed with such depth and range of scholarship. We cannot lay claim however to have undertaken such a 'precise' study of the social and religious context in which our mystics produced their texts. We have only attempted to sketch the change of mood and aspiration between the periods and the changing 'tongues' which frame our theme. Our theme has been the tradition of 'discernment of spirits' as it develops out of the experiences of individuals who have journeyed along the mystic road. But at the same time we hope our study has given some 'human weight' to the attempts of mystics to exchange the

---

1 Peter Brown, *The Body and Society. Men, Women and Sexual Renunciation in Early Christianity*, London: Faber & Faber, 1990 (first published New York: Columbia University Press, 1988), 446.

warmth of human relationships for a more lasting warmth in the divine touch and its ecstatic denouement in the spiritual marriage and 'the living flame of love'.

There is something 'forbidding' about the heroic self-sacrifice which the mystic journey seems to demand. This is despite the reassurances which the mystics provide about the compensations and the ultimate fulfilment which may be achieved. Moreover, the achievement of the mystics often seems not so much an encouragement but a mirror in which we may see displayed our own deficiencies of love. To read their texts is to be reminded of the divine longing and our own matching but inchoate desires for recognition. The mystics in church history cannot be ignored however much we may wish to overlook them. We find ourselves asking whether their experiences of the divine love which we see reflected before us are real or whether they are 'an illusion'. If we decide the experiences are 'real' we can scarcely ignore their message; if they are illusions, many of the moral imperatives which still inform our hopes for an unselfish society are also perhaps quixotic delusions. Our theme about the way the mystics authenticate what is happening to them, is a challenging one; one which carries 'human weight' and may stir the 'warm red blood', even today.

When we attempt to unfreeze the texts of the mystics, what then do we discover? Certainly people who describe a *via amoris*. Can we be sure that they have really trodden that road and experienced the ultimate goal? This is not really the historical question we have been exploring, but our story may perhaps suggest an answer. The texts themselves are the evidence that the authors believed they had experienced something of surpassing value which has influenced them. Through their preservation the texts have influenced others who come after them. It is this influence, the creativity of a living tradition, and the manner in which it has been appropriated that has been our subject. What seems to be evident is that the task of appropriation has not been dependent on particular influences, although sometimes these appear to be dominant but on active participation in a complex religious culture which finds its focus in an institutional church but a church which surpasses itself as an institution to become a communion with a living spirit, a spiritual community informed by a mystical tradition. Part of that culture is the cumulative experience we have called 'discerning the spirits' in which the participants 'feel' the 'stirring' of the spirit and seek to identify and join that which beckons them to participate in its being. In becoming aware of the 'real', they also become aware of its illusory 'shadow' which leads nowhere. Paradoxically it is often the 'will o' the wisp' of the shadow which leads them 'to turn' to understand the reality which is foreshadowed.

'Turning' is a key concept. Kenneth Burke in his illuminating study, the *Rhetoric of Religion*, analyses the use of the term by Augustine of Hippo in the *Confessions* in relation to his 'conversion'. Augustine refers to 'God having converted him

[Augustine] to Him' (*conversisti enim me ad te*)[2]. He must have felt that some power beyond, and yet within him, had turned him in order for him to be turned. The 'conversion' occasion was when he heard the child chanting 'tolle lege' and he opened the Bible at *Romans* 13:13-14 and read:

> Not in rioting and drunkenness, not in chambering and wantonness, not in strife and envying; but put ye on the Lord Jesus Christ and make not provision for the flesh, to fulfil the lusts therof[3].

Suddenly all 'shadows' of doubt dispersed (*cum fine huisce sententiae quasi luce securitatis infusa cordi meo omnes dubitationis tenebrae diffugerunt*). The 'turning' is primarily an intellectual rather than a moral conversion as light is infused into the intellect and suddenly things and conduct are seen from a different perspective. Augustine regards this as an opening of the mind in which the mystic veils are removed (*remoto mystico velamento*)[4] . The Bible is said to express itself in 'words most open' (*verbis apertissimis*) while at the same time preserving the dignity of the secret. Ambrose had previously 'laid open' the Bible to him by interpreting some things figuratively, but it was not until that moment in the garden that he could conceive of something spiritual except in terms of the body, that is, words with a spiritual content. He interprets the changed perspective as a transference of love from one kind of object to the other[5]. In *De Trinitate* he explains the transference theologically in trinitarian terms as analogous to the love of the Father for the Son. The 'love' is the third person of the Trinity, the Holy Spirit. By analogy the transfer of love between corporeal objects through a spiritual medium is like an opening up of the imagination through the medium of a change in the operating mode from analogical to 'anagogic'.

This Augustinian explanation of the ability of the imagination to change its mode of operation from corporeal to spiritual through a revitalisation of the spiritual senses is an important feature in the development of the tradition of discernment of spirits. The revitalisation is brought about by an external agency working through the senses which feed the memory with different modes of 'image' than it has hitherto been accustomed to receive. The bodily senses are not replaced in the change of operation. They are complemented by the revitalisation of the spiritual senses. The point is important because the images received through the bodily senses continue to provide temptations and weaken the will. So Augustine makes clear his conversion is intellectual rather than moral.

---

2 Kenneth Burke, *Rhetoric of Religion*, University of California Press, 1970, 117, quoting Augustine, *Confessions* viii, xii. He notes a similar passage in Jeremiah 31:18: 'Converte me et convertar'.

3 *Ibid.*, 116 quoting Augustine, *Confessions* viii, xii.

4 *Ibid.*, 61 quoting Augustine, *Confessions*, vi, iv.

5 *Ibid.*, 86, quoting Augustine, *De Trinitate*, v, xi.

The facet of the tradition of discernment of spirits which deals with the moral conversion seems to have been developed by Cassian and John Climacus from the experience of the Desert Fathers and the Alexandrine School of exegists with whose work they were apparently familiar. Peter Brown in his *The Body and Society*, to which we have already referred, makes an interesting comparison between Cassian's and Augustine's views on moral conversion:

> The transparency that John Cassian associated with the gift of 'purity of heart' was shown in the body by the ebbing of the sexual drive. But the gift was won only through a struggle with the heart itself, in the slow and intricate untwisting of the private will. If Augustine disagreed with Cassian, it was not because he believed that the body's instincts were any stronger or more corrupt: rather he held that the most humble details of the body's experience of sexuality …mirrored a failure of the will more drastic and irrevocable than Cassian had been prepared to admit[6].

For Augustine, sexual temptations seemed to continue to surface in his consciousness throughout his life despite his constant battle to purge them. He seemed to doubt that the kind of 'purity' or transparency which Cassian believed could be achieved was possible for the human soul to attain in this life. Augustine's belief made him sceptical that a contemplative 'union' was possible. He came to symbolise the 'active' in the church community whose role was to do 'more' to establish Christ's kingdom on earth by attempting to live as a Christian in a pagan world, cooperating with the abundant graces which were available and which he had himself received, through no merit of his own, in all their abundance.

The 'purity of heart' and the 'dispassion' which both Cassian and Climacus believed could be achieved by the monks, through the graces mediated by meditation on Scripture and a strict regimen of ascetic practice, provided the *sine qua non* for the contemplative life. Without purity or dispassion they agreed with Augustine divine union or divinisation was improbable if not impossible. They both understood the contemplative existence to be a progress in which moral, intellectual and spiritual development proceeded in parallel. However until such time as 'transparency' had been achieved, until the self had, as it were, disappeared, discernment of spirits was likely to be imperfect. They therefore placed emphasis on the role of the spiritual director, as a tutor, in monitoring spiritual development and on humility and obedience in the contemplative in cooperating with the direction. In this interpretation the acquisition of the 'virtue' of discernment is progressive but until such time as the contemplatives are adjudged 'expert' they are to distrust their own judgement in matters of their own experience of spiritual progress and formation.

---

6   Peter Brown, *The Body and Society*, *op.cit.*, 433.

The final contribution which we identified in the formative phase of the experience of discernment was that of the Pseudo-Dionysius. Dionysius was not the founder of the apophatic tradition of spirituality but he was perhaps the most rigorous interpreter of a tradition of exegesis which Gregory of Nyssa's *Life of Moses* was perhaps hitherto the most well-known example. In his *Mystical Theology*, Pseudo-Dionysius, as we have seen, took the intellectual pursuit of divine union to a conclusion from which Augustine had perhaps resiled believing the gulf between creature and creator could not be traversed in this life. Dionysius agreed that the gulf was 'infinite'. The divinity was unknowable in its essence. Much might be affirmed about its nature as he had shown in the *Divine Names* but when all that could be affirmed had been written, the divinity was still unknown in its essence. The paradox of 'knowing' the divinity by 'unknowing' became the ultimate achievement of the apophatic contemplative existence. The divinity was 'known' in the ecstatic union to which the negative way might lead. But it was 'dark' knowledge in which the 'splendour' of the 'vision' which participative union produced was 'blinding' and left the contemplative 'transparent' in the projection of its light through the transfiguration which was the phenomenological characteristic of the experience but yet unaware of its essential nature. Certainly it can be said that Dionysius added an intellectual dimension to the tradition of 'discernment of spirits' by affirming that however much 'discernment' might be sought in the formation of the contemplative, in the final silence the attempt to discern must itself be abandoned. We have seen the *Cloud* Author and John of the Cross wrestling with the practical consequences of these insights for the contemplative in their day.

The late fourteenth-century mystics inherited a form of Christian culture which had thoroughly ingested the idea of mystical experience. The landmarks of this culture we have suggested were exemplified in the works of Dante and Chaucer. The mysterious evocative spirituality of Beatrice and Becket was a reality in the consciousness of the times. It was recognisable to the audiences Dante and Chaucer addressed as a hidden layer of reality which existed within the materiality of the world around them. It is not surprising that there were those both on the Continent and in England who were experiencing these hidden spirits with intensity. None of the English mystics whose experiences we have discussed, seem to have sought out an experience of the divine. They tell us the divine spirit has sought them. Even the *Cloud* Author who appears to be addressing a young man who is wondering whether he should dedicate his whole life to contemplative prayer, is first and foremost concerned with the kind of 'stirring' the young man is experiencing. Julian of Norwich, as a child, had wished for an experience of Christ's suffering so that she might appreciate its magnitude. However, the *Showings* she experienced, when they came, were unexpected and unsought. Walter Hilton goes so far as to suggest he had not consciously experienced the watershed which marks off a 'reformation in faith and feeling' he is discussing. It is something, a gift, the recipient is unaware of until it happens. All these mystics are conscious of the magnetic pull of the divine spirit, and their concern is to guide those who experience its insistence and power.

In fact the unexpected nature of the experience is for all these English mystics the main indication that it is an authentic experience of the divine grace. They warn against the dangers of seeking spiritual graces of an overt physical kind such as those which Richard Rolle was thought to be advocating. There is the same conscious awareness of the reality of evil spirits as Cassian, in particular, warned against. Spirits which led the unwary to destruction, were exemplified by the excesses of some Brethren of Free Spirit and Beguines on the Continent. An authentic experience of the grace of a divine 'touch' was characterised by personal self-effacement and great devotion. Julian is particularly disturbed by the thought that she is the recipient of a prophetic vision which she is expected to make known to her fellow Christians.

On the other hand, all the mystics are equally adamant that a genuine and authentic mystical experience should be cultivated once it becomes evident, first as a powerful stirring and finally as some fulfilling participation in the divine love. The love from first to last is the same, but the experience of its fulfilling intensity has to be cultivated and the recipient guided towards its fulfilment. The quality to be cultivated is a progressively more refined spiritual consciousness. This is the area in which the affirmative and negative ways diverge in their practice.

The *Cloud* Author, as we have seen, is addressing those who are already 'proficients' and are being stirred powerfully towards a 'perfection' of whose demands they are only dimly aware. They have fulfilled the ascetic and meditative regimens of their states in life but have not attained the tranquillity and perfect peace which they had sought in the contemplative vocation. The *Cloud* Author takes them on the final stage of the journey which Dionysius had foreshadowed in his *Mystical Theology*. It is essentially now a passive way, the way of final ascent, according to the *Cloud* Author. The principal worker is the Holy Spirit. So the prospective contemplatives seeking perfection, are instructed how to concentrate their longing by excluding all images from their minds and proceeding in blind faith to offer their whole beings to God. As in the case of Dionysius, discernment is abandoned because God in this participative union remains hidden and unknowable until the contemplative is drawn into the silence of participative union. The nature of the union the *Cloud* Author cannot reveal. Unlike Dionysius, however, he emphasises the consciousness of divine love as the spiritual reality which is experienced. Dionysius it will be recalled, was concerned with the divine 'light' which irradiated and transfigured the human being. For the *Cloud* Author it was an experience of 'union' or spiritual marriage rather than divinisation analogous perhaps, the *Cloud* Author concedes, to the human experience of 'love' but beyond description. The touch of the divinity is one of caring in which the human becomes aware of the joy of being loved and responds in an inexplicable abandonment.

The affirmative way is described by Hilton. He is addressing the needs of actives and contemplatives both lay and religious. The affirmative way is one of reformation, even in its final stages. It is the Augustinian 'turning' first in faith which is both moral and intellectual, and then in faith and feeling. The feeling expresses Augustine's transference of love. In this case, however, the transference is from Christ who has been the guide in the earlier stages, to the Trinitarian godhead, who is recognised in the Holy Spirit as the 'love' of the Father for the Son. Reformation in feeling becomes, as it were, a participation in the love which is the unitive nature of the Trinitarian God. It is perhaps fitting that this unique insight of Augustine of Hippo is expressed by a person who late in life has become an Augustinian canon. The discernment of spirits however has Christ as its touchstone. He is the exemplar of the Divine Spirit and the Christian follows Christ into the darkness of night in which sin is finally cleansed. The Christian emerges with Christ into the divine love which joins Christ to the Father in the light of the new dawn.

Julian recognises the same type of affirmative approach as Hilton. Her experience of the mystic way is christological and her visions of the Crucifixion lead into an understanding of the Trinitarian nature of the Divine being. However, she also recognises that the visions and locutions whose full meaning she discerns through infusions of intuitive insights, are not the usual mode through which divine being is recognised. So in Julian's work we find a very strong emphasis being placed on conformity with Church teaching. The role of the Church in the discernment process is not emphasised to the same degree by either of the other mystics. With them it seems to be taken for granted, though with the *Cloud* Author, in particular, the possibility of an unsympathetic Church response is recognised. 'Actives' he seems to say cannot be expected to understand the 'contemplative' vocation. 'Contemplatives' will have to rely on the guidance of other experienced 'contemplatives' in their work.

When we come to the Spanish mystics of the sixteenth century, we see these traditions of affirmative and negative approaches more rigorously delineated. The teaching on discernment of spirits is correspondingly delineated with greater emphasis by Ignatius of Loyola and with lesser by John of the Cross. As might be expected at a time of crisis in the Church's existence, the role of the Church becomes more prominent as the final arbiter of authenticity.

In the teaching of John of the Cross the passivity of the negative way is more starkly evident because we are aware of his highly developed aesthetic sensibility and his gifts in articulating his experience of divine love in poetic images of surpassing intensity. The stripping away of imagery and the tearing aside of the veils of the world and the self, nevertheless, like the same operations in the *Cloud* Author's teaching, have active and passive components. They involve the contemplative in 'active' passivity as the divine touch dries out the final vestiges of resistance from the natural powers of the soul to bring about the eruption of the flame in which the transfiguration and the radical conversion to a divinely orientated perspective occur. The *Cloud* Author scarcely dares imagine he is living, as it were, the divine life.

John of the Cross is boldly aware not only of his new existence but also of the path he journeyed to achieve it. It has been not so much an incarnational experience as a transfiguration and reincarnation. The reincarnation takes the form of a renewal of the roots of his order on Mount Carmel which like the renewal of the Church itself in his day would only come about through its crucifixion.

He refers to the experience, however, not as a reincarnation but as a spiritual marriage. It takes place in the dimension of 'Night' where the 'living flame of love' is the only evidence of divine existence as it gently heals and cauterises the wounds which the tearing of the 'veils' has created. The world and self are forgotten as the metamorphosis takes place in the final union. The passivity of the human being enables it to see and remember in the Night. Rebirth, as it were, is the product of the spiritual marriage, in a kind of reincarnation. John discerns all this with the senses darkened in a new dimension of sensing, anagogic in intensity and essence but analogical in its imaginative expression.

The contrast between the negative way of John of the Cross and the affirmative way of Ignatius of Loyola seems to be much greater than that between the *Cloud* Author and either of Walter Hilton or Julian of Norwich. The difference perhaps reflects not only the seemingly very different backgrounds and personalities of the mystics themselves but also the greater urgency for renewal of Christian life in their times. Certainly the latter part of the fourteenth century in England seems to have been a period of social, political, economic and religious disorientation. The tensions however were not as pressing as in the sixteenth century, where the disintegration of the Church seemed also to threaten the state and certainly the political ambitions of Charles V and Phillip II of Spain. John of the Cross and Ignatius of Loyola were already living in the world of the Reformation; the fourteenth-century English mystics were hardly more than conscious of its first rumblings in England in the writings of Wycliffe and the Lollard movement and, in the wider community, of 'conciliarism' as a reaction to the Great Schism. Nor were they yet fully aware of the question these developments might pose about the authority and authenticity of the Magisterium itself. In the sixteenth century the Magisterium was itself only too aware, if perversely at times, of the threat to which its authority and authenticity was exposed.

We have suggested that the background of hidalgo and soldier in the formation of Ignatius of Loyola influenced the presentation of his spirituality. On the other hand, we have been careful to observe that the course of his life and work were not formatively influenced by any religious polemical or apologetic intent in regard to the Protestant reformers. On the contrary, his early aspirations were directed to the Moslem threat with which his forebears had struggled for centuries. His ambition was to carry the missionary zeal, which had earlier led to the defeat of the Moslems in Spain, off-shore into the Moslem and Christian heartland on the Eastern littoral of the Mediterranean.

We do not wish to exaggerate the influence of Ignatius' military background at the expense of his religious conversion, but the same characteristics of energy, determination, and organisational skill pervaded his life in both the earlier and later phases. No-one could have been better suited to carry the standard of an active spirituality concerned with promoting Christ's kingdom in its besieged condition in the first half of the sixteenth century.

We have suggested that he approached the task of promoting the Kingdom like a military strategist. The *Spiritual Exercises* are presented like a concise set of orders to a military commander. The essential features are the recognition of the deployment and resources of both one's own troops and the enemy and also of the unforeseen occurrence. In order to be confident in the deployment of one's own strength, it was necessary to get into the very mind of the enemy so that his tactics could be anticipated. More than that, one should appreciate that the enemy was desperate, showed no mercy, and took no prisoners. The battle in which those undertaking the *Spiritual Exercises* were to be engaged was a fight to the death. Before entering such a conflict, however, it was essential to recognise and purge one's own weaknesses.

The contrast between Ignatius and John recalls that between Augustine and Cassian not in its similarity but in the change of intellectual scenario. Augustine and Cassian were at odds about the capacity of the human will to influence its own direction; Cassian being more optimistic than Augustine. Ignatius and John of the Cross were never at odds in a direct sense of course. Yet Ignatius was concerned with influencing others by spelling out the terms of the election which confronted them in all its emotional, sensory and intellectual drama. John did not present a choice. He presented a way; a way which was every bit as hard and difficult as the choice which Ignatius presented but which offered not a vista of additional elections and hardships in defence of the Kingdom, but a fulfilment of surpassing joy in the heart of the Kingdom.
The difference was not about grace and its relationship to the human will as with Augustine and Cassian which was essentially 'theological', but about spiritual fulfilment; on the one hand in participative love, and on the other in service. Where we may ask do the fourteenth-century English mystics fit into this changing emphasis in the discernment of spiritual direction? Something of both the earlier and later emphases seem to be apparent in the teaching. The issues surrounding the relationship of grace and the human will are still pervasive but human will is of lesser consequence than divine love. The later emphasis on the complementary natures of love and service is only partly evident. Hilton is beginning to wrestle with the problem of spiritual fulfilment as recognised in the contemplative tradition, but as it might be transposed to the life of an active whether secular or lay. The tension is apparent in the mystery surrounding the transference of love from Christ as the active exemplar, to the Trinity in its contemplative unity. Between the writing of Books one and two of the *Scale of Perfection* he seems to have worked out his solution. The *Cloud* Author does not seem to recognise a complementarity between love and service. Rather

he recognises a progression from service to unitive love. Julian's message does not fit into an either/or mould. Her message is about the continuity and nature of divine love and the need to trust that it will lead to human fulfilment. Moreover, the teaching of the Church is not at odds with her message; there are simply two orders of existence, spiritual and temporal and they exist together in the lives of each individual. The Church provides the means through which each individual may find fulfilment providing they 'seek' trustfully.

To the extent that the tradition of discernment of spirits traverses the search for spiritual fulfilment in the human being, we may recognise a 'Departure', a stop along the journey and an 'Arrival'. The arrival, of course, is not the end of the journey but it marks an important junction in the historical development of the tradition beyond which the tradition does not take active and contemplative forks. The journey now proceeds not perhaps in union but in parallel, the one aspect complementary to the other[7].

Peter Brown, as we noted at the beginning of this 'Epilogue', refers to 'the strange tongue of a long-lost Christianity'. Yet a church which can produce in 1993 an Encyclical which echoes in its opening words the Dionysian theme of the unspeakable 'Veritatis Splendor' is not entirely 'lost' even if the 'tongue' seems strange to some[8]. The Encyclical attempts to join itself to a tradition of moral teaching which it traces from its seminal source in the past. Whether its 'word' is heard in the babel of this age is another matter and this may be Peter Brown's point. As we have seen 'discerning' the 'strange tongue' according to the mystical tradition is 'discerning the spirit' of 'love' as 'real', and yet beyond human expectations of 'reality', as it makes itself felt in individuals in communion with the spirit in the Church. The 'communion' occurs within the 'cultural ambiance' which binds the imagination of the individual, analogically and anagogically, to the origins of its being. The mystics of the late fourteenth century in England and of the sixteenth in Spain no less than those in preceding and following periods appropriate the experience of the past when they attempt to discern the spirits which make their lives in a Church which 'teaches with authority' neither comfortable nor comfortless, joyful nor joyless, neither hurtless nor hurtful. Their experience, as it is transmitted by their texts, we may recognise even today, unfrozen and coursing with 'warm red blood':

> We are born with the dead;
> See, they return, and bring us with them[9].

---

7   See for example Jean-Pierre de Caussade S.J. and his *Abandonment to Divine Providence*, trans. John Beavers, New York: Doubleday, 1975, which seems to embrace the Ignatian concept of divine providence and the 'abandonement of self' of John of the Cross.

8   *Veritatis Splendor. Encyclical Letter of John Paul II on certain Fundamental Questions of the Church's Moral Teaching*, Homebush, N.S.W.: St Pauls, 1993.

9   T.S. Eliot, 'Four Quarters. Little Gidding V' in *Collected Poems 1909-1962*, London: Faber and Faber, 1983, 222.

SELECT BIBLIOGRAPHY

Primary Sources

Ancrene Riwle, Eng. trans. M.B. Salu with intro. by G. Sitwell O.S.B., Orchard Books, 1955.

Anselm, St., *Tractatus de Concordia Praescientia et Praedestinationis nec non Gratiae Dei cum Libero Arbitria* (PL. 158.522).

Aquinas, Thomas, *Works* in the 'VIVES' ed. S.E. Fretté and others, 34 vols, Paris, 1871-80.

Aristotle, *Metaphysica*, Trans. John Warrington, London: Dent, 1956.

Augustine of Hippo: The following translations have been used: The Latin texts in *Corpus Scriptorum Ecclesiasticorum Latinorum*, Vienna, 1866 ff. and in *Patrologia Cursus Completus*, Series Latina, Ed. J.P. Migne, Paris, 1844-1864, Vols 32-47, are shown in brackets.
- *Confessions*, Trans. E.B. Pusey, London: J. Dent & Sons Ltd. (Everyman edition), 1953. (CSEL 33, 1-388 and PL. 32, 659-868)
- *The City of God*, Trans. J. Healy, Ed. R.V.G. Tasker, London: J.M. Dent & Sons Ltd. (Everyman edition), repr. 1950. (CSEL 40, I.3-660; 40, II.1-670 and PL. 41, 13-804)
- Augustine, *Earlier Writings*, Ed. J.H.S. Burleigh, Philadelphia: Library of Christian Classics, Westminster Press, 1953, contains:
 - *Soliloquia* (PL. 32, 869-904)
 - *De Magistro* (PL. 32, 1193-1220)
 - *De Libero Arbitrio* (PL. 32, 1221-1310)
 - *De Vera Religione* (PL. 34, 121-172)
 - *De Utilitate Credendi* (CSEL, 25, 3-48 and PL. 42, 63-92d)
 - *De Fide et Symbolo* (CSEL, 41, 3-32 and PL. 40, 181-196)
 - *De Diversis Questionibus* (PL. 40, 11-100)
- Augustine, *Later Works*, Ed. John Burnaby, Philadelphia: Library of Christian Classics, Westminster Press, 1955, contains:
 - *The Trinity*. Books VIII-XV (PL. 42, 819-1098)
 - *The Spirit and the Letter* (CSEL 60, 155-229 and PL. 44, 201-246)
 - *The Homilies on the First Epistle General of St John* (PL. 35, 1379ff.)
- *Expositions on the Book of Psalms* (*Enarrationes in Psalmos*), Ed. from the six volumes of the Oxford Translation by A. Cleveland Coxe, 1888, Nicene and Post-Nicene Fathers, First Series, Vol. viii. (PL. 37, 1033-1968)
- *De Doctrina Christiana* (PL. 34, 14-122)
- *Epistolae*, 1-270 (CSEL Vols 34, 44, 57, 58 and PL. 33, 61-1162)
- *Sermones*, 1-363 (PL. 38, 23-1484; 39, 1493-2354)
- *De Quantitate Animae* (PL 32, 1035-1080)

- *Quaestiones Evangeliorum Ex Matthaeo et Luca II* (PL. 35.1321-1364)

Baker, Augustine, *Holy Wisdom*, Ed. G. Sitwell, London, 1964.

Bernard of Clairvaux, *Sancti Bernardi Opera*, Ed. J. Leclercq, C.H. Talbot, H.M. Rochais, Rome, 1957, 1958, 1963, Vols 1-3.
----- *De Diligendo Deo*, Trans. 'On the Love of God' by Religious of the Community of St Mary the Virgin, London and Oxford, 1950.

Boethius, *De Consolatione Philosophiae*, Ed. Ludovicus Bieler, Turnholti Bredols (CCSL 94), Trans. S.J. Tester, London: Heinemann, 1973.

Bonaventure, St., Crit. Ed. of his *Works* by the Franciscans of Quaracchi, 10 vols, 1882-1902 (Eng. trans. of his works J. de Vinck, 5 vols, Patterson, N.J., 1960-70).

Book of Holy Men, Latin trans. of Pelagius and John The Deacon as Books V and VI of Rosweyd's *Vitae Patrium*, Ed. J.P. Migne PL. LXXIII Cols 851-1022, entitled *Verba Seniorum*.

Bridget of Sweden, *Revelations*, Ed. C. Durante, 2 vols, Rome, 1628 and a 15th Cent. Eng. Selection of Extracts, ed. P. Cummings, E.E.T.S. clxxviii, 1929.

Cassian, John, *Cassiani Opera Omnia*, Ed. A. Gazet, Douai, 1616, Reprinted J.P. Migne, PL XLIX-L.
----- *Collationes*, Crit. Ed. M. Petschenig in CSEL xiii, 1886 (Fr. trans. E. Pechery, O.S.B., Paris: *Sources Chrétiennes*, xlii, liv, lxiv, 1955-9).
----- *Conferences*, Eng. trans. Colin Luibheid, New York: Paulist Press, 1985.
----- *De Institutis Coenobiorum*, Crit. Ed. M. Petschenig in CSEL xvii, 1888 (Fr. trans. J.C. Guy, S.J., *Sources Chrétiennes* CIX, Paris, 1965).

Cervantes, M. de, *Don Quixote de la Mancha*, Trans. C. Jarvis, Ed. E.C. Riley, Oxford University Press, 1992.

The Chastising of God's Children and the Treatise of Perfection of the Sons of God, Ed. J. Bazire and E. Colledge, Oxford: Blackwell, 1957.

Chaucer, Geoffrey,
1. Middle English
- *The Canterbury Tales*, Ed. A.C. Cawley, London: J.M. Dent, 1958, repr. 1991.
2. Modern English
- *The Canterbury Tales*, Trans. N. Coghill, Penguin Books, 1977.
- *Troilus and Criseyde*, Trans. N. Coghill, Penguin Books, 1971.

Climacus, John, *The Ladder of Divine Ascent*, Eng. trans. Archmandrite Lazarus Moore, London: Faber & Faber, 1959 (*Scala Paradisi*, ed. Matthew Rader, Paris, 1633; PG. lxxxviii, Cols 569-1209).
----- *The Ladder of Divine Ascent*, Eng. trans. Colin Luibheid and Norman Russell, London: S.P.C.K., (Classics of Western Spirituality), 1982.

Cloud Author,
1. Middle English Versions
- *The Cloud of Unknowing and Related Treatises* (*The Book of Privy Counselling*; *The Epistle of Prayer*; *The Epistle of Discretion*; *Hid Divinity*; *Benjamin Minor, the Study of Wisdom*; *Of Discerning Spirits*), Ed. P. Hodgson, Salzburg, Austria: Institut für Anglistik und Amerikanistik, Exeter: Catholic Records Press, 1982.

- *The Cloud of Unknowing and the Book of Privy Counselling*, Ed. P. Hodgson, E.E.T.S., O.S. 218 (1944, 1958, 1973).
- *Deonise Hid Diuinity*, (Contains also *A Tretyse of þe Stodye of Wysdome þat Men Clepen Beniamyn, A Pistle of Preier, A Pistle of Discrecioun of Stirings; A Tretis of Discrescyon of Spirites*), Ed. P. Hodgson, E.E.T.S. O.S. 231, London, 1955, 1958.
2. Some modernised Versions in English
- Johnston, W., *The Cloud of Unknowing and the Book of Privy Counselling*, New York, 1973.
- McCann, J., *The Cloud of Unknowing and Other Treatises* (*The Epistle of Privy Counsel, Denis Hid Divinity* and a commentary on *The Cloud* by Fr. Augustine Baker), London, 1924, sixth and revised edition 1952, Reprinted 1960.
- Wolters, C., *The Cloud of Unknowing and Other Works* (*Epistle of Privy Counsel, Dionise Hid Divinite, Epistle of Prayer*), Penguin Books, 1978.
- Wolters, C., *A Study of Wisdom* (*Epistle of Prayer, Epistle of Discretion of Stirrings, Benjamin Minor*), Fairacres, Oxford: S.L.G. Press, 75, 1980.

Dante Alighieri, *The Divine Comedy*, Trans. D.L. Sayers and B. Reynolds, Penguin Books, 1955, 1962 (Also trans. C.H. Sisson, Carcarnet New Press, 1980 - unrhymed verse.).
----- *Works*, Temple Classics edition (Dent) in 6 vols [Text and Prose trans. on opposite pages] contain the *Commedia* 3 vols, and *Vita Nuova* and *Canzoniere* 1 Vol., and 2 vols contain *Convivio* and Latin Works in English.
----- *The Letters of Dante*, Ed. Paget Toynbee, Oxford: Clarendon, 1920.
----- *Vita Nuova*, Trans. with Intro. by Mark Musa, Oxford: Oxford University Press, 1992.

Erasmus, Desiderius, *Christian Humanism and the Reformation. Selected Writings*, Ed. John C. Olin, New York: Harper Torchbooks, 1965.
----- *The Praise of Folly*, Trans. Leonard F. Dean, Chicago, 1946.

Flete, William, *De Remediis Contra Tentationes*, Ms Bodleian Library, Bodley 43, Oxford.

Francisco de Osuna, *The Third Spiritual Alphabet*, Trans. and intro. by Mary E. Giles, New York: Paulist Press, 1981.

Gerson, J., *Omnia Opera*, Ed. L.E. Dupin, 5 vols, Antwerp, 1706 (Modern ed. P. Glorieux, Paris, 1960ff.).

Gregory of Nyssa, *Works*, Ed. J.P. Migne, P.G., xliv-xlvi (Fr. trans. *Vita Moysis* and *De Hominis Opificio*, ed. J. Daniélou, S.J. *Sources Chrétiennes*, i and vi, 1942-43; Eng. trans. *Life of Moses* by E. Ferguson and A.J. Malherbe, London, 1979).

Gregory the Great, *Homiliae in Hiezechilem Prophetam*, Corpus Christianorum, Series Latina, cxlii, Turnholti, 1971 (Homilies on Ezekiel).
----- *Moralia in Job*, Corpus Christianorum, Series Latina, Libri i-x, cxliii (undated), Libri xi-xxii, 1979, Libri xxiii-xxxv, 1985 (Morals, or Morals on Job), ed. Adriaen, CCSL 143, 143A. Turnhout, 1979; Books XXIIIff., in PL. 76.
----- *Liber Regulae Pastoralis*, Trans. 'Pastoral Care' by Rev. H.S. Bramley, London: Parker & Co., 1874 (Latin Source, PL 77, 13-128).
----- *The Dialogues*, Ed. Mittermüller, 1880.

Guigo, Il, *The Ladder of Monks* (*Scala Claustralium*) and *Twelve Meditations* (*Meditationes*), Trans. E. Colledge, O.S.A. and J. Walsh, S.J. New York: Doubleday, Image Books, 1978.

Hilton, Walter,
- *Scale of Perfection*, Editions of Books 1 and 2, based respectively on MSS Cambridge University Library Additional 6686 and British Library 6579 are being made for the Early English

Text Society. S.S. Hussey is editing Book 2 and Book 1, edited by the late A.J. Bliss, is being prepared for press by M.G. Sargent. A translation, based on the above MSS, by J.P.H. Clark and R. Dorward, New York, Mahwah: Paulist Press, 1991, has been used in this book. The other translation of this work referred to is named *Ladder of Perfection* by Leo Sherley-Price, Penguin Books, 1957, repr. 1986.

- *Mixed Life,* in Jones D. ed., Minor Works of Walter Hilton, London, 1929, which also includes lightly modernised texts of *Qui Habitat, Bonum Est* and *Benedictus* (the authorship of the last two is disputed).

- *Eight Chapters on Perfection* and *Angels' Song*, Trans. R. Dorward from editions of F. Kuriyagawa and T. Takamiya, Fairacres, Oxford: SLG Press, 1983.

- Latin Writings, *Walter Hilton's Latin Writings*, Ed. J.P.H. Clark and C. Taylor, 2 vols, Salzburg, Analecta Cartusiana 124, 1987 (Contains texts of all known Latin works by Hilton, together with Middle English trans. of *Epistola ad Quemdam Saeculo Renuntiare Volentem* and the Commentary on the lost *Gilbertine* letter).

Hugh of St Victor, *Opera*, Ed. J.P. Migne P.L. clxxv-clxxvii (Eng. trans. of *Selected Spiritual Writings*, Sr Penelope C.S.M.V. Classics of the Contemplative Life, 1962).

Ignatius of Loyola,
- *Autobiography of St Ignatius*, Trans. Joseph N. Tylenda as *A Pilgrim's Journey*, Wilmington, Delaware: Michael Glazier, 1985.

- *Inigo: Discernment Log-Book. The Spiritual Diary of St Ignatius Loyola*, Trans. Joseph A. Munitz, London, 1987.

- *MHSJ, Chronicon Societatis Jesu Auctore Joanne de Polanco*, 6 vols, Madrid, 1894-8.

- *MHSJ, Fontes Documentales de S. Ignatio de Loyola: Documenta de S. Ignatii Familia et Patria Iuventute, Primis Sociis*, Rome, 1977.

- *MHSJ, Monumenta Ignatiani* in the following series:
    - *I. Epistolae et Instructiones S. Ignatii*, 12 vols, Madrid, 1903-11.
    - *II. Exercitia Spiritualia. S. Ignatii Eorumque Directoria*, 2 vols, Madrid and Rome, 1919 and 1955.
    - *III. Sancti Ignatii Constitutiones Societatis Jesu*, 4 vols, Rome 1934-8, 1948.
    - *IV. Scripta de Santo Ignatio,* 2 vols, Madrid, 1904, 1918 (Includes *Vita Ignatii Loyolae: P. Ribadeneira*, Naples, 1572).

- *MHSJ, Fontes Narrativi de S. Ignatio de Loyola et de Societatis Jesu initiis*, 4 vols, Rome, 1943-60.

- *MHSJ, Monumenta (Epistolae) P. Hieronymii Nadal*, 6 vols, Madrid and Rome, 1898-1964 (Letters of Fr. Jerome Nadal).

- *MHSJ, Monumenta Lainii*, 8 vols, Madrid, 1912-17 (Letters of Fr. Diego Lainez).

- Rahner, Hugo, *Saint Ignatius Loyola: Letters to Women*, Freiburg, Edinburgh and London, 1960.

- Tylenda, J.N. S.J., Ed. *Counsels for Jesuits: Selected Letters and Instructions of Saint Ignatius Loyola*, Chicago: Loyola University Press, 1985.

- *The Spiritual Exercises of St Ignatius*, Trans. Louis J. Puhl, Chicago: Loyola University Press, 1951.

- *Saint Ignatius of Loyola: The Constitutions of the Society of Jesus*, Trans. George E. Ganss, St Louis, 1970.

Jacob of Voraigne, *Legenda Aurea (Golden Legend)*, Ed. T. Graesse, Dresden and Leipzig, 1846 (Caxton's trans. repr. by W. Morris and F.S. Ellis, 3 vols, London, 1892; Modern Eng. version by F.S. Ellis in Temple Classics, 7 vols, 1900).

John of the Cross,
- *San Juan de la Cruz, Obras Completas*, 2nd Edicion, Madrid: Editorial de Espiritualidad, 1980.
- *Vida y Obras Completas de Juan de la Cruz*, 4a Edicion, Madrid: Biblioteca de Autores Cristianos, 1960.
- *The Complete Works of St John of the Cross*, Trans. and ed. E. Allison Peers, Wheathampstead, Herts, 1974.
- *The Collected Works of St John of the Cross*, Trans. Kieran Kavanaugh, O.C.D. and Otilio Rodriguez, O.C.D. Washington: I.C.S. Publications, 1979.
- *The Poems of St John of the Cross*, The Spanish Text and trans. Roy Campbell, London: The Harvill Press, 1951.
- *Selected Writings*, Ed. and intro. Kieran Kavanaugh, O.C.D. New York, Mahwah: Paulist Press (Classics of Western Spirituality), 1987.

Julian of Norwich,
  1. Middle English Version
- *A Book of Showings to the Anchoress, Julian of Norwich*, Ed. Edmund Colledge, O.S.A. and James Walsh S.J., Toronto: Pontifical Institute of Medieaval Studies, 1978 (Part One: Introduction and Short Text; Part Two: The Long Text).
- *Julian of Norwich, Revelations of Divine Love* (Long Text), Ed. Marion Glasscoe, University of Exeter, 1976.
  2. Modernised Mediaeval Versions
- Colledge, E., O.S.A. and Walsh, J, S.J., *Julian of Norwich, Showings*, Trans. from their Crit. Text, Classics of Western Spirituality, New York: Paulist Press, 1978 (Short and Long Texts).
- Wolters, C., *Julian of Norwich, Revelations of Divine Love*, Penguin Books, 1966 (with many reprints), Long Text only.

Kempe, Margery,
  1. Middle English Version
- *The Book of Margery Kempe*, Ed. Sanford Brown Meech and Hope Emily Allen, E.E.T.S. OS. 212, 1940 (from British Library Additional MS 61823).
  2. Modernised Version
- *The Book of Margery Kempe*, Ed. W. Butler-Bowden, Oxford: The World Classics, 1954.
- *The Book of Margery Kempe*, Trans. B.A. Windeatt, Penguin Books, 1985.

Ludolph of Saxony, *Vita Christi*, Lyons, 1554.

Marsilius of Padua, *Defensor Pacis*, Crit. Ed. C.W. Previté-Orton, Cambridge, 1928.

Pascal, B., *Pensées. Notes on Religion and other Subjects*, Ed. L. Lafuma, trans. J. Warrington, London: J.M. Dent, 1972.

Plato, *The Republic*, Trans. A.D. Lindsay, London: J.M. Dent & Sons Ltd., repr. 1954.
----- *The Symposium*, Trans. W. Hamilton, Penguin Books, 1951.
----- *The Last Days of Socrates* (*The Apology, Crito* and *Phaedo*), Trans. H. Tredennick, Penguin Books, 1954.

Plotinus, *Enneads*, Trans. Stephen McKenna, Rev. by B.S. Page, London, 1969 (P. Henry and H.A. Schwyzer, ed., Plotini Opera, 3 vols, Paris and Brussels, 1951-73).

Porete, Margaret, *Le Miroir des Simples Âmes*, Ed. R. Guarnieri in *Il Movimento del Libero Spiritu*, Archivo Italiano per la Storia della Pietà, Rome, 1968, 243-382.

----- *The Mirror of Simple Souls: A Middle English Translation*, Ed. Marilyn Doiron, with an Appendix on Glosses by E. Colledge and R. Guarnieri, Archivo Italiano per la Storia della Pietà, Rome, 1968.

Possidius, 'Life of St Augustine' in *Western Fathers*, Trans. and ed. F.R. Hoare, London: Sheed and Ward, 1954.

Pseudo-Dionysius the Areopagite, *Celestial Hierarchy*, Crit. Ed. G. Heil, Fr. trans. M. de Gaudillac, Sources Chrétiennes, lviii, 1958.
----- *Ecclesiastical Hierarchy, Divine Names, Mystical Theology, Letters*, Ed. J.P. Migne, P.G. iii and iv (a repr. of B. Corderius S.J., 2 vols, fol. Antwerp 1634).
----- *Dionysiaca*, Ed. P. Chevalier O.S.B., Recueil donnant l'ensemble des traductions latines des ouvrages attribués au Denys de l'Aréopage, 2 vols, Paris, 1937-50.
Eng. trans. of his works:
- J. Parker, *The Works of Dionysius the Areopagite*, 2 vols, London, Oxford, 1897-99.
- *Divine Names* and *Mystical Theology* by C.E. Rolt, Translations of Christian Literature, Series 1, Greek Texts, 1920.

Richard of St Victor, *Opera*, Ed. J.P. Migne PL. cxcvi 1-1378.
----- *Benjamin Minor*, Eng. trans. S.V. Yankowski, Ansbach, 1960.

Rolle, Richard, *Incendium Amoris*, Ed. M. Deanesly, Manchester, 1915 and trans. C. Wolters as *Fire of Love*, Penguin Books, 1972.
----- *English Writings*, Ed. H.E. Allen, Oxford, 1931.
----- *Melos Amoris*, Ed. E.J.F. Arnauld, Oxford: Blackwell, 1957.
----- *Prose and Verse*, Ed. S.J. Ogilvie-Thomson, EETS, OS 293, 1988.
----- *The English Writings*, Trans. and ed. Rosamond, S. Allen. Classics of Western Spirituality, Paulist Press, 1989.

Rupert of Deutz, *De Trinitate*, PL. 167, and *Les Oeuvres du Saint Esprit. Intro. et Notes*, J. Griboment, Text Etabli et Traduit E. de Solms, Paris: Editions du Cerf, 1967-70.

Ruysbroeck, Jan van, *The Adornment of the Spiritual Marriage, The Sparkling Stone, The Book of Supreme Truth*, Trans. C.A. Wynschenk, London, 1916.

Shakespeare, W., *The History of Troilus and Cressida*, Ed. Daniel Selzer, New York: Signet Classics, 1988.

Teresa of Avila, *Works*, Crit. ed. Silverio de Santa Teresa O.C.D., 6 vols, Burgos, 1915-19; *Letters*, 3 vols, 1922-24, in 'Biblioteca Mistica Carmelitana' i-ix (Eng. trans. E.A. Peers, *Works*. 3 vols, 1946 and *Letters*. 2 vols, 1951).
----- *The Collected Works of St Teresa of Avila*, Trans. Kieran Kavanaugh and Otilio Rodriguez, Washington D.C.: ICS Publications, 1985.
----- *Autobiography*, Eng. trans. J.M. Cohen, Penguin Classics, 1957.

The Book of the First Monks, Trans. Michael Edwards, Boars Hill, Oxford: Teresian Press, 1985.

The Jerusalem Bible, London: Darton, Longman & Todd, 1966.

Thomas à Kempis, *The Imitation of Christ*, Trans. Leo Sherley-Price, London: Penguin Books, repr. 1956.

Veritatis Splendor. Encyclical Letter of John Paul II on Certain Fundamental Questions of the Church's Moral Teaching, Homebush, N.S.W.: St Paul's, 1993.

Virgil, *The Aeneid*, Ed. Mynors, Classical Texts, Oxford, 1969.

----- *The Aeneid*, Trans. W.F. Jackson Knight, Penguin Books, 1958.

William of St Thierry,
  - *De Contemplando Deo* (PL.184: 365-380), The Works of W. of St. T.: Vol. I, 'On Contem-
  plating God', 'Prayer', 'Meditations', Trans. Sr. Penelope [Lawson]kk CF.3, Spencer, 1971.
  - *De Natura et Dignitate Amoris* (PL.184: 379-408) (*The Nature and Dignity of Love*), Trans.
  T.X. Davis, CF.30, Kalamazoo, 1981.
  - *Expositio Super Cantica Canticorum* (PL.180: 475-546), The Works of W. of St. T.: Vol. II.
  'Exposition on the Song of Songs', Trans. Sr Columba Hart, CF.6; Spencer, 1970.
  - *Speculum Fidei* and *Aenigma Fidei* (PL.180: 365-398; 397-440), 'The Mirror of Faith', Trans.
  T.X. Davis, CF.5; Kalamazoo, 1974; and 'The Enigma of Faith', Trans. J.D. Anderson, CF.9;
  Kalamazoo, 1974.
  - *Epistola ad Fratres de Mont-Dei (Epistola Aurea)* (PL.184: 307-354), CF 12 'The Golden
  Epistle: A Letter to the Brethren at Mont Dieu', Trans. T. Berkeley, OCSO, Kalamazoo,
  Michigan: Cistercian Publications Inc., 1980.
  - *Vita Bernardi* (PL.185: 225-268, ed. J.P. Migne, Paris, 1855).

Wright, T. ed., *The Knight de la Tour-Laudry: a Book for Daughters*, E.E.T.S. (O.S.) xxxiii, 1968.

Secondary Literature:

A Benedictine of Stanbrook, *Mediaeval Mystical Tradition And St John Of The Cross*, London:
  Burns & Oates, 1954.

Adam, A., *Guillaume de Saint-Thierry. Sa vie et ses oeuvres*, Bourg, 1923.

Adolfo de la Madre Dios and Others, 'Espagne, Âge d'Or' in *Dict.Sp.* Vol. 4.2, 1961, Cols 1127-
  1178.

Ahern, B., 'The Use of Scripture in the Spiritual Theology of St John of the Cross' in *Catholic
  Biblical Quarterly* 14, Jan. 1952.

Albrecht, Carl, *Psychologie des Mystischen Bewusstseins*, Bremen, Germany: Carl Schuenemann
  Verlag, 1951.
----- *Das Mystische Erkennen*, Bremen, Germany: Carl Schuenemann Verlag, 1958.

Allen, J.J., *Don Quixote: Hero or Fool?* Gainsville, Fla. Pt.1, 1969; Pt.2, 1979.

Allport, Gordon, *Pattern and Growth in Personality*, New York, 1961.
----- *Becoming*, New Haven: Yale University Press, 1960.

Alonso, J.F., 'Espagne' in *D.H.G.E.* XV, 1963, Cols 892-944.

Anderson, M.D., *Drama and Imagery in English Mediaeval Churches*, Cambridge, 1963.

Arbesmann, R.A., 'The Concept of 'Christus Medicus' in St Augustine' in *Traditio* 10, 1954, 1ff.

Asselin, D.T. S.J., 'Christian Maturity and Spiritual Discernment' in *Notes on the Spiritual Exercises of St Ignatius of Loyola*, Ed. David L. Fleming S.J., St Louis, Mo.: Review for Religious,
  1985.

Aston, M., 'The Impeachment of Bishop Despenser' in *BIHR*, xxxviii, 1965, 127-48.
----- 'Lollardy and Sedition' in *Past and Present*, xvii, 1960, 1-44.

Aumann, Jordon, O.P., *Spiritual Theology*, London: Sheed and Ward, 1980.

Ayton, A. and Davis V., 'Ecclesiastical Wealth in England in 1086' in *SCH*, xxiv, 1987.

Bainton, Roland H., *'Here I Stand', a Life of Martin Luther*, New York: The New American Library, 1950.

Baker, D.N., *Julian of Norwich's 'Showings': From Vision to Book*, Princeton, New Jersey: Princeton University Press, 1994.

Baldwin, A.P., 'The Tripartite Reformation of the Soul in 'The Scale of Perfection', 'Pearl' and 'Piers Plowman'', in *The Mediaeval Mystical Tradition in England*, Papers read at Dartington Hall, July 1984, ed. Marion Glasscoe (Hereafter abbreviated as *M.M.T. in Eng.*, followed by the date).

Balthasar, H.U. von, *Herrlichkeit: Eine Theologische Ästhetik*, Bd. 3. Einsiedeln, 1961-1969.

Barthes, Roland, *Sade, Fourier, Loyola*, Trans. R. Miller, New York: Hill and Wang; 1976, first published 1971 (Paris: Editions du Seuil).
----- *S/Z*, Trans. Richard Miller, London: Jonathan Cape, 1974.

Bataillon, M., *Erasme et l'Espagne: Recherches sur l'Histoire Spirituelle du XVIe Siècle*, Paris, 1937.

Bell, D.N., *The Image and Likeness: The Augustinian Spirituality of William of St Thierry*, Kalamazoo: Cistercian Publications, 1984.

Benedicta [Ward], Sr, S.L.G., 'Julian the Solitary' in *Julian Reconsidered*, Fairacres, Oxford: SLG Press, Convent of the Incarnation, 1988.

Benson, J.F., 'Consciousness of Self and Perceptions of Individuality' in *Renaissance and Renewal*, Ed. R.L. Benson, G. Constable with C.B. Lanham, Cambridge M.A.: Harvard University Press, 1982.

Berlière, Dom W., 'Les Ordres de Citeaux et l'Ordre Benedictine au XIIe Siècle', *Revue d'Histoire Ecclésiastique*, Vol. I, 1900; Vol. II, 1901.

Boase, R., *The Troubadour Revival*, London, 1978.

Bourquin, G., 'The Dynamics of the Signans in the Spiritual Quest' (*Piers Plowman, the Mystics and Religious Drama*) in *M.M.T. in Eng.*, 1982.

Bouyer, L., *La Spiritualité de Cîteaux*, Paris, 1954; trans. E.A. Livingstone as 'The Cistercian Heritage', London, 1958.
----- *A History of Christian Spirituality, Vol. 1: 'The Spirituality of the New Testament and the Fathers'*, Trans. Mary R. Ryan, Burns & Oates, 1968; reprinted 1982.
----- 'Mysticism. An Essay on the History of the Word' in *Understanding Mysticism*, Ed. Richard Woods, O.P. Garden City, N.Y.: Doubleday, 1980.

Bradley, R., 'Christ the Teacher in Julian's *Showings*: the Biblical and Patristic Traditions' in *M.M.T. in Eng.*, 1982.
----- 'The Speculum Image in Mediaeval Mystical Writers' in *M.M.T. in Eng.*, 1984.

Brandsma, T. O.Carm., 'Carmes' in *Dict. Sp.* Vol. 2, 1953, Cols 156-71.

Bridbury, A.R., 'The Black Death' in *Econ. HR*, xxvi, 1973, 577-92.
----- 'Before the Black Death' in *Econ. HR*, xxx, 1977, 393-410.

Brodrick, J. S.J., *Saint Ignatius Loyola: The Pilgrim Years 1491-1538*, New York: Farrar, Straus and Cudahy, 1956.

Brooke, C.N., *The Twelfth Century Renaissance*, London: Thames and Hudson, 1969.

Brooke, Dom Odo, *Studies in Monastic Theology*, Cistercian Publications, 1980 (Cistercian Studies Series No.37).

Brou, A., *Saint Ignace, Maître d'Oraison*, Paris, 1925.

Brown, P., *Augustine of Hippo. A Biography*, London: Faber & Faber, 1967.
----- *Religion and Society in the Age of St Augustine*, London: Faber & Faber, 1973.
----- *Cult of the Saints. Its Rise and Function in Latin Christianity*, London: S.C.M. Press, 1981.
----- *The World of Late Antiquity*, London: Thames and Hudson, 1971.
----- *The Body and Society. Men, Women and Sexual Renunciation in Early Christianity*, London, Boston: Faber and Faber, 1990 (first published, 1988, New York: Columbia University Press).
----- 'Religious Coercion' in *History* xlviii, 1963.

Brueggeman, Walter, *The Prophetic Imagination*, Fortress Press, 1978.

Bruno de Jésus-Marie, *Saint John of the Cross*, Ed. Benedict Zimmerman, New York: Sheed and Ward, 1932.

Bryant, Christopher, S.S.J.E., *Jung and the Christian Way*, London: Darton, Longman and Todd, 1983.

Bucke, Richard, *Cosmic Consciousness*, New York: E.P. Dutton, 1969.

Bultmann, Rudolph, 'Christian Faith and History' from *The Presence of Eternity*, Harper & Row, 1957 (reprinted under the title 'History and Eschatology', Edinburgh University Press).

Burke, E.M., 'Grace' in *N.C.E.* Vol. 6, New York: McGraw Hill, 1967.

Burke, Kenneth, *Rhetoric of Religion*, University of California Press, 1970.

Burnaby, J.E., *Amor Dei: A Study of the Religion of St Augustine*, London, 1938.

Burrell, Fr. David B., *Exercises in Religious Understanding*, Notre Dame, Indiana: University of Notre Dame Press, 1976.

Butler, Abbot C., *Western Mysticism: The Teaching of Augustine, Gregory and Bernard on Contemplation and the Contemplative Life*, London, 1967.

Bynum, Caroline Walker, *Holy Feast and Holy Fast: The Religious Significance of Food to Medieval Women*, Berkeley and Los Angeles: University of California Press, 1987.
----- *Jesus as Mother: Studies in the Spirituality of the High Middle Ages*, Berkeley: University of California Press, 1982.

Cabassut, A., 'Une dévotion médiévale peu connue' in *R.A.M.*, Vol. 25 (1949).

Cappuyns, M., 'Cassien' in *D.H.G.E.* XI, 1949, Cols 1319-48.

Caraman, Philip, S.J., *Ignatius Loyola. A Biography of the Founder of the Jesuits*, San Francisco: Harper & Row, 1990.

Caussade, Jean-Pierre de, *Abandonment to Divine Providence*, Trans. John Beevers, New York: Doubleday, 1975.

Cayré, F., *La Contemplation Augustienne: Principes de la Spiritualité de S. Augustin*, Paris, 1927.

Ceglar, S., *William of St Thierry. The Chronology of his Life with Study of his Treatise 'On the Nature of Love', His Authorship of 'The Brevis Commentatio', the 'In Lacu' and the 'Reply to Cardinal Mathew'*, Ann Arbor: University Microfilms, 1971.

Chadwick, Henry, *Early Christian Thought and the Classical Tradition*, Oxford, 1966 (Reprinted 1987).
----- *The Early Church*, Penguin Books, 1967.
----- *Augustine*, Oxford: Oxford University Press, 1986.

Chadwick, Owen, *John Cassian: A Study in Primitive Monasticism*, Cambridge, 1968 (Second edition).

Chambers, R.W., *On the Continuity of English Prose*, London, 1932.

Chardin, Teilhard de, *The Divine Milieu*, New York: Harper, 1960.
----- *The Phenomenon of Man*, New York: Harper, 1965.
----- *The Vision of the Past*, New York: Harper, 1966.

Chein, Isidor, 'The Image of Man' in *Journal of Social Issues*, 18:4, 1962.

Cheyney, Edward, *Dawn of a New Era, 1250-1453*, New York: Harper & Bros, 1936.

Chollet, A., 'Discernment of Spirits' in *D.T.C.* Vol. 4.B (1939) Cols 1375-1415.

Clark, J.P.H., 'The Lightsome Darkness - Aspects of Walter Hilton's Theological Background' in *Downside Review*, Vol. 95, 1977.

Clark, J.P.H., 'The Cloud of Unknowing, Walter Hilton and St John of the Cross; a Comparison' in *Downside Review*, Vol. 96, 1978.
----- 'Walter Hilton and 'Liberty of Spirit'', in *Downside Review*, Vol. 96, 1978.
----- 'Action and Contemplation in Walter Hilton', in *Downside Review*, Vol. 97, 1979.
----- 'Image and Likeness in Walter Hilton', in *Downside Review*, Vol. 97, 1979.
----- 'Intention in Walter Hilton', in *Downside Review*, Vol. 97, 1979.
----- 'Augustine, Anselm and Walter Hilton', in *M.M.T. in Eng.*, 1982.

Clark, J.P.H., 'Late Fourteenth Century Cambridge Theology and the English Contemplative Tradition' in *M.M.T. in Eng.*, 1992, 1-16.

Clay, R.M., *The Hermits and Anchorites of England*, London: Methuen, 1914.

Coleman, J., *English Literature in History 1350-1400: Mediaeval Readers and Writers*, London: Hutchinson, 1981.

Coleman, T.W., *English Mystics of the Fourteenth Century*, London: Epsworth Press, 1938.

Colledge, E., *The Mediaeval Mystics of England*, New York: Charles Scribner & Sons, 1961.

Collings, Ross, O.C.D., *John of the Cross*, Collegeville, Minnesota: Liturgical Press, 1990.

Colunga, E., O.P., *'Intellectualistas y misticos en la Teologia española en el siglo XVI'* in *Ciencia Tomista* 9 and 10 (1914), 201-21; 377-94: and 223-42 respectively.

Congar, Yves M.-J., *Tradition and Traditions: An Historical and a Theological Essay*, trans. Part 1 M. Naseby, Part 2 T. Rainborough, London: Burns & Oates, 1966.

Constable, Giles, *Three Studies in Mediaeval Religious and Social Thought*, Cambridge University Press, 1995.

Constant, G., 'Alumbrados' in *D.H.G.E.* II, 1914, Cols 849-853.

Cooper, A., O.M.I., *Julian of Norwich. Reflections on Selected Texts*, N.S.W.: St Paul Publications, 1986.
----- *The Cloud. Reflections on Selected Texts*, Homebush, N.S.W.: St Paul Publications, 1989.

Copleston, F., *A History of Philosophy*, Vol. 2, Mediaeval Philosophy Part I, Augustine to Bonaventure, New York: Doubleday, 1962.

Copleston, F., *A History of Philosophy*, Vol. 3, Late Mediaeval and Renaissance Philosophy Part I, Ockham to the Speculative Mystics, New York: Doubleday, 1963.
----- *Aquinas*, Penguin Books, 1953.

Couilleau, Guerric, 'Jean Climaque' in *Dict. Sp.* Vol. 8 (1974), Cols 369-89.

Coulson, John, *Religion and Imagination*, Oxford, 1981.

Courcelle, Pierre, *Connais-Toi Toi Même: De Socrate à St Bernard*, 3 vols, Paris, 1974-75.

Cousins, Ewart H., 'Francis of Assisi: Christian Mysticism at the Crossroads' in *Mysticism and Religious Traditions*, Ed. S.T. Katz, Oxford University Press, 1983.

Crisógono de Jésus Sacramentado, *The Life of St John of the Cross*, Trans. Kathleen Pond. London: Longmans, Green & Co., 1958.

Cross, F.L. and E.A. Livingstone (eds), *Oxford Dictionary of the Christian Church*, Oxford, Second edition, 1974; reprinted 1984.

Cugno, Alain, *St John of the Cross: Reflections on Mystical Experience*, Trans. Barbara Wall, New York: Seabury, 1882.

Cumont, F., 'Le Mysticisme astral dans l'antiquité' in *Bulletin de l'Académie Royale de Belgique* (Classe de Lettres) 5, 1909, 256-286.

Dalmases, C. de, *Ignatius of Loyola: Founder of the Jesuits: His Life and Work*, Trans. J. Aixalá, S.J., St Louis: Institute of Jesuit Sources (first published 1982), 1985.

Daniélou, J., *Platonisme et Théologie Mystique*, Paris: Edition Montaigne, 1944.
----- 'La Vision Ignatienne du monde et de l'homme' in *R.A.M.* Vol. 26, 1950, 5-17.

D'Arcy, M.C, S.J., *The Mind and Heart of Love*, New York: Holt, 1947.

Davies, Oliver, *'God Within': The Mystical Tradition of Northern Europe*, London: Darton, Longman and Todd, 1988.
----- 'Transformational Processes in the work of Julian of Norwich, and Mechtild of Magdeburg' in *M.M.T. in Eng.*, 1992, 39-52.

Davies, R.G., 'After the Execution of Archbishop Scrope' in *BJRL*, lix, 1976-77, 40-74.

Davis, Charles, *Dante and the Idea of Rome*, Oxford: Clarendon Press, 1957.

Deanesly, M., *A History of the Mediaeval Church, 590-1500*, London: Methuen, 8th ed. 1954.
----- *The Lollard Bible*, Cambridge, 1920.

Déchenet, J.M., *William of St Thierry: The Man and His Work*, Trans. Richard Strachan, Spencer: Cistercian Publications, 1972 (Cistercian Studies Series No.10).
----- 'Les Maîtres et les Modèles: Guillaume de St Thierry' in *La Vie Spirituelle* 53, Paris, 1937.

----- 'A Propos de la Lettre aux Frères du Mont-Dieu' in *Collectanea Ordinis Cister-ciensium Reformatorum*, 5, 1938.

Deikman, Arthur, 'Deautomatization and the Mystic Experience' in *Altered States of Consciousness*, Ed. Charles Tart. Garden City, N.Y.: Doubleday, 1969, 32.

Dening, Greg, *Performances*, Melbourne University Press, 1996.

D'Entreves, A.P., *Dante as a Political Thinker*, Oxford: Clarendon Press, 1952.

Derrida, J., 'Structure, Sign and Play in the Discourse of the Human Sciences' in *Writing and Difference*, Trans. A. Bass, London, 1978, 278-93.

Dickens, A.G., *The Age of Humanism and Reformation: Europe in the Fourteenth, Fifteenth and Sixteenth Centuries*, Englewood Cliffs, New Jersey, 1972.

Diehl, P.S., *The Mediaeval European Religious Lyric: An Ars Poetica*, University of California Press, 1985.

Dobson, R.B. (ed.), *The Peasants Revolt of 1381*, Trans. from Latin and Norman French, London: Macmillan, 1970, 2nd Edition, 1983.

Doran, Robert, S.J., *Subject and Psyche: Ricœur, Jung and the Search for Foundations*, Washington D.C.: University Press of America, 1977.
----- 'Subject, Psyche and Theology's Foundations', *Journal of Religion* 57/3, July, 1977, 267-87.

Doyle, A.I., 'A Survey of the Origins and Circulation of Theological Writings in English in the 14th, 15th and early 16th Centuries with special consideration of the part of the clergy therin', Diss. 2301-2, Cambridge University, 1953,

Drabble, H. (ed.), *The Oxford Companion to English Literature*, Oxford University Press, 5th Ed. 1988.

Dudden, F.H., *Gregory the Great: His Place in History and Thought*, 2 vols, London, 1905.

Dudon, P., S.J., *Saint Ignace de Loyola*, Paris, 1934.
----- *Saint Ignatius of Loyola*, Trans. William J. Young, S.J., Milwaukee, Bruce, 1949.

Duffy, Eamon, *The Stripping of the Altars, Traditional Religion in England c.1400-c.1580*, New Haven and London: Yale University Press, 1992.

Durkheim, E., 'The Social Foundations of Religion' in *Sociology of Religion*, Ed. R. Robertson, Penguin Books, 1969.

Eco, Umberto, *Art and Beauty in the Middle Ages*, Trans. Hugh Bredin, New Haven and London: Yale University Press, 1986 (Third Printing 1988).

Egan, Harvey J., S.J., *What Are They Saying About Mysticism?* New York/Ramsey: Paulist Press, 1982.
----- *Christian Mysticism, the Future of a Tradition*, New York: Pueblo Publishing Col., 1984.
----- *The Spiritual Exercises and the Ignatian Mystical Horizon*, St. Louis: Institute of Jesuit Sources, 1976.
----- 'Christian Apophatic and Kataphatic Mysticisms' in *Theological Studies*, Sept. 1978, 399-426.

Eliot, T.S., *Collected Poems 1909-1962*, London: Faber and Faber, 1963, repr. 1983.

Elliott, Ralph W.V., 'Chaucer's Clerical Voices' in *Mediaeval English Religious Literature*, Eds Gregory Kratzmann and James Simpson, Cambridge: D.S. Brewer, 1986, 146-155.

Ellis, Roger, 'Author(s), Compilers, Scribes, and Bible Texts: Did the Cloud-Author translate *The Twelve Patriarchs?*' in *M.M.T. in Eng.*, 1992, 193-221.

Elton, G.R., *Reformation Europe, 1517-1559*, London: Collins, 1967 (first published 1963).

Emden, A.B., *Biographical Register of the University of Cambridge to 1500*, Cambridge, 1963.

Erikson, Erik, *Insight and Responsibility*, New York, 1964.

Evans, G.R., *Augustine on Evil*, Cambridge: Cambridge University Press, 1982.

Ferrante, Joan M., *The Political Vision of the Divine Comedy*, Princeton University Press, 1984.

Festugière, A.-J., *L'Enfant d'Agrigente*, Paris, 1950.
----- *'La Révelation d'Hermès Trismégiste'*, 4 vols, Paris, 1944-54.
Fisher, Alden, 'Freud and the Image of Man' in *Proceedings of the American Catholic Philosophical Association* 35, 1961.

Fisher, H.A.L., *A History of Europe*, 2 vols, London: Eyre & Spottiswoode, 1949 (first published 1935).

Fitzgerald, R.B., *Community and Conflict: The English Church, 1350-1381*, Ph.D. Thesis, Duke University, 1976, Ann Arbor: University Microfilms, 1979.

Foresti, Fabrizio, O.C.D., *Sinai and Carmel: The Biblical Roots of the Doctrine of St John of the Cross*, Darlington Carmel, 1981.

Forman, Robert K., 'Mystical Experience in the *Cloud*-Literature' in *M.M.T. in Eng.*, 1987.

Forsyth, Neil, *The Old Enemy: Satan And The Combat Myth*, Princeton University Press, 1987.

Foucault, Michel, *L'Ordre du Discours*, Paris: Gallimard, 1971.
----- 'What is an Author?' in *Language, Counter-Memory, Practice*, Trans. S. Simon, Ed. Donald F. Bouchard. Ithaca: Cornell University Press, 1977.

Frank, Erich, 'Role of History in Christian Thought' in *The Duke Divinity School Bulletin*, XIV, 1949.

Fransen, Peter, S.J., *The New Life of Grace*, Trans. Georges Dupon, S.J. London: G. Chapman, 1971.
----- 'Toward a Psychology of Grace' in *Lumen Vitae* 12:1, 1957.

Gabriel de Sainte-Marie-Magdaleine, O.C.D., 'Carmes Déchaussés' in *Dict. Sp.* Vol. 2, 1953, Cols 171-209.

Gabriele di S.M.M. O.C.D., *La Contemplazione Acquista*, Firenze, 1938.

Gadamer, H.-G., *Wahrheit und Methode*, Tübingen: Mohr, 1960.

Garcia-Villoslada, R., *San Ignacio de Loyola: nueva biografia*, Madrid, 1985.

Gardner, H.L., 'Walter Hilton and the Authorship of 'The Cloud of Unknowing'' in *Review of English Studies*, 9, 1933, 129-47.
----- 'The Text of the *Scale of Perfection*'in *Medium Aevum*, 5, 1936, 11-30.
----- 'Walter Hilton and the Mystical Tradition in England' in *Essays and Studies*, 22, 1937, 103-27.

Gatta, Julia, *Three Spiritual Directors for our Times: Julian of Norwich, Cloud of Un-knowing, Walter Hilton*, Cambridge MA: Cowley Publications, 1986.

Geertz, C., 'Religion as a Cultural System' in *The Interpretation of Cultures*, Hutchinson, 1975.

Gilkey, Langdon, 'Dissolution and Reconstruction in Theology' in *Christian Century* 82, 1965.

Gillespie, Vincent, and Ross, Maggie, 'The Apophatic Image: The Poetics of Effacement in Julian of Norwich' in *M.M.T. in Eng.*, 1992, 53-78.

Gilson, E., *The Christian Philosophy of Saint Augustine*, Trans. L.E.M. Lynch, London, 1961.
----- *Dante the Philosopher*, Trans. D. Moore, London: Sheed and Ward, 1948.
----- *The Spirit of Mediaeval Philosophy*, Trans. A.H.C. Downes, New York: Sheed and Ward, 1940.
----- *The Mystical Theology of St Bernard*, Trans. A.H.C. Downes, London, 1940.

Gimello, Robert M., 'Mysticism in its Contexts' in *Mysticism and Religious Traditions*, Ed. Stephen T. Katz, Oxford University Press, 1983.

Glasscoe, M. (ed.), *Mediaeval Mystical Tradition in England*, 5 vols, Exeter: D.S. Brewer, 1980-92.
----- 'Visions and Revisions: A Further Look at the Manuscripts of Julian of Norwich' in *Studies in Bibliography*, 42, 1989, 103-20.
----- *English Mediaeval Mystics: Games of Faith*, London – New York: Longman, 1993.

Green, J.D., 'The Influence of St Augustine on Spirituality in the Mediaeval Church: A Comparative Study of St Gregory the Great, William of St Thierry and Walter Hilton', An unpublished thesis submitted in fulfilment of the requirements for the Degree of Master of Arts in the Department of History, Faculty of Arts, University of Melbourne, 1987.

Green, V.V.H., *The Later Plantagenets*, London: Edward and Arnold, 1953.

Gribomont, J., 'La Scala Paradisi, Jean de Raitou et Ange Clareno' in *Studia Monastica* ii, 1960, 345-58.

Guarnieri, R., 'Frères du Libre Esprit' in *Dict. Sp.* Vol. 5, 1964, Cols 1241-68.

Guibert, Joseph de, S.J., *The Jesuits, Their Spiritual Doctrine And Practice, A Historical Study*. Trans. William J. Young, S.J., Ed. George C. Ganss, S.J. Chicago: Institute of Jesuit Sources, 1964 (Original title: *La Spiritualité de la Compagnie de Jésus. Esquisse historique*, Rome, 1953).
----- *Saint Ignace. Mystique*, Toulouse, 1950.

Guinard, P., *El Greco: Biographical and Critical Study*, Trans. J. Emmons, Lausanne, Skira, 1956.

Guitton, J., *Essay on Human Love*, Trans. M. Channing-Pearce, London, 1951 (First published Paris: Aubier, 1948 as *Essai sur l'Amour Humain*).

Guy, J.C., *Jean Cassien, Vie et doctrine spirituelle*, Paris, 1961.

Hesterman, J.C., *Inner Conflict of Tradition: Essays in Indian Ritual, Kingship and Society*, Chicago, 1985.

Haight, Roger, S.J., *The Experience and Language of Grace*, New York: Paulist Press, 1979.

Happold, F.C., *Mysticism*, Penguin Books, 1963.

Hardy, Richard, *Search for Nothing: The Life of St John of the Cross*, New York: Crossroad, 1982.

Haring, D.G. (ed.), *Personal Character and Cultural Milieu*, 3rd ed., Syracuse N.Y., 1956.

Harnack, A., *History of Dogma*, 3rd ed., trans. James Miller, London: Williams and Norgate, 1898; and New York: Russell and Russell, 1958.

Haskins, C.H., *The Renaissance of the Twelfth Century*, Harvard University Press, 1939 (first published 1927).

Haughton, Rosemary, *Transformation of Man: A Study of Conversion and Community*, London, Dublin, Melbourne: Geoffrey Chapman, 1967.

Heath, Peter, *Church and Realm 1272-1461: Conflict and Collaboration in an Age of Crises*, Fontana Press, 1988.

Heer, F., *The Mediaeval World*, Trans. J. Sondheimer, London: Weidenfeld and Nicholson, 1962.

Henry, P., *La Vision d'Ostie*, Paris, 1938.

Hick, J., *Evil and the God of Love*, London: Collins, 1974.

Hilton, R.H. and Ashton, T.H. (eds), *The English Rising of 1381*, Cambridge, 1984.

Hobsbawm, E. and Ranger, T. (eds), *The Invention of Tradition*, Cambridge: Cambridge University Press, 1983.

Hocking, W., 'The meaning of Mysticism as seen through its psychology' in *Understanding Mysticism*, Ed. Richard Woods O.P. Garden City, New York: Doubleday, 1980.

Hocking, W., *The Meaning of God in Human Experience*, New Haven: Yale University Press, 1963.

Hodgson, P., *Three Fourteenth Century English Mystics*, Longmans, Green & Co. for the British Council and National Book League, 1967.

Hogg, J., 'The Latin Cloud' in *M.M.T. in Eng.*, 1984.

Hollis, C., *Saint Ignatius*, London: Sheed and Ward, 1931.

Holmes, U.T., *A History of Christian Spirituality: An Analytical Introduction*, Minneapolis: Seabury Press, 1980.

Hudson, A.M., 'Lollardy: the English Heresy' in *SCH* xviii, 1982, 261-83.
----- *The Premature Reformation: Wycliffite Texts and Lollard History*, Oxford, 1988.

Hügel, Baron von, *The Mystical Element of Religion*, 2nd ed. London, 1923.

Hughes, Gerard, *God of Surprises*, London: Darton, Longman and Todd, 1985; repr. 1986.

Hughes, Jonathan, *Pastors and Visionaries. Religion and Secular Life in Late Mediaeval Yorkshire*, Woodbridge, Suffolk: Boydell Press, 1988.

Huizinga, J., *The Waning of the Middle Ages*, London: Penguin Books, 1965 (first published 1924).

Hussey, S.S., 'Walter Hilton, Traditionalist' in *M.M.T. in Eng.*, 1980.

Huxley, Aldous, *The Doors of Perception and Heaven and Hell*, London: Penguin Books, 1959.
----- *Grey Eminence*, New York, 1941.

Inge, W.R., *Christian Mysticism*, New York: Scribner's, 1899.

Iparraguirre, Ignacio, 'Viajes de Iñigo de Loyola anteriores a 1518' in *AHSJ*, Vol. 26, 1957, 230-51

James, William, *The Varieties of Religious Experience*, New York: New American Library, 1958.

Jantzen, Grace, *Julian of Norwich*, London: S.P.C.K., 1987.

Javelet, Robert, *Image et Ressemblance au Douzième Siècle: De Saint Anselm à Alain de Lille*, 2 vols, Strasbourg, 1967.

Johnston, W., S.J., *The Inner Eye of Love: Mysticism and Religion*, London: Collins, 1978.
----- *The Mysticism of the Cloud of Unknowing*, Wheathamstead, Herts: Anthony Clarke, 1980.
----- *The Mirror Mind: Spirituality and Transformation*, London: Collins, 1981.

Johnston, W., S.J., *Silent Music. The Science of Meditation*, London: Collins, 1974.
----- *The Still Point*, New York: Harper & Row, 1970.

Joliffe, Peter S., *A Check-List of Middle English Prose Writings of Spiritual Guidance*, Toronto: Pontifical Institute of Mediaeval Studies, 1974.

Kamen, H., *The Spanish Inquisition*, London: Weidenfeld and Nicholson, 1965.

Katz, Stephen T. (ed.), *Mysticism and Philosophical Analysis*, New York: Oxford University Press, 1978.
----- 'Languagae, Epistemology, and Mysticism' in above work.
----- (ed.), *Mysticism and Religious Traditions*, Oxford University Press, 1983.
----- 'The 'Conservative' Character of Mysticism' in above work.

Keller, C.A., 'Mystical Literature' in *Mysticism and Philosophical Analysis*, Ed. Steven Katz, Oxford: Oxford University Press, 1978.

Kelsey, Morton, *Discernment; A Study in Ecstasy and Evil*, New York: Paulist Press, 1978.

Kieckhefer, R., *Unquiet Souls: Fourteenth Century Saints and Their Religious Milieu*, University of Chicago, 1984.

King, T.M., *Teilhard's Mysticism of Knowing*, New York: Seabury Press, 1981.

Knight, Stephen, 'Chaucer's Religious Canterbury Tales' in *Mediaeval English Religious Literature*, Eds Gregory Kratzmann and James Simpson, Cambridge: D.S. Brewer, 1986, 156-66.
----- 'Geoffrey Chaucer' in *Re-Reading Literature* Series, Ed. T. Eagleton, Oxford, 1986.

Knowles, M.D. and Hadcock, R.N., *Mediaeval Religious Houses, England and Wales*, London: Longmans, 1953.

Knowles, M.D., *The English Mystical Tradition*, London, 1961.
----- *The English Mystics*, London: Burns and Oates, 1927.
----- 'Becket. St. Thomas' in *N.C.E.*, Vol. 2, 1967, 212-14.

Knowles, M.D. and Russell-Smith, J., 'Walter Hilton' in *Dict. Sp.* Vol. 7, 1969, Cols 525-530.

Knox, R.A., *Enthusiasm: A Chapter in the History of Religion with Special Reference to the xviith and xviiith Century*, Clarendon Press, 1950.

Kratzmann, Gregory and Simpson, James (eds), *Mediaeval English Religious and Ethical Literature*, Cambridge: D.S. Brewer, 1986.

Ladner, G.B., *The Idea of Reform: Its Impact on Christian Thought and Action in the Age of the Fathers*, Cambridge, Mass.: Harvard University Press, 1959.

Lagorio, Valerie M., 'New Avenues of Research in the English Mystics' in *M.M.T. in Eng.*, 1980.
----- 'Variations on the Theme of God's Motherhood in Mediaeval English Mystical and Devotional Writings' in *Studia Mystica* 8 (Summer 1985), 15-37.

Lagorio, V.M. and Bradley, Ritamary, *14th Century English Mystics: A Comprehensive Annotated Bibliography*, New York, 1981.

Larkin, William J. Jr., *Culture and Biblical Hermeneutics*, Grand Rapids, Michigan: Baker Book House, 1988.

Lash, Nicholas, *Newman on Development: The Search for an Explanation in History*, London: Sheed and Ward, 1975, Ed. 1979.

Laveille, Mgr., *Sainte Thérèse de L'Enfant Jésus*, Lisieux, 1926.

Lawrence, C.H. (ed.), *The English Church and the Papacy in the Middle Ages*, London: Burns & Oates, 1965.
----- *Mediaeval Monasticism, Forms of Religious Life in Western Europe in the Middle Ages*, London and New York: Longman, 1984.

Lea, H.C., *A History of the Inquisition in Spain*, 4 vols, New York, 1922.

Le Cler, Joseph, *The Two Sovereignties*, London: Burns, Oates and Washbourne, 1952.

Leclercq, Jean, 'Modern Psychology, and the Interpretation of Mediaeval Texts' in *Speculum* 48, 1973, 476-90.
----- *The Love of Learning and the Desire for God. A Study of Monastic Culture*, Trans. C. Misrahi. New York: Fordham University Press, 1961.

Leclercq, J., Vandenbroucke, F., Bouyer, L., *The Spirituality of the Middle Ages*, New York: Seabury Press, 1982.

Leech, Kenneth, 'Hazelnut Theology: Its Potential and Perils' in *Julian Reconsidered*, Fairacres, Oxford: S.L.G. Press, 1988.

Leff, Gordon, *The Dissolution of the Mediaeval Outlook*, New York: New York University Press, 1976.
----- *Heresy in the Later Middle Ages: The Relation of Heterodoxy to Dissent c.1250 - c.1450*. Manchester: Manchester University Press, 1967.

Lentricchia, Frank and McLaughlin, Thomas (eds), *Critical Terms for Literary Study*, Chicago and London: University of Chicago Press, 1990.

Lerner, R.E., *The Heresy of the Free Spirit in the Later Middle Ages*, Berkeley: University of California Press, 1972.

Leturia, Pedro de, *Iñigo de Loyola*, Trans. A.J. Owen S.J. Reissued Chicago: Loyola University Press, 1965 (originally Syracuse: Le Mayne College Press, 1949).

Le Vené, R.A. (ed.), *Culture and Personality: Contemporary Readings*, Chicago, 1975.

Levi-Strauss, C., *Totemism*, Boston, 1963.

Lewis, C.S., *The Discarded Image: An Introduction to Mediaeval and Renaissance Literature*, London, 1964.
----- *Allegory of Love. A Study in Mediaeval Tradition*, London: Oxford University Press, Geoffrey Cumberledge, Repr. 1953.

Llewelyn, Robert (ed.), *Julian: Woman of our Day*, London: Darton, Longman and Todd, 1986.
----- *With Pity Not With Blame*, London: Darton, Longman and Todd, 1983.

Llorca, B., *Die Spanische Inquisition und die Alumbrados*, Berlin-Bonn, 1934.

Lonergan, B., *Insight: A Study of Human Understanding*, London: Darton, Longman and Todd,
    1957, Edition 1983.
----- *Method in Theology*, London: Darton, Longman and Todd, 1972; repr. second edn, 1975.
----- *Grace and Freedom: Operative Grace in the thought of St Thomas Aquinas*, Ed. J. Patout
    Burns, S.J., London: Darton, Longman and Todd, 1971.

Lonergan, B., *Understanding and Being: An Introduction and Companion to Insight*, Ed. Elizabeth
    A. and Mark D. Morelli, New York and Toronto: Edwin Mellen Press, 1980 (Halifax Lectures,
    1958).

Lorenzo, B., 'The Mystical Experience of Julian of Norwich with reference to the Epistle to the
    Hebrews (ch.ix): Semiotic and Psychoanalytic Analysis', trans. Yvette Le Guillou, in *M.M.T.
    in Eng.*, 1982.

Lossky, Vladimir, *The Mystical Theology of the Eastern Church*, Trans. Fellowship of St Alban
    and St Sergius, Cambridge and London: James Clark & Co., 1957, Repr. 1973.
----- 'La Notion des 'Analogies' chez le Pseudo-Denys l'Areopagite' in *AHDLMA*, 5 (1930), 279-309.

Lottin, Dom, *Libre Arbitre et Liberté depuis Saint Anselm jusqu'à la Fin du XIIIe Siècle*, Louvain,
    1942-60.

Louth, A., *The Origins of the Christian Mystical Tradition from Plato to Dionysius*, Oxford, 1985
    (first published, 1981).
----- *Discerning the Mystery, An Essay on the Nature of Theology*, Oxford: Clarendon Press, 1983.
----- *The Wilderness of God*, London: Darton, Longman and Todd, 1991.

Lubac, H. de, *A Brief Catechesis on Nature and Grace*, Trans. Br. Richard Armandez F.S.C. San
    Francisco: Ignatius Press, 1984.
----- *Splendour of the Church*, London: Sheed and Ward, 1956; second edition 1979, repr. 1986.
----- *Exégèse Médiévale: Les Quatre Sens de L'Ecriture*, 4 vols, Paris: Aubier, Editions Montai-
    gne, 1959-64.
----- *La Foi Chrétienne: Essai sur la Structure du Symbole des Apôtres*, Paris, 1969.

Lucien-Marie de Saint Joseph, O.C.D., *L'expérience de Dieu. Actualité du Message de Saint Jean
    de la Croix*, Paris, 1968.

Luscombe, D.E., *The School of Peter Abelard – The Influence of Abelard's Thought in the Early
    Scholastic Period*, Cambridge, 1969.

Mâle, Emile, *L'Art Religieux de la Fin du Moyen-Age en France*, Paris, 1931.

Malevez, Père, 'La Doctrine de l'Image et de la Conaissance Mystique chez Guillaume de St Thier-
    ry' in *Recherches de Science Religieuse*, Vol. xxii, 1932.

Manion, M., 'Women in the Catholic Tradition' in *Christian Spiritual Theology: An Ecumenical
    Reflection*, Ed. Noel J. Ryan, Melbourne: Dove Communications, 1976.

Maréchal, Joseph, *Studies in the Psychology of the Mystics* (*Etudes sur la Psychologie des Mysti-
    ques*. 2me éd. Paris, 1938), Trans. Alger Thorold, London: Burns, Oates and Washbourne,
    1927.
----- 'Application des Sens' in *Dict. Sp.* Vol. 1, Paris, 1937, Cols 810-28.

Maritain, Jacques, 'St John of the Cross, Practitioner of Contemplation; Todo y Nada, ' in *The Degrees of Knowledge*, Trans. G.B. Phelan, New York: Charles Scribner & Sons, 1959, 310-83.
----- 'The Natural Mystical Experience and the Void' in *Understanding Mysticism*, Ed. Richard Woods, O.P., Garden City, N.Y.: Doubleday, 1980.

Markus, R.A., *Christianity in the Roman World*, London: Thames and Hudson, 1974.
----- ''Imago' and 'Similitudo' in Augustine' in *Revue des Etudes Augustiniennes*, Paris, 10, 1964, 125-43.

Maslow, A.H., *Toward a Psychology of Being*, New York, 1968, Second Edition.
----- *The Farther Reaches of Human Nature*, Penguin Books, 1976.

Maven, Alexander, 'The Mystic Union: A Suggested Biological Interpretation' in *The Highest State of Consciousness*, Ed. John White, Garden City, N.Y.: Doubleday, 1972.

Mavrodes, G., 'Real v Deceptive Mystical Experiences' in *Mysticism and Philosophical Analysis*, Ed. S.T. Katz, New York: Oxford University Press, 1978, 235-58.

McCool, Gerard, 'Rahner's philosophy of the human person' in *Theological Studies* 22, 1961.

McEntire, Sandra, 'The Doctrine of Compunction from Bede to Margery Kempe' in *M.M.T. in Eng.*, 1987.

McFarlane, K.B., *John Wycliffe and the Beginnings of English Non-Conformity*, London: English Universities Press, 1952.

McGinn, Bernard, *The Growth of Mysticism*, New York: Cross Road, Vol. 1: *The Foundations of Mysticism*, 1991; Vol. 2: *The Growth of Mysticism*, 1994.

McHardy, A.K., 'The Alien Priories and the Expulsion of Aliens from England in 1378' in *SCH*, xii, 1975, 133-41.

McIntire, C.T. (ed.), *God, History and Historians*, Oxford University Press, 1977.

McKisack, M., *The Fourteenth Century*, Oxford, 1959.

McNab, B., 'Obligations of the Church in English Society: Military Arrays of the Clergy, 1369-1418' in *Order and Innovation in the Middle Ages: Essays in Honour of Joseph R. Strayer*, Eds. W.C. Jordan, B. McNab and T.F. Ruiz, New Jersey, 1976, 293-314.

McNiven, P., 'The Betrayal of Archbishop Scrope' in *BJRL* liv, 1971-72, 173-213.

Meissner, William W., S.J., *Foundations for a Psychology of Grace*, Glen Rock N.J.: Paulist Press, 1960.
----- *Ignatius of Loyola: The Psychology of a Saint*, New Haven and London: Yale University Press, 1992.

Melchior de Ste-Marie, O.C.D., 'Carmel (Ordre de Notre Dame du Mont-Carmel)' in *D.H.G.E.* XI, 1949, Cols 1070-1104.

Merriman, R.B., *The Rise of the Spanish Empire in the Old World and the New*, 4 vols, New York, 1918-34.

Merton, Thomas, *The Ascent to Truth*, London: Burns and Oates, 1976.
----- *The Asian Journal of Thomas Merton*, London, 1974.

Mierlo, J. van, S.J., 'Begardisme' and 'Beguinages' in *D.H.G.E.*, VII (1934), Cols 426-41 and 457-73.

Minnis, A., 'The Sources of the *Cloud of Unknowing*: A Reconsideration' in *M.M.T. in Eng.*, 1982.

Molinari, Paul, S.J., *Julian of Norwich, the Teaching of a 14th Century English Mystic*, London: Longmans, Green & Co., 1958.

Monceaux, P., *Histoire de la Littérature Latine Chrétienne*, Paris, 1924.

Moore, Peter, 'Mystical Experience, Mystical Doctrine' in *Mysticism and Philosophical Analysis*, Ed. Steven T. Katz, New York: Oxford University Press, 1978.

Moore, Peter, 'Christian Mysticism and Interpretation: Some philosophical issues illustrated in the study of Mediaeval English Mystics' in *M.M.T. in Eng.*, 1987.

Morel, Georges, *Le Sens de l'Existence selon S. Jean de la Croix*, 3 vols, Paris: Aubier, 1960-1.

Mueller-Vollmer, Kurt (ed.), *The Hermeneutics Reader*, Basil Blackwell, 1986.

Murdoch, Iris, *Sovereignty of the Good*, London, 1976.

Neumann, Erich, 'Mystical Man' in *Eranos Jahrbuch* 30, 1968, 375-415.

Newman, J.H., *An Essay in Aid of a Grammar of Assent*, Notre Dame, London: University of Notre Dame Press, edition 1986.
----- *Apologia Pro Vita Sua*, London: Sheed and Ward, edition 1987.
----- *An Essay on the Development of Christian Doctrine*, London, 1890.
----- *The Via Media of the Anglican Church, Illustrated in Lectures, Letters and Tracts Written Between 1830 and 1841*, 2 vols, London, 1891.

Nicolas, Antonio T. de, *Ignatius de Loyola: Powers of Imagining* (A philosophical hermeneutic of Imagining through the Collected Works), State University of New York Press, 1986

Nieva, Constantino, 'The *Cloud of Unknowing* and St John of the Cross' in *Mount Carmel* 26, 1978, 79-89.
----- *This Transcending God*, London: The Mitre Press, 1971.

Nuttin, Joseph, *Psychoanalysis and Personality*, New York, 1962.

Nygren, Anders, *Agape and Eros*, Trans. P.W. Watson, London, 1957.

Olphe-Galliard, M., 'Cassien' in *Dict.Sp.* Vol. 2, 1953, Cols 214-76.

Oman, C., *The Great Revolt of 1381*, 2nd ed., Oxford, 1969.

Otto, R., *The idea of the Holy*, Trans. J.W. Harvey, Oxford University Press, 1924 and Penguin Books, 1959.

Owens, Claire Meyers, 'The Mystical Experience: Facts and Values' in *The Highest State of Consciousness*, Ed. John White, Garden City, N.Y.: Doubleday, 1972.

Owst, G.R., *Literature and Pulpit in Mediaeval England*, Cambridge, 1933.

Palgrave, F.T. (ed.), *The Golden Treasury*, London & Glasgow: Collins, 1861.

Palliser, M.A. O.P., *Christ, Our Mother of Mercy. Divine Mercy and Compassion in the Theology of the Shewings of Julian of Norwich*, Berlin and New York: Walter de Gruyter, 1992.

Panofsky, E., *Renaissance and Renascences in Western Art*, London: Paladin Books, 1970 (first published Almquist and Wiksell, 1963).

Pantin, W.A., *The English Church in the Fourteenth Century*, Cambridge, 1955.

Park, Tarjei, 'Reflecting Christ: The Role of the Flesh in Walter Hilton and Julian of Norwich' in *M.M.T. in Eng.*, 1992, 17-38.

Parr, James A., *Don Quixote: An Anatomy of Subversive Discourse*, Newark, Del., 1988.

Peers, E. Allison, *Spirit of Flame. A Study of St John of the Cross*, London: SCM Press, 1943.
----- 'The Historical Problem of Spanish Mysticism' in *St Teresa of Jesus and other Essays and Addresses*, London, 1953, 139-52.

Pegon, J., 'Discernment of Spirits' in *Dict.Sp.* Vol. 3, 1957, Cols 1222-91; and in *N.C.E.* Vol. 4, 893-95.

Pelikan, J., *The Christian Tradition. A History of the Development of Doctrine*, Chicago and London:
- Volume 1, 'The Emergence of the Catholic Tradition' (100-600), 1971.
- Volume 3, 'The Growth of Mediaeval Theology' (600-1300), 1978.
- Volume 4, 'Reformation of Church and Dogma' (1300-1700), 1984.

Pelphrey, Brant, *Christ our Mother. Julian of Norwich*, London: Darton, Longman and Todd, 1989.
----- *Love Was His Meaning: The Theology and Mysticism of Julian of Norwich*, Salzburg: Institut für Anglistik und Amerikanistik, Universität Salzburg, 1982.

Penner, Hans M., 'The Mystical Illusion' in *Mysticism and Religious Traditions*, Ed. S.T. Katz, New York: Oxford University Press, 1983.

Peters, Willem A.M., 'St Ignatius in England' in *The Month*, n.s., Vol. 16, 1956, 22-9.
----- 'Richard Whitford and St Ignatius' visit to England', *AHSJ*, Vol. 25, 1956, 328-50.

Petersen, J.M., *The Dialogues of Gregory the Great in their Late Antique Cultural Background*, Toronto: Pontifical Institute of Mediaeval Studies, Studies and Texts 69, 1984.

Pike, Nelson, 'On Mystic Visions as Sources of Knowledge' in *Mysticism and Philosophical Analysis*, Ed. S.T. Katz, New York: Oxford University Press, 1978, 214-34.

Poncelet, A., 'Vie Ancienne de Guillaume de Saint-Thierry' in *Mélanges Godefroid Kurth*, Liège, 1908, 1, 85-96.

Portalié, E., *A Guide to the Thought of St Augustine*, Trans. A.J. Bastian, S.J., Chicago, 1960.

Pourrat, P., *La Spiritualité Chrétienne, Des Origines de l'Eglise au Moyen Âge*, 2 vols, Paris, 1919.

Powicke, F.M., *Christian Life in the Middle Ages*, Oxford: Clarendon Press, 1935.

Prescott, A.J., 'Judicial Records of the Rising of 1381,' London University Ph.D. thesis, 1984.

Prince, Raymond and Savage, Charles, 'Mystical States and the Concept of Regression' in *The Highest State of Consciousness*, Ed. John White, Garden City, N.Y.: Doubleday, 1972.

Puech, H.Ch., 'La ténèbre mystique chez le Pseudo-Denys l'Aréopagite et dans la tradition patristique' in *Études Carmélitaines*, XXIII (2), Paris, 1938, 33-53.

Purcell, M., *The First Jesuit: St Ignatius Loyola (1491-1556)*, Chicago: Loyola University Press, 1981 (Originally published 1957, Newman Press, Westminster Md.).

Quinn, Peter A., 'Ignatius Loyola and Gian Pietro Carafa: Catholic Reformers at odds' in *Catholic Historical Review*, Vol. 67, 1981, 386-400.

Rahner, Hugo, *Ignatius the Theologian*, Trans. Michael Barry, London: Geoffrey Chapman, 1990 (originally published 1964 as 'Ignatius von Loyola als Mensch und Theologe').

----- *Ignatius the Man and the Priest*, Trans. J. Coyne, Rome: CIS, 1977.

----- *The Vision of St Ignatius in the Chapel of La Storta*, Rome: CIS, 1979.

----- *St Ignatius of Loyola: A Pictorial Biography*, Trans. John Murray, S.J., Chicago: Regenery, 1956.

----- *The Spirituality of St Ignatius Loyola. An Account of Its Historical Development*, Trans. F.J. Smith, S.J. Westminster, Md: The Newman Press, 1953.

Rahner, Karl, *Foundations of Christian Faith. An Introduction to the Idea of Christianity*, Trans. William V. Dych, London: Darton, Longman and Todd, 1978.

----- *Mission et Grâce*, Vol. 1. Trans. Charles Maller, Paris and Tours: Maine, 1962.

----- 'Concerning the Relationship between Nature and Grace' in *Theological Investigations* I, Baltimore: Helicon Press, 1961.

----- 'The Logic of Concrete Individual Knowledge in Ignatius Loyola' in *The Dynamic Element in the Church*, New York: Herder and Herder, 1964.

Rahner, Karl, S.J. and Paul Imhof, S.J., *Ignatius of Loyola*, New York: Collins, 1979.

Ravier, A., *Ignace de Loyola fonde sa Compagnie de Jésus*, Desclée de Brouwer, 1974.

Redfield, R., 'The Social Organisation of Tradition' in *Peasant Society and Culture. An Anthropological Approach to Civilisation*, Chicago, 1956.

Reeves, Marjorie, 'Dante and the Prophetic View of History' in *The World of Dante*, Ed. Cecil Grayson, Oxford: Clarendon Press, 1980, 44-60.

Ricœur, Paul, *Interpretation Theory: Discourse and the Surplus of Meaning*, Fort Worth, Texas, 1976.

Ricœur, Paul, 'The Hermeneutical Function of Distinciation' in *Hermeneutics and the Human Sciences: Essays on Language, Action and Interpretation*, Ed. and trans. John B. Thompson, Cambridge, 1981, 131-144.

----- *Temps et Récit*, Paris, 1983 (Published in English as *Time and Narrative*, 2 vols, trans. K. McLaughlin and D. Pellauer, Chicago: University of Chicago Press, 1984).

----- 'Consciousness and the Unconscious' in *The Conflict of Interpretations: Essays in Hermeneutics*, Ed. Don Ihde, Evanston: North Western University Press, 1974.

Riehle, W., *The Middle English Mystics*, Trans. Bernard Standring, London: Routledge & Kegan Paul, 1981.

Riley, E.C., *Don Quixote*, London, 1986.

Roemer, Judith, O.S.F., 'Discernment in the Director' in *Notes on the Spiritual Exercises of St Ignatius of Loyola*, Ed. David L. Fleming, S.J. St Louis, Mo: Review for Religious, 1985.

Rogers, D., 'Psychotechnological Approaches to the teaching of the *Cloud*-Author and to the *Showings* of Julian of Norwich' in *M.M.T. in Eng.*, 1982.

Roques, R., *L'Univers Dionysien: Structure hiérarchique du monde selon le Pseudo-Denys*, Paris, 1954.

----- 'Contemplation' and 'Denys' in *Dict. Sp.* Vol. 2.B 1953, Cols 1785-87, 1885-1911; Vol. 3, 1957, Cols 244-86.

Rousseau, Phillip, *Ascetics, Authority and the Church*, Oxford, 1978.

Rousselot, P., *Pour l'Histoire du Problème de l'Amour au Moyen Âge*, Münster i.W. 1908; reprinted Paris, 1933.

Ruiz, Federico, *Saint Jean de la Croix mystique et maître spirituel*, Trans. de l'Espagnol par Marie-Agnès Haussièttre, Paris: Les Editions du Cerf, 1994.

Russell, Bertrand, *A History of Western Philosophy*, London: George Allen & Unwin, Ltd., 1946.

Russell, J.B., *The Devil: Perceptions of Evil from Antiquity to Primitive Christianity*, Ithaca, 1977.
----- *Satan: The Early Christian Tradition*, Ithaca, 1981.
----- *Lucifer: The Devil in the Middle Ages*, Ithaca and London: Cornell University Press, 1984.

Russell-Smith, J., 'In Defense of the Veneration of Images' in *Dominican Studies*, Vol. vii, 1954, 180-214.
----- 'Walter Hilton' in *Pre-Reformation English Spirituality*, Ed. James Walsh, S.J. New York: Fordham University Press, 1966, 182-97.

Ryder, Andrew, 'The English and Spanish Mystics', Diss. University of Lancaster, U.K., 1976.

Sandquist, T.A., 'The Holy Oil of St Thomas of Canterbury' in *Essays in Mediaeval History* presented to Bertie Wilkinson, Ed. T.A. Sandquist and M.R. Powicke, Toronto, 1969, 330-44.

Sargent, M.G., 'A New Manuscript of 'The Chastising of God's Children'' in *Medium Aevum*, 46, 1977.
----- 'The organisation of the Scale of Perfection' in *M.M.T. in Eng.*, 1982.

Saussure, F. de, *Cours de Linguistique Générale* (1916), Ed. Tullio de Mauro, Paris 1981, Eng. trans. Wade Baskin, New York, 1959.

Sayers, Dorothy L., *Introductory Papers on Dante*, London: Methuen, 1954.
----- *Further Papers on Dante*, London: Methuen, 1957.

Sayles, G.O., *The Mediaeval Foundations of England*, London: Methuen, 1948.

Sayre, H., 'Performance' in *Critical Terms for Literary Study*, Ed. F. Lentricchia and T. McLaughlin, Chicago: University of Chicago Press, 1990.

Schlier, Heinrich, 'L'Homme d'après la prédiction primitive' in *Essais sur le Nouveau Testament*, Trans. I. Liefooghe, Paris, 1968.

Sikka, Sonya, 'Transcendence in Death: A Heideggerian Approach to Via Negativa in The Cloud of Unknowing' in *M.M.T. in Eng.*, 1992, 179-192.

Sitwell, G., 'Contemplation in *The Scale of Perfection*' in *Downside Review*, Vol. 67, 1949, 276-90; and Vol. 68, 1950, 21-34, 271-89.

Smalley, Beryl, *The Study of the Bible in the Middle Ages*, Oxford, 1964.
----- 'Ecclesiastical Attitudes to Novelty c.1000 - c.1250' in *Church, Society and Politics*, Ed. Derek Baker, *Studies in Church History* 12, Oxford, 1975.
----- *Studies in Mediaeval Thought and Learning: From Abelard to Wyclif*, London: Hambleden Press, 1981.

Smart, Ninian, 'Understanding Religious Experience' in *Mysticism and Philosophical Analysis*, Ed. Stephen T. Katz, New York: Oxford University Press, 1978, 10-21.
----- *The Religious Experience of Mankind*, London, 1969.
----- 'Myth and Transcendence' in *The Monist*, Vol. 50, No.4, Oct. 1966.

----- 'The Purification of Consciousness and the Negative Path' in *Mysticism and Religious Traditions*, Oxford University Press, 1983.

Smith, Herbert F., S.J., 'Discernment of Spirits' in *Notes on the Spiritual Exercises of St Ignatius of Loyola*, Ed. David L. Fleming, S.J. St Louis, Mo.: Review for Religious, 1985.

Smith, John E., 'William James' Account of Mysticism: A Critical Appraisal' in *Mysticism and Religious Traditions*, Ed. Stephen T. Katz, Oxford University Press, 1983.

Smith, J.H., *The Great Schism, 1378*, London: Hamilton, 1979.

Southern, Richard, *The Mediaeval Theatre in the Round. A Study of the Staging of the Castle of Perseverance and Related Matters*, London: Faber, 1957.

Southern, R.W., *The Making of the Middle Ages*, London: Hutchinson's University Library, 1953, repr. 1967.
----- *Western Society and the Church in the Middle Ages*, Vol. 2 in the Pelican History of the Church Series, Penguin Books, 1970.

Speaight, R., *Teilhard de Chardin: A Biography*, London: Collins, 1967.

Spradley, James and McCurdy, David W., *Anthropology: The Cultural Perspective*, New York: Wiley, 1975.

Stace, Walter T., *The Teachings of the Mystics*, New York: New American Library, 1960.
----- *Mysticism and Philosophy*, New York: Macmillan, 1960.

Steggink, Otger, *Experiencia y Realismo en Santa Teresa y San Juan de la Cruz*, Madrid: Editorial de Espiritualidad, 1974.

Stein, Edith, *The Science of the Cross. A Study of St John of the Cross*, Ed. Dr L. Gelber and Fr. Romaeus Leuven, O.C.D., trans. Hilda Graef. Burns and Oates, 1960.

Stock, Brian, *Listening for the Text: On the uses of the past*, Baltimore and London: Johns Hopkins University Press, 1990.
----- *The Implications of Literacy: Written Language and Models of Interpretation in the Eleventh and Twelfth Centuries*, Princeton and New Jersey: Princeton University Press, 1983.

Stormon, E.J., 'The Spirituality of St Augustine'; 'The Spirituality of St Bernard'; and 'The English Mystics' in *Christian Spiritual Theology. An Ecumenical Reflection*, Ed. N.J. Ryan, S.J. Melbourne: Dove Communications Pty.Ltd., 1976.

Strayer, J.R. (ed.), *Dictionary of the Middle Ages*, New York: Charles Scribner & Sons, 1989 (Vol. 9: '*Mystery Cults*' by Joscelyn Godwin; Vol. 8: '*Mystery Plays*' by Richard Beadle).

Streng, F.J., 'Language and Mystical Awareness' in *Mysticism and Philosophical Analysis*, Ed. S.T. Katz, New York: Oxford University Press, 1978.

Sullivan, J.E. *The Image of God: The Doctrine of St Augustine and its Influence*, Dubuque, 1963.

Sumner, M.O., 'St John Climacus, the psychology of the Desert Fathers' in *The Guild Lecture* No.83 of the Guild of Pastoral Psychology, Jan. 1953.

Suzuki, D.T., *Introduction to Zen Buddhism*, London, 1961.

Tanner, N.P., *Popular Religion in Norfolk with Special Reference to the Evidence of Wills, 1370-1532*, Unpubl. D.Phil. Thesis, Oxford, 1973.

Taylor, H.O., *The Mediaeval Mind: A History of the Developments of Thought and Emotion in the Middle Ages*, London, 1911.

Terrien, S., *The Elusive Presence*, New York, 1978.

Thomas, H., *Spanish and Portuguese Romances of Chivalry*, Cambridge, 1920.

Thompson, A.H., *The English Clergy and Their Organisation in the Later Middle Ages*, Oxford, 1947.
----- 'The Pestilences of the Fourteenth Century in the Diocese of York' in *Archaeological Journal* lxxi, 1914, 97-154.

Thompson, C.P., *The Poet and the Mystic: A Study of the Cantico Espiritual of San Juan de la Cruz*, Oxford: Oxford University Press, 1977.

Thornton, M., *English Spirituality: An Outline of Ascetical Theology According to the English Pastoral Tradition*, London, 1963.

Thurston, H., *The Physical Phenomenon of Mysticism*, London, 1952.

Tierney, B., *Foundations of Conciliar Theory*, Cambridge: Cambridge Studies in mediaeval life and thought, new series iv, 1955.

Tracey, David, *The Analogical Imagination: Christian Theology and the Culture of Pluralism*, London: S.C.M. Press Ltd., 1981.

Trevelyan, G.M., *English Social History*, London, 1944.

Trinkaus, Charles, *In Our Image And Likeness: Humanity and Divinity in Italian Humanist Thought*, 2 vols, Chicago and London, 1970.

Trueman Dicken, E.W., *The Crucible of Love. A Study of the Mysticism of St Teresa and St John of the Cross*, London: Darton, Longman & Todd, 1963.

Ullman, W., 'Thomas Becket's Miraculous Oil' in *Journal of Theological Studies*, viii, 1957, 129-33.
----- *Mediaeval Foundations of Renaissance Humanism*, London, 1977.
----- *A History of Political Thought: The Middle Ages*, London: Penguin Books, 1965.
----- *The Growth of Papal Government in the Middle Ages: A Study of the Ideological Relation of Clerical to Lay Power*, London: Methuen, 2nd ed., 1962.

Unamuno y Jugo, M. de, *La Vida de Don Quijote y Sancho* (1905), Trans. A. Kerrigan *Our Lord Don Quixote and Sancho*, with related Essays and an Intro. by W. Starkie, Princeton, N.J.: Princeton University Press, 1967.
----- *Del Sentimento Tragico de la Vida*, Trans. A. Kerrigan, *The Tragic Sense of Life in Men and Nations*, Intro. S. de Magriaga, Ed. and annotated by A. Kerrigan and M. Nolick, Princeton, N.J.: Princeton University Press, 1972.

Underhill, Evelyn, 'The Peace of Will, Intellect and Feeling in Prayer' in *Essentials of Mysticism*, 1920, Repr. New York: A.M.S. Press, 1976.
----- *Mysticism: A Study in the Nature and Development of Man's Spiritual Consciousness*, London: Methuen & Co. Ltd. (1st ed. 1911); 17th ed. 1949.
----- *The Mystics of the Church*, London: James Clark [n.d.].

Van der Meer, F., *Augustine the Bishop. The Life and Work of A Father of the Church*, Trans. E. Battershaw and G.R. Lamb, London: Sheed and Ward, 1961 (2nd Impression, 1978).

Vansteenberghe, E., 'Schisme d'Occident' in *D.T.C.* Vol. 14 (pt. 1, 1939), Cols 1468-92.

Vernet, F., *Mediaeval Spirituality*, Trans. Benedictines of Talacre, London and St Louis, 1930.

Viller, M. and Pourrat, P., 'Abandon' in *Dict. Sp.* Vol. 1, 1940, Cols 1-49.

Vilnet, J., *Bible et Mystique chez Saint Jean de la Croix*, Bruges: Desclée de Brouwer, 1949.

Völker, W., *Kontemplation und Ektase bei Pseudo-Dionysius Areopagita*, Wiesbaden, 1958.

Vries, Piet Penning de, S.J., *Discernment of Spirits According to the Life and Teachings of St Ignatius of Loyola*, Trans. W. Dudok van Heel, New York: Exposition Press, Eng. Trans. 1973.

Walsh, James, S.J. (ed.), *Pre-Reformation English Spirituality*, New York: Fordham University Press, 1966.

Warren, W.L., 'A Reappraisal of Simon Sudbury' in *JEH* X, 1959, 139-52.

Watson, K., 'The Cloud of Unknowing and Vedanta' in *M.M.T. in Eng.*, 1982.

Watson, Nicholas, 'The Trinitarian Hermeneutic in Julian of Norwich's *Revelation of Love*' in *M.M.T. in Eng.*, 1992, 79-100.

Weigel, Gustave, 'Theology and Freedom' in *Thought* 35, 1960.

White, John (ed.), *The Highest State of Consciousness*, Garden City, N.Y.: Doubleday, 1972.

White, Victor, *God and the Unconscious*, Cleveland: World Publishing Co., 1961.
----- *Soul and Psyche*, New York: Harper & Row, 1960.

Wicksteed, P.H., *From Vita Nuova to Paradiso*, London: Longmans, 1922.

Williams, Charles, *The Figure of Beatrice*, London: Faber, 1943.

Williams, Rowan, *Wound of Knowledge: Christian Spirituality from the New Testament to St John of the Cross*, London: Darton, Longman and Todd, 1979; repr. 1981.

Windeatt, Barry (ed.), *English Mystics of the Middle Ages*, Cambridge University Press, 1994.

Wöhrer, F., 'An Approach to the Mystographical Treatises of the *Cloud*-Author through Carl Albrecht's 'Psychology of Mystical Consciousness'' in *M.M.T. in Eng.*, 1984.

Wolfe, Rosemary, *The English Mystery Plays*, London: Routledge & Kegan Paul, 1972.

Woods, Richard O.P. (ed.), *Understanding Mysticism*, Garden City, New York: Doubleday, 1980.
----- *The Meaning of God and Human Experience*, New Haven: Yale University Press, 1963.

Workman, H.B., *John Wyclif.* 2 vols, Oxford, 1926.

Zaehner, R.C., *Mysticism Sacred And Profane*, New York: Oxford, 1961.
----- *Concordant Discord. The Interdependence of Faiths*, Oxford: Clarendon, 1970.
----- *Hindu and Muslim Mysticism*, London, 1960.
----- *At Sundry Times*, London, 1958.